15.95

Author
Christine Routier-Le Diraison

Translation
Anthony Roberts

Adaptation
Mary Hyman, Alexandra Tufts-Simon

With special thanks to:
W. Sureerat, Associate Director of the Tourism Authority of Thailand in Paris, and D. Elouard.

Photo credits: **Hoa-Qui:** G. Boutin, p. 101; De Wilde, pp. 12, 18, 21, 33, 36, 45, 49, 53, 56, 65, 73, 76, 84, 97, 126, 132, 136, 149, 153, 161; Presse-Sport, p. 176; M. Renaudeau, pp. 29, 60; C. Vaisse, p. 25; C. Valentin, pp. 41, 93, 145 — **Hans Petersen,** pp. 156, 169 — **C. Routier-Le Diraison,** p. 105.

This edition published in the United States and Canada in 1988 by
Prentice Hall Press
A division of Simon & Schuster, Inc.
Gulf + Western Building
One Gulf + Western Plaza
New York, New York 10023

PRENTICE HALL PRESS is a trademark of Simon & Schuster, Inc.

This guide is adapted from *en Thailande,* published by Hachette Guides Bleus, Paris, 1988.

© Hachette Guides Bleus, Paris, 1988
English translation © Hachette Guides Bleus, Paris, 1988
Maps © Hachette Guides Bleus, Paris, 1988.
All rights reserved. No part of this publication may be reproduced, stored in a retrieval system or transmitted in any form, or by any means, electronic, mechanical, photocopying, recording or otherwise, without the prior consent of Hachette Guides Bleus.

Library of Congress Cataloging-in-Publication Data
Routier-Le Diraison, Christine
Frommer's touring guide to Thailand.
Translation of: En Thailande.
Bibliography: p. 181
Includes index.
1. Thailand — Description and travel —
1976 — Guide-books
I. Title.
DS563.R6813 1988   915.93'0444   88-2533
ISBN 0-13-331208-9

Printed in France by Aubin Imprimeur, Ligugé

FROMMER'S TOURING GUIDE TO THAILAND

PRENTICE HALL PRESS

NEW YORK

HOW TO USE YOUR GUIDE

- Before you leave home, read the sections 'Planning Your Trip' p. 10, **'Practical Information'** p. 17, **'Thailand in the Past'** p. 38, and **'Thailand Today'** p. 57.
- The rest of the guide is for use once you are there. It is divided into large sections discussing either a **large city** (e.g., Bangkok, Chiang Mai), an **itinerary** (e.g., Bangkok to Chiang Mai) or a **region** (e.g., the Northeast).
Each of these sections contains practical information specific to the area being discussed (access, accommodation, restaurants, useful addresses, etc.), followed by what to see: sights, monuments, etc.
- Each chapter includes a **general map of the area** in question. Those featuring Bangkok and Chiang Mai contain a map of the city, which corresponds to a **grid reference** [(B5), (C1), etc.] included after each address, with the exception of those that are off the map.
- At the back of the guide is a **Useful Vocabulary** listing the most common or useful Thai terms with their English translations, p. 178. There is also a short **Bibliography** of works on Thailand, p. 181.
The **Index** includes not only place names and monuments but also practical information contained in each chapter.

SYMBOLS USED

Places of interest, monuments, museums, works of art

- ★★★ not to be missed
- ★★   very interesting
- ★   worth a look

Hotel classifications

- ▲▲▲▲ Luxury hotel
- ▲▲▲   First-class hotel
- ▲▲   Moderately priced hotel
- ▲   Inexpensive hotel

MAPS

General map of Thailand, 8-9.
Bangkok, 80-81.
Floor plan of the National Museum, 107.
Ayutthaya, 118.
Northern Thailand, 137.
Chiang Mai, 141.
The Ko Samui Archipelago, 160.
Phuket, 168.

CONTENTS

Introducing Thailand 7

Planning Your Trip 10
When to go, 10 - Getting there, 10 - Entry formalities, 11 - Import and export regulations, 11 - Health, 12 - Money, 13 - What to take, 13 - Before you leave: some useful addresses, 15.

Practical Information 17
Accommodation, 17 - Business hours, 18 - Changing money, 18 - Do's and don'ts, 19 - Emergencies, 20 - Festivals, 20 - Food and drink, 23 - Language, 26 - Metric system and electricity, 26 - Organizing your time, 26 - Post office and telecommunications, 27 - Press, 28 - Safety precautions, 28 - Shopping, 29 - Time, 32 - Tipping, 32 - Toilets, 32 - Tourist information, 32 - Transportation, 33.

Thailand in the Past 38

Thailand Today 57

Bangkok 78
Getting the most out of Bangkok, 79 - Practical information, 82.
Visiting Bangkok, 98 - Organizing your time, 98 - The principal sections of Bangkok, 99 - The temples of Bangkok, 99 - The Palace, 104 - The National Museum, 106 - Old Thai houses, 112 - The markets, 113 - Chinatown: red and gold, 115 - Bangkok seen from the klongs, 115.

Outside Bangkok 117
Ancient cities and monuments, 117 - Ayutthaya, 117 - Bang Pa In, 119 - Nakhon Pathom, 120 - Ancient City, 121.
The beaches, 121 - Bang Saen, 122 - Pattaya, 122.
Other attractions, 123 - Damnoen Saduak floating market, 123 - Crocodile farm, 124 - Rose garden, 124 - The Bridge over the River Kwai, 124 - Nam Tok and the River Kwai, 125.

Bangkok to Chiang Mai via the Fallen Cities 126
Practical information, 126.
Exploring the fallen cities, 127 - Ayutthaya, 127 - Lopburi, 127 - Phitsanulok, 128 - Sukhothai, 129 - Kamphaeng Phet, 131 - Si Satchanalai, 133 - Lampang, 134.
Some other northern itineraries, 135.

Chiang Mai 137
Practical information, 138.
Visiting Chiang Mai, 144 - The temples of Chiang Mai, 144 - Doi Suthep, 145 - Chiang Mai Museum, 146 - Craftsmen's villages, 146 - Old Chiang Mai, 147 - Tribal Research Centre, 147.
Outside Chiang Mai, 147 - To the south, 147 - To the north, 148.
Mae Sariang and Mae Hong Son, 150 - Practical information, 150 - The itinerary, 150.
By pirogue from Chiang Mai to Chiang Rai: along the Kok River, 151 - Practical information, 151 - Going down the river, 152.
Chiang Rai and the Golden Triangle, 153 - Practical information, 153 - Exploring the Golden Triangle, 154.

Southern Itinerary: the Eastern Seaboard 155
Practical information, 157.
Along the coast, 157 - Hua Hin: the royal beach, 157 - Prachuap Kiri Khan, 158 - Ko Samui, 159 - Songkhla, 162.

Phuket 165
Practical information, 166 - The beaches, 170.

Outside Phuket, 171 - Phangnga Bay, 171 - Ko Phi Phi: Swallow's Nest Island, 172.

The North-east: Toward the Laotian Border 173
Practical information, 174.
Along the Khmer trail, 174 - Pimai, 174 - Phnom Rung, 175 - Muang Tham Palace, 175 - Surin: the gathering of the elephants, 175 - Khao Yai National Park, 177.

Useful Vocabulary 178

Bibliography 181

Index 182

Thailand in brief

Location: Asia, 5 928 mi/9 484 km from London.

Frontiers: 2300 mi/3700 km long (Kampuchea, Laos, Burma, Malaysia).

Coasts: 1600 mi/2600 km.

Land Area: 198,000 sq mi/514,000 sq km.

Population: 51 million (growth rate 2% per year).

Capital: Bangkok (population 6 million).

Principal religion: Theravâda Buddhism.

Official language: Thai.

Principal international language: English.

Government: Constitutional monarchy.

Administrative divisions: 75 provinces, each administered by a governor.

Principal resources: Tourism, agriculture (rice), tin, processing industries.

INTRODUCING THAILAND

To Western eyes, the image of Thailand has often been romanticized. It is time to set the record straight.

Today, Thailand is an efficient and attractive holiday destination, with revenues from tourism surpassing those yielded by the annual rice crop. The ancient jungle cities, beaches fringed by coconut palms, processions of monks, dancing girls in city bars, palaces, bamboo cabins, elephants, poppy fields, temples, wonderful food, and charming people are all there to be discovered ... but their enchantment is that of a real nation with a distinctive and vigorous culture all its own.

Thailand is Asia-made-easy, with excellent communications, modern hotels, a high-quality tourist infrastructure, and probably the most gracious service in the world. You can approach it according to your budget and your preferences.

Thailand personifies the ancient wisdom of Asia, with a background of 2500 years of Buddhism. Here passions are muted and tolerance is the order of the day. Thailand's temples are open to all. They are oases of peace in a tumultuous world. Inside, a feeling of timeless tranquillity is imparted by the scent of incense and jasmine, the glint of gold and lacquer and the presence of the silent Buddhas and saffron-robed monks.

However, the 15 mi/25 km between Bangkok's airport and the city centre will soon dispel any lingering illusions about the so-called Venice of the Orient. Bangkok is a maelstrom of traffic, bright lights and deafening noise. With fascination, you will gaze from your taxi at the incomprehensible signs on the walls of the buildings, the varnished tiles of the temple roofs against a monsoon-laden sky, and the crowds surging along the streets and sidewalks. Suddenly, the driver screeches to a halt at a traffic light, opens the door of his taxi, and emits a long stream of saliva. Stop. This is Asia.

It's all real: the temples, the skyscrapers, the wretched floating abodes, the garden-girt palaces, and the smiles and frowns, which sometimes get mixed up in the presence of foreigners. Bangkok is the focal point of modern Thailand. A more traditional Thailand is to be seen in the countryside, among the peasants, the rice-paddies, the buffalo, and the colourful hill-tribe populations.

THAILAND

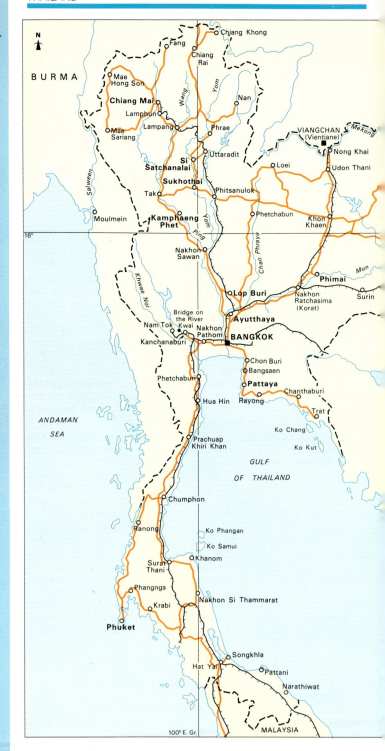

Distances from Bangkok

Ayutthaya	51 mi/
(by train: 1 h 20)	86 km
Bang Saen	63 mi/
	106 km
Chanthaburi	191 mi/
	319 km
Chiang Mai	420 mi/
(by train: 14 h)	700 km
(by plane: 1 h)	
Chiang Rai	494 mi/
	823 km
Chumphon	276 mi/
(by train: 9 h)	460 km
Haadyai	748 mi/
(by train: 19 h)	1 247 km
(by plane: 1 h 15)	
Hua Hin	138 mi/
(by train: 4 h)	230 km
Kanchanaburi	75 mi/
(by train: 2 h 30)	126 km
Khon Khaen	267 mi/
(by train: 8 h 30)	445 km
(by plane: 1 h)	
Lampang	362 mi/
(by train: 11 h 30)	604 km
Lamphun	400 mi/
(by train: 13 h 30)	667 km
Nakhon Pathom	33 mi/
	56 km
Nakhon Phanom	441 mi/
	735 km
Nakhon Ratchasima ..	153 mi/
(by train: 5 h)	256 km
Nakhon Si Thamma-	682 mi/
rat	1 137 km
(by train: 16 h 45)	
Nan	447 mi/
	745 km
Pattaya	84 mi/
	140 km
Phetchaburi	75 mi/
(by train: 4 h)	126 km
Phitsanulok	299 mi/
(by train: 7 h)	498 km
(by plane: 40 min)	
Phuket	553 mi/
(by train: 1 h 10)	922 km
Rayong	125 mi/
	208 km
Songkhla	780 mi/
	1 300 km
Trad	232 mi/
	387 km
Ubon Ratchathani ...	388 mi/
(by train: 10 h 30)	647 km
(by plane: 1 h 45)	
Udon Thani	337 mi/
(by train: 10 h 30)	562 km
(by plane: 1 h 35)	
Yala	837 mi/
(by train: 20 h)	1 395 km

N.B. Times for lengths of trips by train or plane are approximate. These depend on the number of stops.

PLANNING YOUR TRIP

WHEN TO GO

The weather in Thailand is nearly always hot, particularly in lowland areas where the climate is humid and tropical. Seasonal variations depend on the monsoon, which lasts for about five months, from June to Oct. Rather than the endless deluge we may imagine, the monsoon is characterized by uncertain weather (thunderstorms alternating with clear skies). Travel and tourism in Thailand remain perfectly feasible during the 'rainy season'.

Broadly speaking, the mountains of the north, the north-eastern plateau and the central plains experience more variation in seasonal temperatures than the low-lying peninsular zone. For example, in Chiang Mai the temperature can reach 95° F/35° C in summer (Mar.-May) and drop to 46° F/8° C in winter (Nov.-Feb.). By contrast, Bangkok and the peninsular zone experience heat and tropical humidity throughout the year.

Thailand is best visited between Nov. and Feb. when the weather is generally neither too hot nor too rainy and when many of the traditional festivals take place. Since it's the height of the tourist season, it means higher prices and less room in hotels and planes.

Weather chart

	J.	F.	M.	A.	M.	J.	J.	A.	S.	O.	N.	D.
Average temperature F.	90	91	93	95	93	91	90	90	90	88	88	88
Hours of sun daily	8	8	8	10	8	6	5	5	5	6	7	8
Days of rainfall	1	2	3	4	13	14	15	15	17	13	4	1
Sea temperature F.	79	81	81	82	82	82	82	82	82	81	81	81

GETTING THERE

By air

More than 30 international airlines operate flights to Bangkok's Don Muang Airport. You can also fly from Malaysia directly to Hat Yai or Phuket in Southern Thailand or from Hong Kong to Chiang Mai in the north. Thai Airways International has flights from London to Bangkok via Frankfurt, Copenhagen, or Delhi (flight time: approx. 13 hours), while British Airways offers several direct weekly flights (approx. 12 hours).

If you are starting from North America, all Thai Airways International flights leave from Seattle and stop over in Tokyo (17 hours, Seattle to Bangkok). United Airlines flies from New York, San Francisco, and Los Angeles with a stopover in Tokyo (21 hours from New York, 17 from Los Angeles or San Francisco).

Thai Airways International also services Australia with flights from Sydney and Melbourne via Singapore (14 hours).

Note : You must pay an airport tax for all departures from Bangkok (150 ฿ for international flights, 20 ฿ for local flights).

For more detailed flight information, contact your local travel agent.

By sea
Few tourists can afford to spend a month traveling to their holiday destinations, but if you are in no hurry, it is possible to reach Bangkok by sea. Several freighters operate from Europe and the United States and ships from Hong Kong, Japan, and Singapore regularly stop in Bangkok. There is also a boat between Perlis, Malaysia, and Satun, Thailand. Inquire from a local travel agent for more details.

By land
The only land route currently open to Thailand is from Malaysia; no access is possible from Burma, Laos, or Kampuchea. A train leaves Singapore for Bangkok three times a week with connections in Kuala Lumpur and Butterworth. The trip takes two days. Along the three main roads crossing the southern Thai border, taxis and minibuses are available to shuttle tourists to the major towns. If you want to drive back across the border from Thailand to Malaysia, make sure your car is insured, otherwise Malaysian officials can refuse entry.

ENTRY FORMALITIES

Passports and visas
Your passport must be valid for at least six months from your date of entry.
Visas are unnecessary for a stay of up to 15 days on condition that you can show a departure ticket and sufficient funds for your stay. Transit visas (valid 30 days) and tourist visas (60 days) can be obtained from all Thai embassies and consulates. Once inside Thailand, getting your visa extended is time-consuming and costly. It is best to avoid the administrative entanglements by carefully planning the length of your stay beforehand. As a last resort, some people prefer leaving Thailand to obtain another visa in a neighbouring country such as Malaysia or Indonesia.

Vaccinations
No vaccinations are officially required unless you are coming from an infected area. It is prudent, however, to be vaccinated against tetanus, typhoid, and paratyphoid infections before you leave your home country. In the event of a cholera outbreak in South-east Asia, cholera vaccinations may be compulsory; check with your travel agent.

IMPORT AND EXPORT REGULATIONS

As in most countries, Thailand strictly prohibits the importation of narcotics and pornography. Guns must be licensed by the Thai Police Department. Goods you can bring with you duty-free include 200 cigarettes, a litre of alcohol, a movie camera, and a still camera. There is no limit to the number of rolls of film that you can bring in.

Plants
Should you wish to export local plants or seeds in your baggage when you leave, make sure that you receive the appropriate authorization from your country of destination.

Pets
Pets must be vaccinated and in good health. The Thai authorities require certificates to this effect, as well as an entry permit which is available upon arrival at the airport.
Do not attempt to export animals without carefully studying the law. Many, like flying squirrels, yellow-bellied weasels, and wild cats, may not be taken out of the country. For further information, contact the Immigration Office, Soi Suan Phlu, Sathorn Tai Rd., Bangkok, Tel: 286

Young priest learns to drape his robe.

9176 or 286 9230. In addition, remember that the country you will be leaving for may not allow the animals to enter. US and UK regulations concerning the importation of animals are very strict; ask your travel agent for information.

▬ *HEALTH*

Thailand is a reasonably safe country from the standpoint of health. The larger cities all have excellent hospital facilities and many Thai doctors speak English, having studied in the United States. Nonetheless, all visitors to Thailand should take some preliminary precautions to avoid contracting malaria or suffering from digestive difficulties.

Malaria

This disease is transmitted by the anopheles mosquito and is endemic to

What to take

many regions of Asia — particularly the north and west of Thailand. The best precaution against it is to take preventive medication, which should be started at least one week before the trip and continued for at least three weeks after returning home. To keep away mosquitos, sprays and creams are usually ineffective; the best prevention is a regular dosage of vitamin B1, which gives the skin an odour the mosquitos seem to hate. If, however, you prefer to use electric fumigators, don't forget to take along an adapter for American or British plugs.

Stomach problems

These are common among tourists and are usually due to the change of climate and diet. The local pharmacist will advise you as to the best medication.

There is no really foolproof defense against the amoebas that cause digestive problems, but if you avoid drinking tap water and eating raw vegetables, you run almost no risk at all. Most hotels provide purified water. You may find it useful in certain situations (such as staying the night in a remote village) to carry hydrochlorazone water-purifying tablets. Otherwise there's no cause for panic: As you will quickly discover, the Thais are an almost obsessively clean people.

First-aid kit

This should contain aspirin, bandages, an antiseptic, vitamins C and B1, all-purpose antibiotics, and medicine for seasickness. If you are under treatment, take your medicine with you; although Bangkok pharmacies are well-supplied, it is not always easy to make yourself fully understood. Medicines which contain narcotic drugs should be accompanied with a doctor's prescription to avoid any problems you might have bringing them into the country.

■ MONEY

Currency

The Thai currency (Baht, abbreviated to ฿) cannot be purchased abroad. European currencies may be exchanged in Bangkok, but in the provinces it is best to carry US dollars. For greater security, keep most of your money in traveler's checks, which also command a more favourable exchange rate than cash. Small US dollar denominations can come in handy. There is no limit on the importation of traveler's checks and letters of credit. On the other hand, cash exceeding US $2000 must be declared on entry (see also 'Changing money' p. 18).

Your budget

In Thailand, as in most Asian countries, there is a considerable difference between local living standards and those of the average tourist, who can spend in one week what the average Thai spends in six months, or even one year. For one thing, Western-style food, if you must have it, is roughly six times as expensive as the local cuisine. And if you don't haggle before you buy, your souvenirs will cost you as much as they would in a department store back home.

The cost of your trip, therefore, will depend greatly on your style of traveling. If you want to live in modern comfort, you will need between US $60 and US $80 (£35 to £45) per day. If you are willing to live as the Thais do, US $20 to US $30 (£12 to £18) should be quite enough to cover hotels, food, and transportation.

■ WHAT TO TAKE

Clothing

There is no need to take a large quantity of clothes. Most hotels have express cleaning services. Moreover, Thai tailors are excellent — and capable of making shirts, dresses, and suits in record time. All Western styles worth copying have been copied in Thailand and are sold there at very low prices: for example, shirts bearing the insignia of a crocodile. For your own comfort, choose cotton rather than nylon or other synthetic fabrics that might either stick to your skin in hot, humid weather or take time to dry after a sudden downpour.

Light casual clothes are recommended. Bangkok nightlife imposes no strict rules of dress, although Thai women usually wear formal clothes in the evening; you may or may not wish to do likewise. Women should avoid plunging necklines and short skirts, even in Bangkok which has a conservative side despite its lively reputation.

Pack at least one wool garment, which you will need in the north and in heavily air-conditioned restaurants and hotels — and don't forget your bathing suit (nudity at beaches is deeply shocking to the Thais). Sandals (plastic or rubber ones for the monsoon season) and a pair of comfortable walking shoes are necessary. Socks should be woolen or cotton. One practical detail: in Thailand, you must take off your shoes to enter a house or temple. Consequently, be sure to take shoes that are easily slipped on and off. The more worn they are, the less likelihood there will be that someone will 'borrow' them outside a temple (this has been known to happen, and sometimes the 'borrowers' are other tourists). There is no need to take a raincoat, even in the rainy season; though torrential, the downpours tend to be short. A locally made oil-paper umbrella will be quite sufficient protection, and you can bring it back as a souvenir.

Luggage

Passengers flying economy class may carry 44 lb/20 kg of baggage without charge; for every excess kilo, allow 1% of the first-class fare. There is no need to load yourself down with bags because Bangkok is a modern city where anything you may conceivably need can be found.

When selecting baggage for the trip, bear in mind the conditions you will face in Thailand. If you plan to visit the northern hill areas, go down the Mae Kok River near Chiang Rai, or ride in local buses, the classic suitcase should be rejected in favour of a duffel-bag (preferably with a shoulder strap). Because there are rickshaws at every station entrance, a backpack will be cumbersome unless you intend to go on a walking tour or trek.

For more leisurely travel, a suitcase of average size should be quite sufficient. Avoid really sumptuous luggage, which may arouse envy. Ideally, you should take two bags: one basic piece and a smaller hold-all for short excursions. Don't forget that heavy, cumbersome bags can spoil your whole trip.

If you plan to stay in economy hotels, a sleeping bag may be a useful asset. People who find it hard to sleep in noisy places are well-advised to bring earplugs; hotels in Thai city centres tend to be exceedingly noisy with traffic, the omnipresent racket of transistor radios, and people in the next room who think nothing of taking a shower at four in the morning.

Photographic equipment

Ultra-violet filters and sun hoods are strongly recommended for Asia. Avoid taking too much heavy equipment, which you will find doubly burdensome to carry around in the heat. A low ASA film is appropriate for Asian light conditions. If you have light-absorbing or telephoto lenses, or if you plan to take pictures at night or in interiors, take a stock of light-sensitive film (Ektachrome high speed or Tri-X). All the commonly known brands of film are available at comparable prices in major Thai tourist centres but there is no guarantee that they have been properly stored at all times. It is best to bring your own stock.

Never leave your camera in the sun or in an overheated place. As in all tropical climates, to prevent moulds it is advisable to carry drying agents like silica gel or baked rice. (These products are only effective when hermetically packed.) Used film should be developed as soon as possible.

Most Thais will pose for you, provided you give them warning. It is considered extremely rude to catch people off guard with a camera. If you detect the slightest hesitancy, it is better not to insist. In some tourist-frequented mountain villages, notably around Chiang Mai, payment will be requested for photographs.

Photographing temple interiors is generally accepted but you should be discreet and avoid interrupting ceremonies.

▰ *BEFORE YOU LEAVE: SOME USEFUL ADDRESSES*

For more detailed information, contact the following Thai embassies, consulates, or Tourism Authority of Thailand (TAT) offices.

Australia
Embassy
Canberra, 111 Empire Circuit, Yarralumla ACT 2600. Tel: (062) 73 1149.

Consulate
Sydney, 56 Pitt St., NSW 2000. Tel: (02) 27 2542.

Tourism Authority of Thailand
Sydney, 56 Pitt St., NSW 2000. Tel: (02) 27 7549.

Canada
Embassy
Ottawa, 85 Range Rd., KIN 8J6. Tel: (613) 237 0476.

Tourism Authority of Thailand
For Eastern Canada, contact the New York office below. For Western Canada, contact the Los Angeles office below.

Great Britain
Embassy
London, 29-30 Queen's Gate, SW7 5JB. Tel: (01) 589 2944.

Consulates
Birmingham, c/o Smith Keen Cutler Exchange Bldg., Stephenson Place B24NN. Tel: (021) 643 9977.
Liverpool, 35 Lord St., 2. Tel: (051) 227 2525.

Tourism Authority of Thailand
London, 9 Stafford St., WlX 3FE. Tel: (01) 499 7670.

United States
Embassy
Washington, 2300 Kalorama Rd., NW, DC 20008. Tel: (202) 483 7200.

Consulates
Chicago, 35 East Wacker Dr., III 60601. Tel: (312) 236 2447.
Los Angeles, 801 N. La Brea Ave., CA 90038. Tel: (213) 937 1894.
New York, 53 Park Place, 10007. Tel: (212) 732 8166.

Tourism Authority of Thailand
New York, 5 World Trade Center, NY 10048. Tel: (212) 432 0433.
Los Angeles, 3440 Wilshire Blvd., CA 90010. Tel: (213) 382 2353.

PRACTICAL INFORMATION

ACCOMMODATION

Hotels

Hotels are plentiful in Thailand and are varied and generally of excellent quality. There are more than 20,000 rooms of all categories available in Bangkok, 10,000 in Pattaya, 5000 in Chiang Mai, and 4000 in Phuket. In the provinces, the tourist circuits are well-furnished with modern, American-style hotels which are relatively cheap (80 ฿ to 200 ฿).

The quality of service in Thai hotels and restaurants, where discretion and courtesy are the rule, is among the best in the world. The orchids placed on your pillow by the house-cleaning staff, the smiling greeting of the bell-hop (who expects no tip), the glass of water served without your asking, the elevator rug with the day of the week written on it — these, and many other details, will make your stay most pleasant and relaxing.

In this guide, hotels are divided into four categories: luxury, first-class, moderately priced, and inexpensive. The prices indicated below are for Bangkok. In Chiang Mai and other provincial cities you can expect to pay about one-third less for equivalent accommodation in each category. Service accounts for 10% of the bill and taxes for 16.5%.

Luxury hotels (▲▲▲▲)

Such hotels, to be found only in Bangkok, are better described as super-luxurious and offer excellent value by European and American standards. The details vary from one establishment to another but all have air-conditioned rooms with private bath, drinking water, and TV, and most include shopping malls, hairdressing salons, bars, discotheques, swimming pools, saunas, and more than one restaurant. Expect to pay between 2000 ฿ and 3000 ฿ per night for a double room.

First-class hotels (▲▲▲)

The hotels in this category are similar to the ones above in terms of comfort and service. The main difference lies in the less-luxurious surroundings which result in a lower price: 900 ฿ to 1500 ฿ per night for a double room.

Moderately priced hotels (▲▲)

This category of hotel provides air-conditioning, private bath, TV, and drinking water, as well as at least one restaurant and a swimming pool. GIs from Vietnam used to form a large proportion of these hotels' clientele and you can expect to find excellent comfort at a very reasonable price: 400 ฿ to 600 ฿ per night for a double room.

Inexpensive hotels (▲)

If your budget is limited, you may decide to opt for this category of accommodation, generally provided by the smaller Chinese-run hotels.

Thai dancer.

These are to be found all over the country. These are no-frills establishments with running water, and your night's stay will cost between 50 ฿ and 100 ฿.

Monasteries and other accommodation

Monasteries will sometimes agree to shelter foreigners. They are only supposed to accept men, but some have relaxed their monastic rules sufficiently to allow women too. You sleep in the *sala,* which is an open building, none too comfortable but free of charge. Be sure, however, to leave a contribution.

You will rarely be allowed to stay in a private house, except perhaps in isolated villages like those of the hilltribes in the north. Negotiation is rendered well-nigh impossible by the language barrier. In all likelihood, if you stay overnight, you will find unexpected residents in your bedroom called *Chin Choks.* A *Chin Chok* is a kind of grey lizard which has the useful habit of gulping down mosquitos.

▰ BUSINESS HOURS

As in all hot countries, the day in Thailand begins early in the morning. Administrative offices are open between 8:30am and 4:30pm, with a break for lunch. It is hopeless, however, to try to resolve a difficult administrative problem after 3pm. Banks are generally open from 8:30am to 3:30pm Mon. to Fri., although certain exchange facilities stay open till 8 or 10pm.

Most shops are open from about 8:30 or 9am until 8 or 9pm, though itinerant vendors pack up their wares at around 7pm. Shop hours are not subject to any legal limitations. Many Chinese stores stay open seven days a week, including holidays. Department stores are open from 10am to 6:30 or 7pm.

There are no strict visiting hours for temples and museums, but, as a general rule, they cannot be entered after 4pm. Entrance is usually free of charge on weekends.

▰ CHANGING MONEY

The Thai Baht (฿) is divided into 100 *satangs*. There are 10 ฿ notes (brown), 20 ฿ notes (green), 100 ฿ notes (red) and 500 ฿ notes (violet). Coin values are 25 *satang* and 50 *satang,* 1 ฿ and 5 ฿. 5 ฿ coins are very similar to 1 ฿ coins, so watch your change.

The Baht is firmly aligned with the US dollar, US $1 being worth approximately 26 ฿, and it fluctuates with the dollar on the currency market. The British pound is worth about 40 ฿, subject to change with the $/£ exchange rate.

Try to avoid changing money too frequently; the process can be lengthy and tedious unless you are changing traveler's checks. You can change at banks (8:30am-3:30pm Mon.-Fri.), at licensed money changers, or in hotels (commission of 5% to 10% on the official rate of exchange). Traveler's checks are convertible into dollar bills or pound notes, but the bank will require a commission. The money changers in Silom Road, Suriwong Road or New Road in Bangkok do not accept traveler's checks but offer higher rates for cash than the banks and hotels. There is no black market for exchanging the Baht.

Always carry small notes and coins to pay for meals, taxis, and other current expenses. The sight of a big note usually causes hopeless panic, because most Thais do not possess the cash necessary to give you back your change.

Credit cards

All credit cards are accepted in most luxury and higher category establishments (hotels, restaurants, shops) in Bangkok, Chiang Mai, and Pattaya. The International Visa card is the easiest to negotiate, since it is accepted at the Thai Farmer's Bank which has more branches all over the country than any other bank.

DO'S AND DON'TS

Conventions and usages in Asia are totally different from our own. In their ignorance of Eastern courtesy, Westerners are frequently viewed by Thais as absolute barbarians. Here are some general rules of behaviour.

General recommendations

Always remove your shoes before entering a temple or a Thai home. People who wear no shoes are expected to wash their feet at the entrance. There is usually a clay pot with a wooden ladle.

The Thais do not shake hands. The usual gesture of welcome (or gratitude) is to join both hands, as if in prayer, and raise them to the forehead or chest while bowing. You will quickly get used to this graceful custom, which is known as the *wai*.

Do not be surprised if you find yourself being addressed by your Christian name (Miss Christine or Mr. John). This is how the Thais commonly address one another, with the prefix *Khun,* which means Mr., Mrs., or Miss. Family names were introduced in Thailand in the early 20th century (under Rama VI), but they are so long and complicated that the Thais seldom use them.

Avoid showing impatience or anger. People will simply laugh at you.

Beware of inadvertently insulting anyone. Thais tend to be phlegmatic, but they hate to lose face. In addition, if you stare at someone it will be interpreted as a kind of provocation.

At restaurants, never snap your fingers or whistle to summon a waiter. A wave of the hand is sufficient.

It is a sign of contempt in Thailand to touch another person's head, the head being considered the noblest part of the human body.

Avoid crossing your legs, because in doing so you may unintentionally point your foot at someone. This is a very serious insult since the foot is viewed as the body's most contemptible member. Also, should you drop a bank note, never put your foot on it to keep it from flying away. This would be an appalling sacrilege because Thai bank notes carry a portrait of the king, who is considered holy (see 'The King' p. 43).

How to behave with monks

Monks should be treated with the utmost respect. Theoretically, women are not allowed to speak to them unless first addressed, and are expected to keep a respectful distance. All contributions must be placed in a collection box, since monks are forbidden to handle them directly. Foreigners are expected to leave a coin or two, particularly if they have caused some minor disturbance.

Visitors should not enter a holy place in shorts or other revealing or unkempt clothes.

It is disrespectful to touch statues or other religious objects on temple grounds; nor should you handle a religious object (such as a Buddha) like a common souvenir. Above all, never pick such an object up by its head.

Sanuk

In Asia, everything happens more slowly. People walk, climb staircases, buy and sell at a more leisurely pace. While in Thailand, try to operate at the same speed. Remind yourself that you're on vacation, and that, in the Thai heat, slowing your pace is advisable for your health.

One Thai habit you should try to adopt as soon as possible is the quest for *sanuk*. *Sanuk* is a term that covers everything pleasant, agreeable or amusing. Life is divided between *sanuk* circumstances and those which are *mai sanuk* (not amusing and to be definitely avoided).

Don't expect all Thais to be punctual. Many rarely have any notion of time. The rendez-vous is a Western institution which is diametrically opposed to the Thai way of looking at things. The person you have arranged to meet may not show at all, for any number of reasons: because of the rain, or because he forgot, or even because a more interesting prospect arose at the last minute. Should a Thai friend offer to drive you to the airport on the day of your departure, offer to meet him at the terminal instead.

EMERGENCIES

In most cases, a call to your hotel desk is the most efficient way to obtain emergency assistance because of the language barrier. However, a bilingual Tourist Police force is attached to the TAT which has offices in all the country's major cities. Through the TAT, fire and ambulance assistance can also be obtained. For help, contact the following TAT offices:

Bangkok Ratchadamnoen Nok Ave. Tel: (02) 282 1143-7.
Chiang Mai 135 Praisani Rd., Amphoe Muang. Tel: (053) 23 5334.
Kanchanaburi Saeng Chuto Rd., Amphoe Muang. Tel: (034) 51 1200.
Nakhon Ratchasima 53/1-4 Mukkhamontri Rd., Amphoe Muang. Tel: (044) 24 3427 or 24 3751.
Pattaya 382/1 Chaihat Rd., South Pattaya. Tel: (038) 42 8750 or 42 9113.
Phitsanulok 209/7-8 Baromatrai Lokanart Rd., Amphoe Muang. Tel: (055) 25 3427 or 25 2743.
Phuket 73-75 Phuket Rd., Amphoe Muang. Tel: (076) 21 2213 or 21 1036.
Songkhla 1/1 Soi 2 Niphat Uthit 3 Rd., Hat Yai. Tel: (074) 24 3747 or 24 5986.
Surat Thani Sala Prachakhom Bldg., Na Muang Rd., Amphoe Muang. Tel: (077) 28 2828 or 28 1828.

FESTIVALS

Although Thailand's religious festivals follow the Buddhist lunar calendar, its civil holidays conform to the Christian year.

The Thais love to enjoy themselves, to meet, mingle and stroll in the streets. They eagerly take advantage of any pretext for rejoicing. The following calendar gives a general outline of festivities: for all specific information, contact the TAT office nearest you before you leave home or in the city you are visiting.

February

Magha Puja is the anniversary of the day when Buddha expounded his doctrines before 1250 of his disciples. Thai Buddhists mark this occasion with processions and rituals in the temples.

The Feast of Phra Buddhabaht is the occasion of a pilgrimage to the Shrine of the Holy Footprint, near Saraburi (85 mi/136 km from Bangkok).

The Chinese New Year is celebrated on the first day of the first lunar month, which is usually in Feb. This is a good time to pay a visit to the Lisu tribe: you will have more fun with them than you would if you stayed in Bangkok (see p. 67).

February-April

The windy season is the period for kite fights. 'Male' kites *(chula)* and 'female' kites *(pakpao)* duel until one falls out of the sky. The game dates back to the middle of the 13th century. In 1690, the astute governor of Ayutthaya used kites as bombers, dispatching explosives by air.

Kite fights take place every afternoon in Sanam Louang, Bangkok's main square, near the Chao Phraya River.

Ordination of a monk.

April

6th: **Chakri Day** commemorates the founding of the reigning dynasty. The king and queen proceed to the Royal Pantheon in Bangkok, which is open to the public only on this occasion.

13th-15th: **Songkran**, an especially popular holiday throughout Thailand, especially at Chiang Mai, combines the Water Festival and the **Thai New Year**. Songkran is essentially a purification rite in which Thais give their houses a thorough cleaning. Offerings of flowers, incense, and candles are made in the temples and Buddha images are sprinkled with water, as are monks and older citizens. In the streets, people throw water on each other in fun and celebration.

May

5th: **Coronation Day** commemorates the coronation of King Bhumibol Adulyadej, the reigning king. The king and queen preside over various ceremonies at the Palace and at the Temple of the Emerald Buddha (Wat Phra Keo) in Bangkok.

Mid-month: The **Ploughing Ceremony** (or **Ceremony of the First Furrow**) is a Hindu festival marking the beginning of the rice planting period. Astrologers predict the quality of the coming rice harvest and Brahmin priests bless samples of seed, which are then distributed among the farmers for good luck. There are also Brahmin processions which accompany a team of magnificently festooned white oxen; the harnessed oxen plough nine furrows in the soil. The king presides over this solemn and impressive ceremony at Sanam Louang Square in Bangkok.

Visakha Puja, which falls on the day of the full moon of the sixth lunar month, is when Thais celebrate the anniversary of Buddha's attainment of Nirvana. His enlightenment is symbolized by the appearance in Thailand's temples of thousands of paper lanterns, specially made for the occasion.

July

Khao Phansa, coinciding with the start of the rainy season, marks the beginning of the Buddhist Lent, which lasts three months. Young Thais usually choose this period for a temporary stay in a monastery.

August

12th: **Queen Sirikit's birthday.** Her Highness Queen Sirikit takes part in various religious ceremonies and gives offerings to monks at the Chitralada Palace, the royal residence in Bangkok.

October

Thot Kathin and the procession of royal barges take place during this month. To celebrate the end of the rainy season, the Thai population and their king present new orange robes to Buddhist monks. Traditionally the king went to the Temple of Dawn (Wat Arun) in sculpted barges majestically floating along the river amid the rhythmic chanting of oarsmen. Unfortunately, the barges are now considered to be too fragile to be brought out and the procession has not been held for many years. There are plans to revive this custom.

9th-14th: **Phra Chedi Klang Nam** takes place at the Pak Nam Pagoda south of Bangkok. On this feast day, the people go out on picnics and watch boat races. They also participate in *chule kathin* in which a monk's robe is manufactured: the raw cotton is woven, dyed, cut out, and sewn together, all in a single day.

23rd: **Anniversary of the Death of King Chulalongkorn** (1910). Various ceremonies are held in front of Chulalongkorn's statue opposite the former National Assembly in Bangkok.

October-November

Loy Krathong (Festival of Lights) falls on the night of the full moon of the twelfth lunar month. This charming festival is among the most spectacular of the Thai year. Throughout the kingdom, thousands of lotus-shaped floats, made of banana leaves and papier mâché and covered with flowers, incense, and lighted candles, are pushed out on the rivers and *klongs* (canals). There is singing and dancing in the towns and villages around the country. The ceremony is particularly beautiful in Sukhothai.

The Chedi Phra Pathom Fair, around the same time, is the occasion for thousands to converge on the **Chedi of Nakhon Pathom** (35 mi/56 km west of Bangkok) to pay homage to the Buddha's relics. A huge fair is held on the site.

November
The Elephant Round-up takes place at Surin (Eastern Thailand). Over 200 elephants parade, reconstruct famous battle scenes, and put on a spectacular show.

December
5th: **King Bhumibol's birthday** is celebrated with great fervour by the entire population of Thailand. Huge ceremonies are held at the Palace and at the Temple of the Emerald Buddha.

Other holidays
Festivals of the minority groups (Chinese, Malays, Indians, etc.) are also worth investigating. Other important dates are United Nations Day, Labour Day, Children's Day, Teachers' Day.... The Thais do not hesitate to shift a holiday that happens to fall on a weekend to the following Monday, and they have even adopted certain Western holidays such as Christmas and New Year.

There are also numerous regional festivals, both lay and religious. These include boat races at Pimai and Nakhon Phanom (Oct.); a cotton fair, with its own elected queen, at Loei (Feb.); the feast of **King Narai** at Lopburi (mid-Feb.); and the buffalo races at Chonburi (mid-Oct.). Check with tourist offices or in newspapers for more information.

FOOD AND DRINK

Food
Thai cooking tends toward extremes, with highly spiced dishes and very sweet desserts. Well-prepared Thai food can be exquisite, the general tone set by a small selection of herbs and spices which are found in most main dishes, such as coriander leaves, coriander root crushed with garlic and pepper, ginger, lemon grass, basil, mint, cardamom, curry spices, and hot peppers. If you come across a piece of red pepper on your plate, be careful: it may be a *prik lueng,* the hottest pepper known to Thai cuisine.

A Thai meal will usually consist of rice accompanied by three to five dishes (beef, pork, chicken, fish, soup). Pickled fish (*nam plaa* in Thai) and shrimp paste are frequently used to strengthen seasonings.

The Thais have adopted certain features of Chinese cooking, and there are distinct echoes of India and Indonesia in some dishes. Perhaps the most popular dish is a local version of Cantonese rice, known as *khao phat:* fried rice with pieces of beef, crab, pork, onions, and eggs. Alone, *khao phat* can make an economical meal (10 ฿-20 ฿).

In restaurants that cater to tourists, menus are written in Latin characters (phonetically transcribed) and explained in English. Prices are generally listed: add between 10% and 15% extra for service. In the case of seafood, prices sometimes refer to the entire fish, rather than individual portions — to be sure, ask the waiter. We recommend that you try as many different dishes as possible; you will seldom be disappointed. A few suggestions:

Lab pladouk yang: catfish smoked with Thai herbs.

Thot man pla: fish deep-fried in butter.

Tom yam koung: prawn soup flavoured with lemon grass; it's the 'Thai national soup', delicious and very spicy.

Kai op saparot: chicken cooked with pineapple chunks and served in a hollowed-out pineapple, excellent.

Neua yang kaoli: slices of marinated beef, cooked at the table.

Ho mok pla tchon: fish flavoured with curry paste and steamed in banana leaves.

The Thais drink a number of sweet concoctions derived from coconut. When reduced to paste, these are charmingly presented in banana-leaf wrappings held in place with toothpick-sized sticks. In general,

Some Thai recipes

You may want to try your hand at a few Thai recipes when you get home. The following are among the most popular (proportions are for four servings).

Sticky Rice

Sticky rice is a special non-irrigated variety of rice common in Northern Thailand and Laos and should be used if possible to accompany Thai dishes. Although not widely available in the West, any large, well-stocked Oriental grocery store should carry it.

Ingredients: 1 cup/200 g sticky rice.

Soak the rice in cold water overnight. The next day, drain the rice, steam it for 30 minutes and serve.

Stuffed Chicken Wings

This dish requires considerable patience and a delicate touch. The result is exquisite.

Ingredients: 8 chicken wings; 2 tbsp each of: crabmeat, dried, black Chinese mushrooms, tinned water chestnuts, soybean vermicelli, *nam plaa* (*nuoc mam* fish sauce), sweet and sour *(hoi sin)* sauce, and flour; 1/4 cup/50 g cooked pork; salt and pepper to taste.

Debone the meaty part of the wings but leave the wingtips on (they are very important for the presentation of the dish). Prepare the stuffing by mixing all the other ingredients in a food processor or heavy-duty blender. Stuff the wings and sew up the ends with kitchen string. Roll in flour, patting off any excess, and fry in very hot oil for ten minutes. Serve very hot.

Steamed Fish

Any fish with firm, white flesh may be prepared in this way. Traditionally, the fish is cooked in fresh banana leaves but aluminum foil may also be used.

Ingredients: 1 lb/500 g boneless fish fillets; 4 tbsp coconut milk; 2 tsp coconut oil (or peanut oil); 1 tsp finely chopped lemon grass; 2 tsp *nam plaa* (*nuoc mam* fish sauce); 2 clove finely chopped garlic; 1 finely chopped hot pepper; 1 diced sweet red pepper; salt and pepper to taste.

Set aside the fish and sweet red pepper. Make a sauce by mixing together all of the other ingredients. Salt and pepper the fish and place one fillet on each of four pieces of leaf or foil. Spread the sauce over the fish, decorate with the diced sweet pepper, then close and seal (if using banana leaves, tie closed with string). Steam for ten minutes and serve (each guest should open the leaf or foil at the table).

Stuffed Pineapple

In this recipe one may use only prawns (shrimp) or pork, if preferred, rather than a mixture of the two. In this case double the measurement of whichever one you are using.

Ingredients: 4 small, ripe pineapples; 1/2 lb/250 g shelled prawns (shrimp); 1/2 lb/250 g diced pork; 3 finely chopped shallots; 1/3 cup/65 g chopped peanuts mixed with a few chopped cashew nuts; 2 tbsp raspberry or wine vinegar; 2 tbsp *nam plaa* (*nuoc mam* fish sauce); fresh mint leaves; salt and pepper to taste.

Stir fry prawns and pork until brown and set aside to cool. Cut the pineapples in half lengthwise. Remove the flesh, dice it, and mix it with all of the other ingredients except for the mint leaves. Stuff half of each hollowed-out pineapple with the mixture, decorate with the mint leaves, then place the other half on top as a cover. Chill until ready to serve.

Coconut flan

This is very light and easy to make.

Ingredients: 2 cups/1/2 l coconut milk; 4 medium eggs; 1 1/4 cups/250 g granulated sugar; 2 tsp taro flour (or cornstarch).

Mix all the ingredients well, pour into a square, low-sided cake pan and bake in a moderate 350 ºF/180 ºC oven for 30 minutes or until set. Allow to cool, cut into squares, and serve.

Street kitchens delight the eye.

however, the sweet Thai desserts are less varied in taste than the main dishes, a characteristic shared with Indian cooking. The lichee mousses, coconut milk flans, and multi-coloured jellies are pleasant but simple.

On the other hand, if you like tropical fruits, Thailand is the place for you. It offers mangos, mangosteens (like small, dark brown apples with red flesh that melts deliciously in the mouth), pineapples, papayas, pomelos (a variety of grapefruit), Chinese oranges, guavas, lichees, *longans* (excellent), *jambuls* (Javanese plums), *chomphu* (which smell like roses), etc. Another curious object you will find in markets at certain seasons is the *durian*, which can grow as large as a human head and is covered with prickly spines. The Thais love *durians* and are willing to pay dearly for them; a good quality fruit may cost 300 ฿, and some of the rarer types are worth anything up to 700 ฿. This represents a considerable investment, given that 2 lb/1 kg of tangerines or grapefruit cost as little as 10 ฿ to 25 ฿ and an average Thai schoolteacher's salary is about 3000 ฿ monthly. Many Westerners are repulsed by the *durian's* strong odour and refuse to taste it.

'Western-style cooking' in Thailand is full of good intentions but is generally unappetizing (exceptions are noted in the restaurant lists provided in the relevant chapters). In Bangkok, however, there is a good selection of other Asian cuisines offered in Chinese, Japanese, Korean, Indonesian, and Indian restaurants.

Drink

American drinks like Pepsi and 7-Up are the rule everywhere except in the remote areas of the country. The fruit juices sold on the street (mainly lime and pineapple) are delicious but it is possible that the water used may not have been filtered. Local beer is excellent and costs 50 ฿ to 90 ฿ a bottle, a small fortune compared to the price of a Pepsi, which may be had for 15 ฿ to 20 ฿. There is also bottled mineral water (Polaris) and soda water. Tea is not a particularly Thai drink but it is often served as a matter of course in Chinese restaurants.

If you're partial to strong liquor, order a glass of Mekhong brand rice whiskey just for the experience. It costs the same as a beer. Some Westerners maintain that the water of the Mekong River is better suited for human consumption than this formidable local whiskey — others disagree.

Hotels serve relatively weak coffee that will not satisfy the thirst of a lover of strong coffee. When you ask for coffee in local restaurants, they will bring you one-third sweetened concentrated milk in two-thirds coffee. If you want straight black coffee (*dam* coffee), the milk will be automatically replaced by sugar, in the same proportions.

You are strongly advised not to drink tap-water or use it to brush your teeth. Mineral water and bottled drinks are plentiful throughout the country.

▬ LANGUAGE

While most Thais speak only Thai, the hotel staff usually have a more or less adequate command of English. You should, however, be careful about this; Thais will often pretend they understand what you're saying out of deference, in order not to disappoint you. You will also find Bangkok full of young volunteer interpreters who can speak a bit of English picked up in school or around American GIs.

Reading can present a further difficulty. Latin characters are sometimes used for street names and shop signs in large towns, and for menus in restaurants frequented by tourists. The rest of the time, gestures, drawings and smiles are the only means of communication. The Thais are rarely put out by the language barrier and always manage to ask how old you are, whether you are married, how many children you have and how much you paid for your watch.

If you want to try to speak the native tongue, the TAT warning should be heeded: 'Naturally, it is an advantage to speak Thai, but be careful about intonations because these can cause highly embarrassing misunderstandings. For example, if you pronounce badly, you may set out to compliment a woman and find you have unintentionally called her a prostitute. If in doubt, abstain.'

▬ METRIC SYSTEM AND ELECTRICITY

Thailand uses the metric system. Some useful conversions: 15 °C = 59 °F, 25 °C = 77 °F, 40 °C = 104 °F; 100 km = 62 mi; 1 l = approx. 1 US quart or 1.8 British pint and 1 kg = approx. 2 lb.

The electrical current works at 220 volts 50 Hz. Most often sockets take American-style flat-pinned plugs but the European round-pin type is also encountered. Adapters and transformers are readily available in the large hotels of the major cities, but if traveling in the provinces it would be wise not to have to rely on electrical appliances: in some areas there are no electrical outlets.

▬ ORGANIZING YOUR TIME

You can either limit yourself to exploring one or two areas in depth, or you can try to visit as much of the country as possible.

The three main tourist zones are:
Bangkok and its surroundings (including Pattaya and the Kwai River).
Chiang Mai and the Golden Triangle (in the north).
Phuket and the coastal beaches (in the south).

The east and north-east of the country have less to offer (apart from Khmer archaeological sites) and are not completely safe.

If you look at the map, you will see that these three poles of attraction are far apart, and that you will have to go through Bangkok in order to reach Phuket from Chiang Mai. Should you wish to visit both the northern ethnic areas and the southern beaches, you might want to make at least one plane trip. Be warned, however, that you can lose a full day getting to and from the airports and waiting for connecting flights.

A two-week trip

Day 1: Departure from North America or Europe.
Day 2: Arrival in Bangkok. Get some rest.
Day 3: Visit Bangkok.
Day 4: Bangkok/Sukhothai (access: see 'Exploring the fallen cities' p. 129).
Day 5: Tour Sukhothai.
Day 6: Sukhothai/Chiang Mai, by road.
Days 7 & 8: Chiang Mai and surrounding area.
Day 9: Chiang Mai/Bangkok by air (preferably a morning flight to ensure a full afternoon in Bangkok).
Day 10: Bangkok/Phuket by air (early in the morning).
Days 11 & 12: Relax in Phuket.
Day 13: Phuket/Bangkok by air (in the morning). Afternoon in Bangkok.
Day 14: Departure from Bangkok.
Day 15: Arrival home.

If your trip cannot be extended beyond two weeks, you may wish to miss out on part of our suggested itinerary in order to visit another part of Thailand which particularly interests you such as Ayutthaya, Lopburi, the Kwai River, Ko Samui, Pattaya, or Chiang Rai. Two weeks — more precisely 12 days — in Thailand is very little, and there's no possibility of seeing everything in that time.

You may be tempted to spend an extra day in Bangkok before you head off into the countryside, but Bangkok is not an easy city for Westerners who need time before they can adapt to it. Your best course is to get away as soon as possible and explore a less stressful Thailand first. After a few days in the Thai provinces, the capital will seem a great deal less threatening.

We suggest that you end your stay at Phuket; in which case you will arrive home tanned and rested. It's up to you, however, to work out your itinerary according to your priorities. Even if you spend a full month in Thailand, you will have to make hard choices. Local travel agencies will help you in such matters as hiring chauffeur-driven cars. You can also seek the advice of the TAT offices.

POST OFFICE AND TELECOMMUNICATIONS

Post Office

The postal system in Thailand is generally efficient. The post offices in most cities are open from 8am to 4:30pm Mon. to Fri. with the exception of the Bangkok General Post Office in New Road which is open from 8am to 8pm. In Bangkok and the larger cities they are also open from 9am to 1pm on Sat.

You can have mail sent either to your hotel or to the Post Restante, General Post Office, New Rd., Bangkok 10100. Remember, Thais write their last name first. In order to avoid confusion in their filing of letters, ask correspondents to print your last name clearly in capital letters. If a letter isn't found under your last name, have the postal official check your first name.

The easiest way to mail letters is to leave them at your hotel desk. If you have the correct stamps to put on them they can also be dropped into one of the many bright red boxes. Allow five days to a week for letters to reach Europe or the US.

Telecommunications

Thai telecommunications have made remarkable progress in recent years. It is now easy to call overseas from Bangkok and Chiang Mai. Toll-free phone booths are even provided for airline passengers in the duty-free zone of the Bangkok airport.

Public phone booths are red and take 1 ฿ coins, the cost of a three-minute local call. Make sure you use a 1 ฿ coin of the correct size, however, because there are three types in circulation. A call to the provinces will cost a minimum of 5 ฿ for three minutes.

To make an international call, dial 100; if you need assistance in making your call, dial 13.

The General Post Office provides 24-hour telegraph and telex services as do most of the major hotels.

▬ PRESS

There are three major English language newspapers published in Thailand: the *Bangkok Post* (morning), the *Nation* (morning), and the *Bangkok World* (evening). Take time to look at these papers. You'll find they contain interesting information on local, economic, and political topics. *Where*, an English-language weekly, is published by the TAT office and distributed to hotels free of charge. It provides general tourist information, along with shop and restaurant addresses. All of these publications are available in Bangkok and Chiang Mai, as is *The International Herald Tribune*. For a guide to the boisterous nightlife in Bangkok, pick up the free bi-monthly *Bangkok after Dark*.

▬ SAFETY PRECAUTIONS

General advice

If you read the English-language newspapers in Thailand, you may well be surprised by the violence they report. There is political conflict (battles between armed rebels and government troops) as well as organized and individual crime. The latter phenomenon is not confined to Bangkok; trouble can arise just as easily in country villages or small towns.

You should always be alert and take basic precautions. Don't carry too much money about with you. Don't carry precious articles (passport, airline ticket, money) in a handbag which can be stolen or forgotten. Don't wear conspicuous clothes or travel with expensive luggage. Deposit your valuables in a hotel safe and be sure to ask for a receipt. Never go alone into isolated areas. Avoid arguments and the company of Mekhong drinkers who have an unpleasant tendency to lose control of themselves after their first bottle.

Drugs

Thais take the subject of drugs extremely seriously and offenders can be immediately imprisoned. Your consulate will not be able to intervene. Never take letters or packages, however harmless-looking, on behalf of people you may meet in Thailand and, when you fly home, try to keep your bags under constant surveillance.

Unsafe areas

You are strongly advised to heed any warnings the Thai authorities may see fit to issue and to keep a close watch on events reported by the press. Keep away from demonstrations in Bangkok as they can suddenly become violent.

Provisionally, the zones to avoid are the following:

In the east — the area between Buri Ram and the Kampuchean frontier.

In the north — isolated villages within the Golden Triangle and along the Mekong. Never venture into this area without a guide.

In the south — avoid traveling by road at night. Pattani, Narathiwat, Yala, and Satun are reputed to be unsafe areas.

Flower garlands sold in the markets are used as offerings in temples.

SHOPPING

You would have to be a most unusual tourist to return from a trip to Thailand empty-handed. All kinds of objects — be they frivolous, useful, or precious — are available here. A wide range of inexpensive souvenirs is also available such as fabrics, jewelry, basketware, ties, pottery, lacquerware, silk-screen paintings, opium weights, wooden statuettes, musical instruments, orchids, masks, straw hats, betel boxes, fighting fish, shadow theatre marionnettes, etc. Although all these things may be found in Bangkok, Chiang Mai is unquestionably Thailand's shopping capital; everything is concentrated in a smaller area, the choice is as great as in Bangkok, and prices are generally lower.

Bargaining

The act of making a purchase in Thailand should be properly relished. It is perfectly normal, even respectable, to discuss the price of an object, and the tourist should engage in the bargaining ritual with tact and perspicacity.

There is nothing harder than to determine the right price; lacking other guidelines, the only remaining criterion is your desire to possess it. Hence the temptation to say 'I'll take it', regardless of price. Do not give in to this urge and you will be rewarded: not only will you pay less, but the very act of buying the object will provide you with an invaluable experience and the respect of the seller. Always establish a framework for the negotiation. Should the initial asking price be divided by two, three, or four? Bear in mind that the standard of living of the average Thai bears no relation whatever to that of the average tourist; a qualified Thai teacher earns about 3000 ฿ per month, and a university professor between 3800 ฿ and 4000 ฿. Remembering this will help you keep a cool head when bargaining. On the other hand, do not suppose that a fine antique can be had for a handful of rice.

You will often be pitted against local dealers with long experience in trading with tourists. Don't be discouraged; strategy is all-important. One of the elementary laws in the art of bargaining is that of showing no special interest in the particular object you are after. It's even advisable to open the proceedings by discussing an article which you are not remotely interested in buying. This approach will enable you to gauge how far your dealer is prepared to lower the asking prices. No good bargain was ever made in haste; so do not hesitate to give full rein to the competition. Some luxury boutiques may refuse to bargain, though you should always try, but in the markets, street stalls and even in middle category hotels, haggling is standard practice.

You can learn a lot about prices by discreetly observing the Thais in action. You will discover that if you offer the same price as the Thais with enough authority, no one will dare to charge you 'tourist prices'.

What to buy?

Antiques

There is no shortage of genuine antiques in Thailand. Bronzes of the Dvaravati period (6th-11th centuries) are fairly common, small and easily transported. There are also countless Buddha statuettes in brass, wood, and stone along with Buddha hands, copperware, Chinese and Thai porcelain, opium pipes and scales, ivories, paintings, and miscellaneous cult objects.

It is advisable, however, to avoid buying Thai antiques unless you have studied Thai art in some depth (a visit to the Bangkok National Museum or to an antique store such as the House of Siam, 8 North Sathorn Rd. might be helpful). Most of the wooden statues on sale date from the 19th century, earlier pieces having been destroyed or placed in museums. In Chiang Mai, there are factories that specialize in the mass production of 'antiques'. These articles are often just as beautiful as the originals.

In Thailand, the antique market is dominated by Burmese pieces smuggled in from the north. There is no antique trade within Burma, where the government forbids the export of religious objects.

You will need special authorization from the Thai Fine Arts Department to take out of Thailand certain antiques or works of art, notably Buddha statuettes. Without it, your purchases will be mercilessly confiscated at customs. Information on how to obtain an authorization is available at the Bangkok National Museum (Tel: 224 1370, 224 1402). Do not trust the advice of dealers; they have been known to report their clients to the customs authorities, then recover the object in question for subsequent resale.

Brass
Brass has been used for several centuries in Thailand as a material for making Buddhas, religious objects, and bowls. More recently, techniques have been modernized for the production of functional and decorative objects including plates, salad bowls, and cutlery. The cutlery may be made entirely of metal, or have rosewood, ivory, or buffalo-horn handles. In principle, Thai brass cutlery is treated to prevent blackening when in contact with food, but the process is by no means perfect and cutlery of this type may require frequent cleaning.

Celadon
The ancient and complex process of glazing pottery was widely practiced during the Sukhothai period. The art has been revived in the Chiang Mai area and is used today in the manufacture of lamps, crockery, vases, and ashtrays. A distinctive characteristic of celadon is its delicate green-jade patina.

Fabrics
Silk: Thai silk is hand-woven, with a texture so fine that it is scarcely visible to the naked eye. Plain-coloured and cameo silks come in the richest Indian fabrics, made of a material so sleek that it seems almost phosphorescent. Silks cost between 200 ฿ and 350 ฿ per yard/90 cm depending on thickness and quality. It can have up to three wefts. If it is to preserve its glistening veneer, silk must be washed in warm water (or dry-cleaned) and ironed on its reverse side only.

Silk ties, scarves, cushion covers, and clothes may also be purchased. It is advisable to have clothing made to measure, because ready-made clothes are not always very well cut. Most shops that sell fabrics will also make clothes or you can try one of Bangkok's innumerable tailors. They are often less expensive than the stores because their prices are negotiable.

If you bring your pattern with you, you can have your garment made with great accuracy and speed (between one and four days). You will find the work to be of very good quality; prices vary between 100 ฿ and 300 ฿ for a shirt or a short dress. Thai traders are also prepared to sell clothes by lots.

Cotton: Handwoven cotton is used for a variety of objects such as table cloths, cushions or patchwork stuffed animals in the form of turtles, crocodiles or elephants. Indonesian batik, which is hand-printed by a wax process, is sold in some Bangkok stores, though the best selection may be had at Hat Yai in Southern Thailand. In Chiang Mai, designers outdo each other in the creation of clothing and accessories using embroidery patterns from the Meo, Yao, Akha or Lisu hilltribes.

Jewelry
Precious stones: Sapphires, rubies, topazes, emeralds, and blue and white zircons are plentiful. These stones can be bought cut or uncut, mounted or by unit. You are unlikely to find fabulous bargains for gems unless you are a connoisseur. The guarantees of authenticity have absolutely no legal value. The main centre for precious stones is Chanthaburi, about 125 mi/200 km from Bangkok.

Silver: Silver objects are skillfully worked by Thai craftsmen, though visitors may prefer uncut jewelry such as the Meo women wear. You will also find rings, bracelets, pendants, belts, and tea services at reasonable prices. Jewelry, like clothes, can be made to order. Antique pieces, especially those from minority groups of Northern Thailand, are often of very high quality, though with prices to match.

Lacquerware
Lacquerware, one of Thailand's oldest crafts, still flourishes in the Chiang

Mai area. Boxes, bowls, glass coasters, and even plates are lacquered, with gold-leaf appliqués on a black background. A new technique, using eggshells, has been revived.

Teak
This dense, warm-toned wood which goes with virtually any style, is used for making salad bowls, hors d'œuvre dishes, cutlery, plates, and boxes of all sizes. Thai craftsmen will even make furniture from photographs or drawings and send it to you in meticulous packing. Prices are reasonable.

Wickerwork
Thai furniture is a harmonious marriage between bamboo and rattan and can make a room look thoroughly original. The only problem is getting it all home. Shops will often arrange for transport, but offer no guarantee of arrival. Wickerwork should be bought in street markets, where it may be had for rock-bottom prices.

The list of worthwhile buys given above is far from exhaustive. There are also theatre masks, dolls, orchids, miniature *samlors*, kites, *tak-raws* (wicker balls used for a game that bears a slight resemblance to soccer), and pirated copies of Western products (e.g., shirts bearing the crocodile insignia, leatherwork). In short, there is good shopping for the tourist in Thailand.

TIME

Thailand Standard Time is 7 hours ahead of Greenwich Mean Time (GMT plus 7). Time differences are: 7 hours ahead of London, 12 hours ahead of New York, 15 hours ahead of Los Angeles, and 3 hours behind Sydney.

TIPPING

The practice of tipping in Thailand is fairly recent and by no means systematic. Most hotels and restaurants add a 10% service charge and any extra tip is entirely optional. You can always show your satisfaction by distributing tips to waiters, porters, hairdressers, guides, etc., but if you do, remember to give roughly what you would at home. A tip of 1 or 2 ฿ will be viewed as an affront.

In the provinces and anywhere outside the main tourist areas, tips are practically unknown and are often perceived as humiliating.

TOILETS

There are no public toilets in Bangkok. In an emergency, go into a restaurant, cinema, or shop: everyone will understand. Thai toilets generally do not have running water (they operate by the bucket system). The words to use are *Hong Nam* for bathroom and *Suam* (pronounced *Soo-um*) for WC. People generally ask for the *Hong Nam*. It will be immediately understood that your purpose is not to take a bath.

TOURIST INFORMATION

The TAT is indispensable. It provides information of all kinds and publishes useful maps and documents (the best maps are provided at Shell and Esso gas stations). TAT is not a travel agency and does not organize tours.

Bangkok 4 Rajdamnern Nok Ave. Tel: (02) 282 1143-7 or 282 0073. The office is close to a boxing stadium on the broad avenue leading from Wat Phra Keo to the National Assembly building. To make it easier for people to find their way around, the main axes of Bangkok are often divided into sectors: *Nok* (outer), *klang* (central) and *nay* (inner).

Chiang Mai 135 Praisani Rd. Tel: (053) 235.334.

Hat Yai 190/6 Nipat Uthit Rd. Tel: (074) 245.986.

Earthenware jars, of Chinese origin, are used for holding drinking water.

Kanchanaburi Saengchoto Rd. Tel: (034) 511 200.
Nakhon Ratchasima (Korat) 2102/2104 Mittaparb Rd. Tel: (044) 243 427.
Pattaya Chai Hat Rd. Tel: (038) 418 750 or 419 113.
Phuket 73-75 Phuket Rd. Tel: (076) 212 213 or 211 036.
Phitsanulok 209/7-8 Surasi Trade Center, Boromtrailokarat Rd. Tel: (055) 252 742.
Surat Thani 5 Talat Mai Rd. Tel: (077) 282 828.
Songkhla 1/1 Soi 2 Niphat Uthit Rd. Tel: (174) 243 747.

TAT offices are open weekdays from 8:30am to 4:30pm. and on Sat., Sun., and holidays from 8:30am to 1pm. The TAT is licensed to deliver visa extensions on Sun. and holidays.

TRANSPORTATION

Plane

If your time is limited, you should use the domestic airline, Thai Airways, to get around the country — don't forget that Thailand stretches over 1250 mi/2000 km from north to south.

Thai Airways office hours are: 8:30am-4:30pm Mon. to Fri.; 9am-noon and 1pm-4:30pm Sat., Sun., and holidays. Flights are scheduled several times a day from Bangkok to all the major cities of Thailand.

North: Phitsanulok, Phrae, Nan, Lampang, Chiang Mai, Chiang Rai, Mae Hong Son.
North-east: Kon Kaen, Udon, Loei, Ubon, Nakhon Phanom.
South: Phuket, Trang, Hat Yai, Pattani, Surat Thani, Nakhon Si Thammarat, Penang.

Thai Airways, 6 Larn Luang Rd., Bangkok 2. Tel: (02) 280 0090 or 280 0070 Mon. to Fri.; 281 1737 or 281 1989 Sat., Sun., and holidays. A new airline, Bangkok Airways, will soon offer direct flights to Ko Samui. Inquire at tourist offices for information.

Train

The Thai rail network serves four regions:
North — to Chiang Mai.
North-east — Korat and Nong Kai, on the Laotian frontier.
East — Ubon Ratchathani and the Kampuchean frontier.
South — Songkhla, Malaysia, and Singapore.

The trains are comfortable, relatively fast, and punctual (a fact worthy of note in a country where precision is by no means a dominant feature). Rail transportation is considerably more expensive than the bus but has the advantage of being relatively unaffected by bad weather. During the monsoon, roads are frequently flooded.

If you are thinking of taking a long rail trip, you should reserve your seat in advance. There are three classes on Thai trains. First class is air-conditioned, as is second class on some express trains. For night travel, there are sleeping cars and comfortable berths, even in second class. In addition to the major train routes, there are many branch lines which will bring you closer to a more traditional Thailand. The food on Thai trains is undistinguished.

Bangkok has two mainline stations: Bangkok (Hualampong) and Thonburi (Bangkok Noi), on the other side of the river. For all information on schedules and reservations, inquire at the State Railway, Hualampong (on the corner of Rama IV Rd. and Rong Muang Rd.). Tel: (02) 223 7010 or 223 7020, from 5am to 10pm.

Bus

Thai bus drivers like to extract every ounce of speed from their machines. On long trips, they can clock 65 mi/100 km per hour, stops included, which is quite a performance. From time to time the driver will let go of his steering wheel and join his hands at his forehead in a salute to a roadside Buddhist shrine. If you still want to give it a try, you will be rewarded by the congenial atmosphere which prevails aboard.

For long journeys, opt for deluxe coaches with individual seats and air-conditioning; the three-person benches on the local buses are cramped.

Bangkok has three main bus stations:
North (and north-east) Station — Talat Mo Chit, Pahol Yothin Rd. Tel: 279 4484-7.
South Station — Khonsong Sa Tai, Charan Sanitwong Rd. Tel: 411 0511 and 411 0112 (for ordinary buses) and 411 4978-9 (for air-conditioned buses).
East Coast Station — Ekamai, Kukhumvit Rd. Tel: 392 2521 or 396 2504.

There is a fourth bus station with air-conditioned buses only, traveling to all destinations:
Air Coach City Terminal, Pahol Yothin Rd. Tel: 279 4484-7.

In the country, you will find mini-buses (or maxi-taxis) known as *song-teos* (which means two bench). These are Japanese pickup trucks with two benches fixed lengthwise behind the cab. They are easy to get in and out of (except for those carrying three cages full of chickens). *Song-teos* are used for short hauls (from town to village) and stop on request anywhere along their route. Fares are very inexpensive.

Boat

Thailand boasts many thousands of miles of waterways. You can go practically anywhere in the country by boat, even to the Bangkok airport. If you opt for this means of transportation, you will rediscover the natural rhythm of traditional Thailand, all too often masked by the surface bustle of the cities. Markets, temples, villages, and schools are all on the banks of rivers or *klongs* (canals). Motorboats and *hang yaos* (literally long-tail boats) are not romantic but are efficient. The *hang yao* is powered by a noisy, polluting truck or motorcycle engine to which is attached a long shaft that serves both as a rudder and as a throttle. Hence its name.

In Bangkok alone there are no less than 22 regular boat and ferry services offering trips for tourists. All are listed in an excellent guide *By Boat Through the Canals and Rivers of Thailand* (Vol. 1), by Véran. Volume 2 lists itineraries outside Bangkok. For a few baht, this guide will show you how to reach the Christian quarter of Thonburi, the floating markets of Bangkok, the temples of old Thailand, and a surprising 'torture museum'. It also lists many floating markets, gardens of orchids, the birthplace of the 'Siamese twins' who gave their name to the well-known birth anomaly, and many other curious facts and places. The guide may be purchased at the Duang Kamol Co. Ltd., a large bookshop on Siam Square, Soi 4, Rama 1, Bangkok. Tel: 251 6335-6 or 250 1262.

Samlor: pedal and motor power

Samlor is a generic term meaning 'three wheels' and used to designate any three-wheeled vehicle, whether it runs on human effort or gasoline. It has the singular characteristic of always being there before you even hail it. In the country, the *samlor*, with its owner dozing comfortably on the back seat, is an integral part of the scenery around markets and stations.

The *samlor* provides Thailand's cheapest luxury — a permanently available, omnipresent chauffeur. The Thais use them to take the children to school, bring back groceries from the market, transport furniture, etc. For the tourist, they are invaluable. Upon arrival in a strange town, *samlor* chauffeurs can help you find a hotel, a restaurant, or a souvenir shop and they invariably know all the places that will interest tourists. The fare, which is negotiable, will probably be double or triple what the Thais pay but you should be quite happy with the transaction: you will have been spared a tedious waste of time searching for your destination.

The original *samlor*, now disappearing, is none other than the legendary rickshaw: a chair on wheels drawn by a bicycle. One or two passengers may be seated behind, depending on their weight; there is also a sunshade and — luxury of luxuries — a plastic curtain which can be rigged up in the event of a downpour. You can admire the allegorical figures which adorn the *samlor's* coachwork. Common sense dictates getting out of the *samlor* on steep hills; though you may risk offending your driver, the consequences of a torn muscle or tendon would be disastrous for him.

The motorized *samlor* appeared in the 1960s. The chair is drawn by a motorcycle and the decorative motif has been expanded to include more abundant religious imagery. The only people who regret the disappearance of the traditional, non-polluting *samlors* are those who have never had to pedal up a hill with a fat tourist in the back seat.

Bangkok, always in the forefront of Thai progress, has produced yet another type of *samlor*, known as a *tuk-tuk*, this time based on the scooter. (More details about the *tuk-tuk* are given on page 83.)

Car

Car rental

You are not advised to rent a car and drive it yourself in Thailand, for several reasons. Signs are written in Thai characters. Thais in general treat the highway code with minimum respect, and few have insurance. In the event of an accident, the foreigner is usually held responsible and may end up in prison.

Kite-flying contests are held every year during the dry season.

If you're willing to run the risk, you can contact one of the car rental companies on Wireless Road, or a multinational firm like Avis (Tel: 230 397), Hertz (Tel: 256 251) or Inter Car Rent (Tel: 259 223).

In order to rent a car in Thailand, you must have an international driving license. The price of renting a car varies from 450 ฿ to 600 ฿ per day, running costs included, if you travel an average of 65 mi/100 km per day. Air-conditioned cars are 30% more expensive and a down payment of 1000 ฿ to 2000 ฿ is always requested. Third-party insurance, a great deal too expensive for the majority of drivers, is not obligatory.

The Thais drive on the left side of the road. The main roads (which lead either to frontiers or to military bases) are broad and well-maintained. The secondary roads, however, leave much to be desired, especially during the rainy season.

Transportation 37

Hiring a driver

All things considered, it is best to entrust yourself to the care of a Thai driver. Even though you may find his method of driving questionable, he will know all the pitfalls and how to avoid them. All car rental agencies offer this alternative, at a price between 1800 ฿ and 2000 ฿ per day.

Motorcycles

Motorcycle rental is much less common than car rental in Thailand, and is essentially confined to holiday resorts (like Pattaya, Ko Samui, or Phuket) and other tourist centres. It is carried out on a makeshift basis: the vehicles are seldom properly maintained and the user is almost never insured. In short, renting a motorcycle is as risky as renting a car — with added discomfort in the rain.

THAILAND IN THE PAST

LAND OF FREE MEN

In 1939, the kingdom of Siam officially took the name of Muang Thai or 'Land of Free Men', the name by which the Thais refer to their own country. This change of name occurred seven years after the substitution of a parliamentary monarchy for an absolute one and, indeed, the new title was appropriate; all of the country's neighbours had long before succumbed to foreign domination. One of the most distinctive traits of the former kingdom's history had been its careful preservation of its own independence in a part of the world much coveted by the colonial powers of Europe. The British colonized Burma and Malaysia, the French took Laos, Kampuchea, and Vietnam, and the Dutch established themselves in Indonesia; there were also foreign concessions in mainland China and the ambitions of Spain and Portugal had to be reckoned with. As far as Siam was concerned, the colonial powers had to be content with one or two pieces of territory which the Thais shrewdly abandoned. In reality, the existence of a buffer state between the British and the French proved highly convenient and both great powers were secretly satisfied with the arrangement.

Very little information is available for the period prior to the annexation of Thailand by the Khmer kings in the 9th century, and the origin of the country's former name, Muang Sayam (or Siam), is unclear. By the time of Marco Polo's voyages at the end of the 13th century, it was already the practice of the Thais to refer to their own country by the name of the capital city.

The most important cities in the history of Thailand are Sukhothai, Ayutthaya, and Bangkok. Bangkok stands for modern Thailand and its hopes for the future. Sukhothai and Ayutthaya represent decisive stages in the development of Thailand's political identity. Nothing is left of them but sombre ruins (290 mi/466 km and 55 mi/86 km north of Bangkok respectively) marking cataclysmic upheavals in the distant past.

SUKHOTHAI

The name Sukhothai stems from the term *Sukha-udaya*, which means 'dawn of felicity'. The kingdom of Sukhothai, founded in 1238, was the first organized state in Thai history. The Thais took advantage of the decline of the Khmer

Empire by wresting away Sukhothai, the Khmers' principal western city, and making it their own capital.

The Thais adopted a wise policy vis-à-vis the Khmers, taking full advantage of Khmer culture while gradually gaining control of their power structures. The Sukhothai era was marked by the spread of Theravâda Buddhism and the emergence of national awareness. According to inscriptions on a 13th-century stele that is now in the Bangkok National Museum, the kingdom became so prosperous that taxation was abolished altogether. At the same time, Sukhothai saw the emergence of the most beautiful and original of the Thai art forms in the country's history (see 'Eight Golden Ages of Thai Art' pp. 50-53).

Under the reign of Rama Khamheng (1277-1317), who 'invented' the Thai script by adapting the Khmer alphabet to Thai words, Sukhothai authority extended as far as Luang Prabang and Viangchan (Vientiane) in Laos and Pegu in Burma. On Rama's death, the Sukhothai kingdom passed to his son, Lo-Thai, a fervently religious and peaceful man who refused to engage in warfare to protect his estates. During his reign, the kingdom was broken up and another city to the south began to grow in power and influence.

AYUTTHAYA

Sukhothai fell like a ripe fruit into the hands of the princes of Ayutthaya, who proclaimed their own kingdom around 1350. They and their followers concentrated their energy on settling old scores with the Khmers and this culminated in the sacking of Angkor, the Kampuchean capital, in 1431. The kings of Ayutthaya assimilated not only the traditions of Sukhothai but also those of the Khmer Empire with its Hindu influences.

The Ayutthaya royal authority began to assume huge proportions when the Hindu concept of the god-king was adopted. The state embraced a centralizing policy, and the first king of Ayutthaya, Ramathibodi, built up a considerable body of constitutional precedents. Boroma Trailokanat, one of his successors, installed political and administrative structures which lasted for hundreds of years, some surviving until the 19th century.

In terms of art and culture, the Ayutthaya period is considered to be a golden age in which architecture, sculpture, painting, and literature gave ample expression to a very powerful and wealthy civilization.

The city of Ayutthaya was extraordinarily large for its time, with between 500,000 and one million inhabitants by the beginning of the 18th century. It was also highly organized and cosmopolitan, with thousands of foreign residents including Portuguese, English, French, and a thriving Japanese colony.

Behind the pomp of Ayutthaya's court, however, lay the shadow of war, incessantly waged by the kingdom against the Khmers and the Burmese. Finally, in 1767 after a two-year siege, Ayutthaya fell to the armies of Burma. The city was sacked and all its treasures were burned.

The Thais have never forgiven the Burmese for the ruthless destruction of their capital and, even today, the Burmese are said to be very unwelcome in Ayutthaya.

Siam and the West

Siam's first contact with Europe was in 1511 when Affonso de Albuquerque of Portugal arrived there after conquering Malacca on the Malaysian peninsula. In return for arms and ammunition to fight the Burmese then invading Siam, King Ramatibodi II allowed the Portuguese to settle and trade within his kingdom.

The wars with Burma continued for the greater part of the 16th century and it was not until 1584 that King Narsuen (Narsuen the Great) definitively re-established Siamese independence. The capital, Ayutthaya, once again began to prosper. At the beginning of the 17th century the Dutch arrived, establishing their first trading station in 1608 at Ayutthaya. That same year King Ekatotsarot (Narsuen's brother) sent emissaries to The Hague, the first Thais to go to Europe.

The English came a few years later, and King James I and the Thai monarch, Prasattong, carried on a cordial correspondence. English visitors described Ayutthaya (referred to as 'Sia') as being 'as great a city as London'. Finally, in 1665, French Jesuit missionaries arrived and Prasattong's son, King Narai, permitted them to establish a mission in Ayutthaya.

France hoped to convert Siam to Catholicism; in 1673 Louis XIV, France's 'Sun King', wrote a letter to Narai, who was flattered. A few years later, France's interests were further aided by the arrival of Constantine Phaulkon, a Greek employee of the East India Company. He learned the Thai language and rose rapidly in the ranks of Thai society, eventually securing the position of advisor to the king and acting as interpreter between the Thai court and the Western countries represented in Thailand.

Phaulkon, who had converted to Roman Catholicism, fell out of favour with the Dutch and the English. Having allied himself with the French, he secretly plotted with the Jesuits to convert the Siamese to Catholicism. Although King Narai did not change his religion, he was persuaded to strengthen his ties with France, send ambassadors to the French court, and allow the French to establish military bases in Siam.

Other high-ranking Siamese officials were growing uneasy about Phaulkon's influence over the king; his great wealth and the lavish banquets he gave made them doubt his motives and the presence of the French soldiers made them fear a military takeover. In the summer of 1688, King Narai fell ill. Anti-French nationalists confined him to his palace and Phaulkon was arrested and executed. The leader of the revolt, Phra Phetracha, seized the throne, ordering the immediate withdrawal of the French troops and of all the other European powers. For the next century and a half Siam was closed to foreigners. It was not until the 19th century that diplomatic relations were re-established between Siam and the West.

BANGKOK

In 1769, two years after the tragic end of Ayutthaya, the Siamese found themselves a new king and a new capital. The capital was Thonburi, opposite modern Bangkok, on the west bank of the Chao Phraya River. The new king, Taksin, consolidated his position by brute force and used his power to reunify the Thai nation, to recover Chiang Mai, Luang Prabang, and Viangchan (Vientiane), and to drive out the Burmese enemy. Little by little, however, Taksin lapsed into a bloodthirsty mystical delirium which was so unsettling to his entourage that he was forced to abdicate and was finally put to death. The execution was carried out with all the honours due to his rank: Taksin was tied up in a silk bag and beaten to death with sandalwood cudgels.

Taksin's successor, General Chao Phya Chakri, was crowned

Temple of the Emerald Buddha.

king in 1782 as Somdetj Phra Bouddha Yot Fa Chulalok Rama I or more simply Rama I. He was the founder of the Chakri dynasty which still reigns in Thailand today. He moved across the river to Bangkok where he established his capital and undertook the construction of temples and palaces in the Ayutthaya style.

The Burmese had been thorough in their work of destruction: the entire national heritage had to be rebuilt and restored, something which took no less than three generations of monarchs, Rama I, Rama II, and Rama III (1782-1851), to achieve. Throughout this period, the Thai rulers were too busy putting the pieces back together to undertake any serious effort at modernization.

It was not until the reign of Mongkut (Rama IV, 1851-1868) that Thailand was fully re-opened to the West and modern influences (see 'Siam and the West' p. 40). Before his accession, Mongkut had spent 27 years in a Buddhist monastery; he was a highly cultured man, passionately interested in astronomy, and successfully predicted the total eclipse of the sun on April 18, 1868. Mongkut was fluent in English and Latin. To enable his children to achieve the same degree of proficiency, he decided to employ an English teacher, Anna Leonowens, who unfairly misrepresented him as a frivolous despot in her autobiography, which later served as the primary source for *The King and I*.

Mongkut was the first Thai monarch to understand the role of Europe, which enabled him to take the necessary measures to avoid the colonization of Thailand. As soon as he became king, he established full diplomatic relations with the European nations and the United States, thereby opening the road to modernization without the risk of a military takeover.

Mongkut's son and successor, Chulalongkorn, reigned for 42 years (1868-1910) and developed Thai policy along similar lines: extension of educational opportunities, abolition of slavery, administrative reform, and road and railway construction. However, in the late 1880s, Chulalongkorn was forced to give up claims in Laos and Western Kampuchea to the French, and territories in the Malay peninsula to the British, in order to maintain Siam's independence.

Despite a wave of liberal reforms, the Thai monarchy remained absolutist. Chulalongkorn and his English-educated sons who succeeded him, Vajiravudh (1910-1925) and Prajadhipok (1925-1932), were all concerned with improving the welfare of their subjects but felt that the Thais were not ready for democracy. Then the Great Depression brought financial instability to Thailand and on June 24, 1932, a coup d'état abolished the absolute monarchy and forced the king to accept a constitution and a parliament. Pridi Phanomyong, the leader of the coup and head of the People's Party, governed the country until 1934 when he was turned out by the army, which considered him too radical. Pibulsongram (Pibul) took his place. He encouraged Western dress and nationalist sentiments and changed the official name of the country from Siam to Muang Thai or Thailand.

Throughout the Second World War, Thailand's government favoured Japan as a counterweight to the colonial powers surrounding the country. Pibul was forced to step down after the defeat of Japan and Pridi, who had led an anti-Japanese resistance movement, once again headed the government. Then, in 1945, following the mysterious assassination of King Ananda Mahidol (Rama VIII), the elder brother of the present king of Thailand, Pridi was ousted. Pibul returned in 1948 to serve for ten years as premier to Bhumibol Adulyadej or King Rama IX.

DEMOCRACY

Between 1932 and 1958, seven coups d'état and six new constitutions served to maintain the military oligarchy's grip on the Thai government. In 1963, Marshal Thanom Kittikachorn became prime minister; his authoritarian style encountered widespread opposition. During the next ten years, Thanom had to face a difficult economic situation exacerbated by the American withdrawal from South-east Asia and aggravated by an organized opposition and the escalation of subversive activities in the provinces. His response was to cut short the process of liberalization by proclaiming a state of martial law in November 1971.

Within a year, students had begun to organize violent demonstrations against Japan, which was accused of ruining the Thai economy. With the support of various prominent liberals, the student movement demanded a new constitution. The king attempted to mediate, but on October 14, 1973, the confrontation between the students and army turned to open violence. The army leaders sent in tanks and helicopters, and the result was bloody: over 350 dead and 1000 wounded.

In 1974, a new constitution was proclaimed by a short-lived civil government headed by Professor Sanya Dharmasakti. After the disorders of that year (strikes, peasant unrest, anti-Japanese riots, and bloody demonstrations in Bangkok), 1975 produced a short respite in the succession of coups. Meanwhile, the American B52s were evacuated from Thai territory, the last GI left Patpong Road on July 20, and the government established diplomatic ties with Beijing in accordance with the new 'bamboo diplomacy'.

In spite of these changes, the overall situation in Thailand was still unsteady and yet another coup took place in October 1976, leading to the suppression of the right to strike and the heavy censorship of books and newspapers. Once again, a new constitution was imposed (the tenth since 1932); this consisted of only 29 articles, as opposed to 200 articles of the 1974 version. A year later, yet another right-wing government came to power but, after several changes of premier, resigned in February 1980 in failure.

The next leader to attempt a solution to Thailand's ills was General Prem Tinsulanond, who placed himself at the head of a coalition government and, with the king's support, just managed to foil a coup mounted by a group of technocratic colonels (the Young Turks) in April 1981. The 28 young officers who led the coup were later pardoned and brought back into the army in September 1986, a conciliatory gesture no doubt encouraged by the recent slowdown of inflation and the euphoria prompted by a strong recovery of the Thai balance of payments.

The fragility of Thai democracy is the result of a deep political malaise within the country. This malaise is aggravated by incessant warfare along the frontiers, and, despite the gradual strengthening of civil power, the army is still determined to keep control of the kingdom's affairs. Although domestic communist subversion has been heavily eroded (12,000 rebels under arms during the 1970s, compared to only 600 today), the threat from Vietnam is still very real. The growth in the number of refugees from that nation, and the failure of the international community to deal with the problem, also contributes to Thai insecurity. The balance of power which is the declared objective of 'bamboo diplomacy' looks like a dangerous exercise when viewed in the light of the Washington-Beijing and Hanoi-Moscow alliances but Thailand possesses a domestic trump card in the person of its king, who knows how to act with discretion vis-à-vis the civil and military powers in the greater national interest.

THE KING

Somdet Phra Chao Yu Hua Bhumibol Adulyadej, otherwise known as Bhumibol or Rama IX, King of Thailand, is ninth in the line of the Chakri dynasty which has ruled the country since 1782. Bhumibol was born in Cambridge, Massachusetts on December 5, 1927. The king has acquired enormous prestige in the eyes of his countrymen, who respect his power but also his humanity and simplicity. You will be told that Bhumibol is an avid photographer, plays several musical instruments, and even composes music (one of his pieces was included in a Broadway revue in 1950). He also figures at the head of Thailand's 'Who's Who' of literature and journalism (noblesse oblige) for the journal he wrote while visiting Switzerland in 1946. Who really knows the innermost personality of this discreet monarch, with his restrained smile and ever-present dark glasses? On the wall of the post office, at the back of the Chinese shop on New Road, and in almost every little house standing on stilts beside the *klongs* (canals) of Thailand, hangs the solemn official portrait of the royal couple. Loved, respected, rarely questioned despite the vicissitudes of political life in contemporary Thailand, His Majesty King Bhumibol is, at once, the best and least known of his people.

Bhumibol came to the throne almost by accident; he was only the king's second nephew, the child of a student at Harvard Medical School. His family returned to Thailand in 1928 and his father died shortly afterwards. The reigning king, who had no direct heir, decided to send his nephews Ananda and Bhumibol to school in Switzerland. In 1935, he abdicated in favour of the elder of the two, Ananda Mahidol, then only ten years old. While a regency council took care of the affairs of the kingdom, Bhumibol attended his Swiss school, *L'École Nouvelle de la Suisse Romande*. Then came the crisis: his elder brother Ananda was found shot dead. This mystery has never been solved.

Giving up his ambition to be an architect, Bhumibol entered Lausanne University to study law. On August 12, 1949, he became engaged to a lovely 17-year-old princess, Mom Rachawong Sirikit Kitiyakara, whom he had met in Paris two years earlier. According to tradition, the future king of Thailand has to light the funeral pyre of his predecessor, after which his own coronation takes place. In Bhumibol's case, the coronation ceremony was deferred by political events, on the recommendations of the court astrologers, and, finally, by an automobile accident outside Lausanne in which Bhumibol was seriously injured. The coronation finally took place on May 5, 1950, shortly after Bhumibol's marriage to Princess Sirikit; on that day, the king

---

The Thai dynasty

Rama I (crowned in 1782) had 41 children.

Rama II (crowned in 1809) had 73 children.

Rama III (crowned in 1824) had 51 children.

Rama IV (crowned in 1851) had 82 children, although he spent 27 years of his life in a monastery.

Rama V (crowned in 1868) had 77 children.

Rama VI (crowned in 1910) married at the age of 40 and had only one child, a girl, born on the eve of his death.

Rama VII (crowned in 1925) inaugurated the custom of monogamy in Thailand and fathered no children.

Rama VIII (crowned at the age of ten in 1935) died unmarried at 21.

Rama IX, the present monarch (crowned in 1950) has four children.

Threatening statues in temples prevent evil spirits from entering.

ascended his octagonal throne and paid solemn homage to the Emerald Buddha. His first message to parliament was a plea to avoid any Thai involvement in the Indochinese conflict then raging.

The moral authority of the king is immense and his portrait is sacred. Constitutionally, he is the head of state and supreme commander of the armed forces; his person is treated with the utmost respect by all his subjects. At Thai cinemas, every show opens with the royal anthem, for which the entire audience stands at attention while the king's portrait is projected on the screen.

The royal couple have four children, Crown Prince Vajiralongkorn and his three sisters, Princesses Ubol Ratand, Maha Chakri Sirindhorn, and Chulabhorn.

RELIGION AND ART: THE BUDDHA IMAGE

The representation of Buddha is one of the constants of Thai sculpture. As the embodiment of the Master among human beings, the Buddha image is invested with supernatural power. Anyone who orders a work representing Buddha acquires merit; by tradition, the artist's function is that of a technician whose personal inspiration is strictly governed by Buddhist canons. 'Measurements other than those laid down by the canons cannot please the sage,' declared the Indian theorist Sukrâcârya in the 5th century; hence it is crucial that artists conform to the *lakshana* (distinguishing marks) as described in the ancient texts. Buddha has 32 primary distinguishing features and 80 secondary ones. Here are a few examples: the hairs of Buddha grow at the rate of one per year; his skin is smooth and delicate; he has 40 teeth; his taste is supremely refined; his voice is like a songbird's, melodic and divine ... clearly, it is no easy task to represent all these qualities in sculpture and painting.

On the other hand, the portraitist has certain precise physical indications at his disposal: Buddha's cranium is prominent, with an *urna* (mark of divinity) on the brow, his heels protrude and his fingers are long. These characteristics are accompanied by particular attitudes *(mudra)* which are also prescribed by the texts. Essentially these are seated, standing, recumbent, and walking.

In Thailand the 'hero' attitude (*virasana,* with the legs folded one on top of the other) tends to be more common than the 'diamond' attitude (*vajrasana:* with the legs crossed, revealing the two plantar arches).

Conventional Buddha attitudes are completed by a whole range of gestures evoking the various stages of Buddha's life. Among these, 40 have been counted in Thai iconography. If you wish to familiarize yourself with this symbolic language, you will find the cloister of the Marble Temple (Wat Benchamabophit) in Bangkok highly instructive because it contains no less than 52 Buddhas covering a wide range of styles and attitudes. Here are some of the more common ones:

Buddha calling the earth to witness his illumination: seated, legs crossed, left hand resting in lap, palm turned upward, right wrist resting on knee, with fingers pointing earthward.
Buddha in meditation: seated, with legs crossed, hands in lap, palms upward.
Buddha preaching his first sermon (turning of the wheel of the law): standing, left arm alongside body (or raised to chest level), and right hand describing the movement of the wheel.
Buddha calming the oceans: standing, both arms at right angles, hands raised, palms turned outward.
Buddha calming family quarrels: standing, left arm alongside body, and right hand raised.
Sleeping Buddha (attainment of Nirvana): recumbent on one side, head resting on right hand, left hand alongside body, and one foot resting on the other.
Buddha practicing asceticism: seated, cross-legged, hands crossed on chest.

Since the artist's mission is sacred, he must detach himself from his model by meditation. He retains nothing that is inessential, and hence his copy is never slavish. However, if he is to understand the subtle balance between innovation and imitation, he must bear in mind the extraordinary supernatural power of the Buddha statue. In this context, imitation constitutes a guarantee that the merits of one statue will be transferred to the next. For this reason, statues are recovered from disused temples, and the Thais are adamantly opposed to the export of their ancient Buddhas.

THE TEMPLES

There are about 26,000 *wats* in Thailand. The term *wat* was once used to define all religious buildings, but today it is mainly applied to monasteries. Like the clergy, the *wats* are taken care of by the population. In every village and city district, the *wat* is the centre of intellectual, social, and religious life. Foreigners never fail to be astonished when they first encounter the village square atmosphere of the *wat* complex, where local children play soccer, women gossip around stalls selling incense, garlands of jasmine, or folded lotus blossoms, and monks while away the hours talking and smoking.

Visitors can enter the temple, provided they take off their shoes. Apart from the flowers and joss sticks, you can buy wafer-thin gold leaf to gild a Buddha statue (equals one merit). Unfortunately, the restoration of an old *wat* bestows less merit than the building of a new one with the result that ugly, modern, standardized temples are springing up all over the country. Older *wats* are gradually disappearing and, with them, the frescos they contain, the artistic quality and original character of which are uniquely Thai in inspiration. For an example of aesthetically pleasing restoration, go to Bangkok's Wat Phra Keo, where scenes from murals depicting the epic *Ramakien* (Indian *Ramayana*) are painstakingly painted by art students who often work as volunteers.

Wat: The *wat* is the ensemble of religious buildings, usually surrounded by a wall and with several entrances. It includes both religious and functional buildings (monks' quarters, the Buddhist school, a pilgrims' resthouse, etc.).

Wats, like villages, should be observed for their day-to-day activities. Children, homeless people, and animals are permitted to circulate freely. In the villages, schools are almost always in the *wat*. It is relatively easy to approach the monks because they do not live in seclusion from the world: young novices especially are often more than willing to talk to foreigners. With a little luck, one of these may offer you his services as a guide. Do not forget to leave some kind of remuneration in the collection box — the monks depend on charity and alms for money.

The *wat* is an ensemble of different structures, each of which has a precise function. The following definitions may help you find your way around:

Bo: The tree beneath which Buddha received his illumination.

Bot: This is the most sacred building of the *wat,* in which the religious ceremonies take place, including the ordination of monks. Its dimensions vary, but it should be capable of housing at least 21 monks, the minimum required for certain Buddhist ceremonies. The principal statue of Buddha always stands in the *bot.*

Chedi: A reliquary surmounted by a spire, usually with a circular base, containing relics of Buddha or of kings and saints.

Ho Rankang: The belfry of the temple, where the gong that regulates the monks' activities is kept.

Ho Trai: The library of sacred texts.

Kuti: The monks' living quarters.

Mondop: A square building which contains some form of relic and is topped by a pyramid-shaped structure that is frequently decorated with mosaics.

Naga: A five- or seven-headed snake used in statuary (to protect Buddha from rain) or in architecture.

Phra: A respectful name used for Buddha himself, for his images, and for Buddhist monks.

Prang: Differs from the *chedi* (see above) by way of its Khmer-style architecture. A very fine example may be seen at **Wat Arun** in Thonburi.

Sala: An open pavilion, used by the monks for meetings and lectures. Pilgrims are allowed to sleep here, along with temporary guests.

Stupa: A bell-shaped edifice, often with a spire. Same function as the *chedi* (see above).

Viharn: Usually at the centre of the courtyard with much the same function as the *bot.* The *viharn* always contains one or several representations of Buddha.

ARTISTS AND IMITATORS

A people who can spend hours making exquisitely designed necklaces of flowers must have a highly developed aesthetic sense. The Thais have always shown such an inclination. Living as they do at the crossroads between the Indian and Chinese civilizations, they have built up an artistic tradition of their own by borrowing from both. Thai artists are imitators, but highly skilled ones; they will use foreign influences only when they think they can master them. In spite of the diversity of schools and styles in Thai art, the source of inspiration always lies in the same ideal of Theravâda Buddhism. Hence it is a combination of religious and popular art, Buddhist thought being as much a part of the average Thai as his own skin. The artist's main preoccupation is not realism but the dreams, supernatural events, and worldly phenomena that make life so unpredictable. The inspiration is not burdened with heavy rational chains. Freedom of expression ends with images of the Buddha, as we have seen, but once artists are perfectly familiar with the *Ramakien* (the Thai version of the Hindu myth of *Ramayana*) or the *Jataka* (tales of Buddha's 549 former lives), they are unlikely to lack further inspiration.

Powerful Lopburi art conveys the martial spirit of the Khmer kingdom. Head of a god (11th-12th centuries).

Throughout their history, the Thais have excelled not only in sculpture and painting, but also in architecture. The great strength of their art is its capacity to create a link between the terrestrial world and the supernatural. In architecture, their principal building is the *wat*, while in statuary their favourite subject is the Buddha.

Thai art did not affirm itself as a specific form until the Sukhothai period (late 12th century) and reached its zenith with Ayutthaya (14th-18th centuries). The various schools which made it possible to establish a chronology of Siamese art are generally associated with particular periods or regions; the fact that several different schools often existed at the same time is therefore nothing out of the ordinary. You will gradually become familiar with the principal styles, all of which are amply represented at the Bangkok National Museum.

THE EIGHT GOLDEN AGES OF THAI ART

Although chronological frameworks are often imprecise because of the conservative nature of Buddhist art, the following periods are traditionally given as classifications.

Dvaravati (6th-11th centuries)
This Indian-influenced style was originally propagated by the Mons. The Dvaravati kingdom, founded at the end of the 6th century, occcupied what is now Central Thailand. The remains of a score of oval Dvaravati cities have been discovered in the Chao Phraya basin and it has now been proved that the influence of Dvaravati extended north to Lamphun and south to Chaiya. However, little remains of the architecture of this period in which brick and laterite were extensively used along with stucco for decoration.

The main inspiration of Dvaravati art was Theravâda Buddhism, as is shown by a number of Pali inscriptions that have survived from the period. Nevertheless, some Hindu images are also to be found.

The Dvaravati Buddha has an original personality which is distinct from Indian precedents: the most striking example is that of Buddha seated in the 'European' position (i.e., on a chair with legs uncrossed). The ultimate decline of Dvaravati was brought about by Khmer expansion in the 12th century.

Srivijaya (8th-13th centuries)
Historically, this period is closely linked to Indonesian colonization in the Malayan peninsula. The kingdom of Srivijaya grew up on the eastern coast of Sumatra (Indonesia) and expanded as far as the region of Nakhon Si Thammarat in Southern Thailand. Most of the remains from this era are from Chaiya, where Hindu influence widened the scope of inspiration. The favorite subjects were the god Vishnu and Avalokitesvara, a particularly famous *Boddhisattva* (a priest worthy of entering Nirvana but who preferred to stay on earth to help his fellow man).

The masterpiece of Srivijaya art is an 8th-century bust of Avalokitesvara, which is considered to be one of the finest pieces in the Bangkok National Museum. A number of other artifacts from that time have been unearthed at Phangnga, near Phuket.

The school of Srivijaya is notable for its extraordinary mastery of sculpture in the round (free-standing pieces), especially in stone.

Lopburi (7th-14th centuries)
The school of Lopburi corresponds to the period when the Khmers controlled the region. In effect, three great Khmer

monarchs ruled over a part of what is now Thailand at different times: Suryavarman I (1002-1050), Suryavarman II (1113-1150), and Jayavarman VII (1181-1218). These reigns were characterized by different artistic expressions respectively known as Baphuon, Wat Angkor, and Bayon. These gave Lopburi an exceptional cultural dimension. The most important monument from the period is the Pimai complex, which was built during the reign of Suryavarman II. Although the architectural style of Pimai is somewhat massive, the harmonious arrangement of the buildings gives an overall impression of elegance and majesty.

Three other great complexes from the first Lopburi period also deserve mention: Tamuen Thom (Surin province), Phnom Rung, and Muang Tham (Buriram province).

The school of Lopburi reached its zenith during the reign of Jayavarman VII. Its later period (13th-14th centuries) was marked by a progressive separation from Khmer influences.

Sukhothai (late 13th-15th centuries)

The Sukhothai style, which was a dominant source of inspiration for the schools that followed, marked the emergence of a specifically Thai form of art. In less than two centuries, Sukhothai developed an influence that surpassed earlier kingdoms. Three sites give us an idea of its grandeur: Sukhothai itself, Si Satchanalai, and Kamphaeng Phet. The greatest achievement of the Sukhothai school is the 'Walking Buddha', whose graceful bearing confers a kind of supernatural beauty, which is exactly how Buddha is described in the canons. This piece represents a high point in the history of Thai sculpture. The seated representations of Buddha are abundant, with a preference for the attitude known as *Bhumisparsa mudra* (calling the earth to witness).

In spite of his unlovely traits (beak nose, elongated earlobes), the Sukhothai Buddha is seductive because of his serene smile and majestic bearing. Almost nothing is known of the painting of this epoch. We have evidence, however, that ceramic work constituted an important item of trade. The *stele* of Rama Khamheng (the 'inventor' of Thai script) provides a fairly complete description of the city of Sukhothai. In any case, the ruins which have survived have so powerful a presence that it is not hard to imagine the splendour of the original capital.

Lan Na or Chiang Saen (11th-13th centuries)

This was the style particularly associated with Northern Thailand during the Sukhothai period. It emerged at the same time as the kingdom of Lan Na, which was founded at the close of the 12th century and supplanted the last Mon kingdom of Haripunchai (or Lamphun). The style of Lan Na (also called Chiang Saen in reference to one of its capitals on the banks of the Mekong River) was heavily influenced by two powerful neighbours, Burma and Laos. Lan Na architecture used the same procedures as Sukhothai (see the *chedi* Jet Yod at Chiang Mai) with the difference that perishable materials such as wood were often included in its structures. For this reason many original buildings have now vanished, or have been inaccurately reconstructed. The style of the Lan Na *stupas* and of certain reliquaries was borrowed from Pagan (Burma), while the ceramic work owes much to Sukhothai techniques. The Buddha statuettes are sculpted in semi-precious stone and the Emerald Buddha is attributed to this period. Although this famous statue is in fact made of jasper, it has drawn many a covetous eye (see p. 100).

U Thong (12th-15th centuries)

The U Thong style heralds the extraordinary artistic achievements of the Ayutthaya kingdom. Heavily influenced by Khmer art until the 13th century, U Thong gradually blossomed along more creative, independent lines while remaining subordinate to the Dvaravati and Sukhothai schools. Its development was limited to Central Thailand.

The U Thong Buddha is recognizable by its headband and stiffly draped garments. The most common attitude is that of Buddha's victory over Mara.

Ayutthaya (15th-18th centuries)

The Ayutthaya period spans nearly four centuries of Thai history. Ayutthaya drew together all the threads of Thai art which had come before it and its style grew more and more refined as it evolved. Though heavily affected by the whimsy of its successive kings, the art of Ayutthaya absorbed a wide variety of foreign influences, the most unexpected of these being that of France, during the reign of King Narai.

The development of a so-called national style came directly from Sukhothai, with later Khmer additions. The relative coldness of Ayutthaya classical statuary is offset by the sophistication of its techniques and the richness of its decoration (this is especially true of works in bronze and wood). A preoccupation with ornament is evident in the mural paintings (*Jataka* illustrations) and in the lacquerwork, while Ayutthaya architecture provided a basic decorative standard for nearly a million inhabitants, with its *prang* and its new form of square-based or polygonal *stupa*. In short, this was the golden age; a period of decadence was perhaps already approaching when the Burmese sacked Ayutthaya in 1767. Curiously enough, this shattering disaster gave the Thais fresh energy to reconstruct their last paradise: Thonburi and Bangkok would continue in the artistic footsteps of Ayutthaya.

Bangkok (18th-20th centuries)

The Thonburi period (1769-1782) marked an interval between the fall of Ayutthaya and the rise of Bangkok. The artistic renewal of the Thai nation was the work of the Chakri dynasty (still reigning today) and coincided with the founding of a new capital at Bangkok on the east bank of the Chao Phraya River.

An important concern for the builders of Bangkok was the recovery of as many Buddha statues from the ruined monasteries as possible, with a view to preserving the merit they represented. Bangkok's architecture continued in the Ayutthaya tradition but its style became more and more encumbered, as if to prove its superiority to its antecedents. In this sense, Bangkok art was nouveau riche, even flashy. The royal palace was built

Wat Chai.

along with a number of important monasteries (Wat Po, Wat Phra Keo, Wat Suthat, Wat Benchamabophit); all were characterized by tiers of varnished tile roofs, incrustations of porcelain and mother-of-pearl, lacquered doors, gilded or polychrome statues, and mural paintings. The artists who fashioned them used traditional techniques but the growing influence of Europe was beginning to stifle their inspiration. Finally, Thai art sank into dull conformism; the Bangkok style, also called *Ratanakosin,* is perceived as too often sacrificing quality to quantity and this is especially true of its statuary.

CHRONOLOGICAL

DATE	THAILAND
1238	Foundation of Sukhothai, the first organized Siamese State
1296	Foundation of Chiang Mai by King Mengrai
1350	Ayutthaya declared capital city under Ramatibodi I; unification of Siam
1390	Chiang Mai captured by King Ramesuen
1431	Angkor falls under Thai rule: King Boromaraja II
1511	First contacts with Europe (Portuguese navigators)
1569	Ayutthaya falls to the Burmese; Siam becomes a vassal state of Burma
1584	Narsuen overcomes the Burmese and declares Siamese independence
1605-1615	Dutch and English arrive in Siam
1657	Beginning of King Narai's reign
1678-1686	Constantine Phaulkon: the Franco-Siamese alliance
1688	Death of King Narai, execution of Phaulkon. Foreigners expelled and Siam closed to the West
1733-1758	Reign of King Boromakot: Ayutthaya's Golden Age
1767	Burmese destroy Ayutthaya
1769-1782	King Taksin's reign; Burmese conquered. Thonburi becomes capital of Siam
1782-1809	Reign of Rama I; Bangkok declared new capital
1851-1867	Reign of Mongkut (Rama IV); Siam once again open to the West. First steps toward modernization
1868-1910	Reign of Chulalongkorn; slavery abolished; Franco-Siamese war over Laos
1932	Absolute monarchy abolished and constitutional monarchy declared
1939	Siam changes name to Thailand
1942	Thailand enters war on Japanese side
1946	Beginning of reign of Rama IX, present king of Thailand
1963	Military gains control under Marshal Thanam Kittikachorn
1973	Students revolt against military regime
1975	Evacuation of US military bases
1981	Attempted coup d'état put down
1987	Year of Thailand: King's 60th birthday

TABLE OF EVENTS

UNITED KINGDOM	USA
Henry III	
Edward I	
Edward III; the Black Death	
Richard II	
Henry IV	
Henry VIII	Early exploration of America
Elizabeth I	
	Sir Walter Raleigh discovers Virginia (1585)
James I	Settlement of Jamestown (1607)
Cromwell's Commonwealth (1648-1658)	Progressive settlement of the 13 chartered colonies
James II	
Fall of James II; war with France	
George II; Anglo-French War in Canada	Molasses Act; growing unrest in the colonies
George III	Townshend Acts
	Boston Tea Party (1773); War of Independence
	George Washington; Thomas Jefferson
Victoria; fall of Derby's administration	Abraham Lincoln; Civil War (1861-1865)
Gladstone; Edward VIII	Andrew Johnson Grover Cleveland Theodore Roosevelt
George V; Baldwin	Herbert Hoover; the Great Depression
George VI; outbreak of WWII	Franklin Roosevelt
	Battle of Midway
Clement Atlee	Harry S. Truman Korean War (1950-1953)
Queen Elizabeth II; Harold Macmillan	Assassination of John F. Kennedy
Edward Heath	Richard Nixon; end of Vietnam War
Margaret Thatcher	Ronald Reagan

THAILAND TODAY

Every year, millions of visitors come to Thailand. In spite of the nearby Kampuchean problem, with its thousands of refugees and its appalling atrocities, neighbouring Thailand is becoming more familiar to Westerners, although many Thais still know little of the West.

THE LAND

Thailand is, above all, a wet country with the torrential rains of the monsoon, the generous Chao Phraya River surrounded by green rice-paddies, and the providential waters of the *klongs* (canals).

Geographically, Thailand covers an area of 198,000 sq mi/514,000 sq km between Burma (to the west and north), Laos (to the north and east), Kampuchea (formerly Cambodia) to the east, and Malaysia (to the south). The Thai countryside extends over 1250 mi/2000 km. The richest area of the country is the basin of the Chao Phraya River and its tributaries, which is some 250 mi/400 km long from north to south and varies in width between 60 and 95 mi/100 and 150 km.

Half of Thailand is taken up by a savanna-covered plateau (the Korat region) which is divided in two by the Mekong River along the Laotian border. Along the northern and western edges of the country stand the foothills of the Himalayas, which are thickly covered by tropical evergreen forests. The southern peninsula, which is shaped like the trunk of an elephant, is less than 60 mi/100 km wide at its narrowest point, the Kra isthmus. This area, known as Siamese Malaysia, is remarkable for its long beaches of white sand and its forgotten offshore islands, once the haunt of pirates.

The highest population density is concentrated in the plains and around Bangkok. The lower region of the Chao Phraya River delta, together with the capital, contains over half of the country's total population. Since the beginning of the 20th century, the population increase of Thailand has been rapid: in 1905, the population was between six and seven million, increasing to 40 million in 1975 and 52 million today. Bangkok and its sister city, Thonburi, have increased in population from 500,000 to six million inhabitants in less than 30 years. Nevertheless, 85% of

Three quarters of the working population are in agriculture.

Thais still live in small villages; Chiang Mai, the country's second largest city, has only about 180,000 inhabitants.

If you want to know about Thailand you should begin with its countryside: you will find the people there as varied as the landscape.

THE THAI PEOPLE

The people of Thailand are often portrayed as graceful dancers in elegant costumes. The Thais also include ragged peasants, people of Chinese origin dressed in the manner of Hong Kong and Singapore, and Meo women, with their worldly wealth hung about them in the form of heavy silver necklaces.

Over 20 different ethnic groups live together on Thai soil, the result of several different waves of migration from the Central Asian plateaux.

Thailand's real name is *Muang Thai,* meaning 'land of free men'. 'Thailand' is merely an anglicized version of this and the name 'Thai' is a generic term which covers the Thais themselves (the Siamese), the Laotians (close relatives and neighbours), and the Burmese Shans. All these groups originally came from Yunnan in China. The Mons and the Khmers, who dominated the territory from the 6th to the 13th centuries, have, today, been almost entirely absorbed by the Thai peoples, though small, scattered groups of them still survive on the north-eastern plateaux. Other minority pockets still exist: the Laos in the Phetchaburi region, for example, along with the Negroid groups of the south and the 'ghost tribes' of the north, with whom no contact has yet been established. At present the Thais constitute about 80% of the country's population.

In Bangkok, it is very difficult to tell apart Siamese (central plains), Yuans (Northern Thailand), Laos (Mekong region), and Korats (descended from the Khmer invaders). Any of them can be *samlor* (pedicab) drivers, office workers, or pickpockets and, in the confusion of the city, their racial differences are obscured. If we wish to distinguish between the various peoples of Thailand, we must go beyond Bangkok to the mountains of the north, to the *mubans* (rural communes) amid their rice fields and to the fishing villages along the coast.

THE RICE FIELDS OF THAILAND

It is dawn, between 5 and 5:30am. In some 40,000 rural communes, a new day is breaking. The women are the first to stir, preparing a breakfast of rice and vegetables for their families. A little food is set aside for the Buddhist priests; every morning the monks of the *wat* come to accept their daily portion from the peasants. Then the children put on their immaculate uniforms and leave for the village school with their satchels under their arms. None of them know yet if they will have the privilege of a secondary education. In the Thai countryside, people are born to the land and on the land they stay, unless they opt for an uncertain future in the city.

Most peasants do not own the land they work, and any possibility of a rise in their standard of living is hampered by debt. The growth of the population has led not only to an increase in the acreage under cultivation, but also to the formation of large landed estates, which engender the classic problems of absentee landlordism and the exploitation of an oppressed and dispossessed peasant class by middlemen. In the north-east, where the average family income is one eighth that of Bangkok, more than 20% of the peasants have been forced off the land.

Is the Thai peasant unhappy with his lot? Not while there's 'rice in the field and fish in the water'. His life revolves around the growth cycle of the rice plant; he ploughs, plants, irrigates, replants seedlings, harvests, dries, and winnows his crop with the help of his entire family.

Thai villages are traditionally located on river banks. The houses are built on stilts as a precaution against flooding, snakes, insects, and wild animals, and the primary materials used are teak for the frame and dried leaves for the roof. The walls are generally made of woven fronds. The interiors contain practically no furniture and the decoration tends to be limited to a picture of the Thai royal family or a photograph of one of the sons of the house who has gone away to work in a monastery or in a shop. Though electricity is rare, running water is always abundant; the *klong* (canal) serves as a village street, drain, washplace, bath, swimming pool, and fishing hole.

Village days are punctuated by a series of small events: listening to the transistor radio with its news of another world named Bangkok, preparing a younger son to enter a monastery, the birth of a new baby, markets, love affairs, scandalmongering, parties, and the national lottery. While Bangkok is ever-changing, life in the countryside has remained almost the same for centuries.

THE ABACUS ECONOMY

Whether they take place in air-conditioned bank offices or in a New Road merchant's modest booth, most business transactions in Thailand are concluded to the clicking sound of the Chinese abacus. At the latest count, the Chinese population is reckoned at four to five million, three quarters of whom are naturalized Thais. Paradoxically, the only country in Southeast Asia which tried to defend itself against all colonial interference has almost 10% of its population from neighbouring countries, including India, Burma, and Malaysia.

Chinese immigration is a very ancient phenomenon in Thailand. Throughout history, famines, floods and political upheavals in China have driven the poorest and the most adventurous of Chinese people to seek their fortunes elsewhere. In the 17th century, there were already 10,000 Chinese in Siam. Immigration increased in the 19th and 20th centuries, but due to large numbers of Chinese women, the process of assimilation was slowed down and many entirely Chinese families were established.

By comparison with Chinese immigrants who went to other South-east Asian countries, those who chose Thailand may

Water buffalo, man and water are still the best combination for growing rice.

nevertheless be distinguished by their relative success at integrating themselves into the indigenous society. Of course, relations between Thais and Chinese have not always been perfect. While the proclamation of the Chinese Republic provoked almost unanimous enthusiasm among the Chinese of Thailand, it hardly brought about a mass exodus back to the motherland. The expatriates' sympathy for the new regime annoyed Thai nationalists enough to produce a wave of xenophobia against them. Chinese were banned from residing in certain 'strategic' areas, Chinese schools were closed, Chinese letters were censored, immigration was brought to a dead halt, and the Chinese were prevented from working in certain professions. In 1955, things returned to normal, with the restoration of the naturalization law *(jus soli)* whereby all people born in Thailand automatically acquired Thai citizenship.

These temporary difficulties by no means quelled the spirit of enterprise which is the predominant characteristic of Thailand's largest minority community. It is calculated that the Chinese control between 70% and 80% of the kingdom's commerce, notably its main exports (rice, manioc, rubber, wood, and tin). They also have a large share of the fishing, banking, and mining industries, along with small businesses, the national lottery, and the opium trade (see p. 69). The transportation, processing, and export of rice has become a virtual Chinese monopoly. Chinese economic activities are regulated by commercial guilds, associations, and brotherhoods which are a combination of trade unions, information exchanges, social services, and merchant banks.

As far as the Thais are concerned, the Chinese have always chosen to collaborate rather than exclude. Thais are involved in their businesses to such an extent that jealousy is averted. Links with Taiwan are somewhat strained because of the recent improvement in relations between Thailand and China. Obviously, the main goal of the Chinese inhabitants of Thailand is to live in peace and as well as possible. The practice of adopting Thai-sounding names has become widespread, and mixed marriages are now becoming more and more frequent.

Nevertheless, certain Chinese traditions are maintained. In the countryside, huge Chinese cemeteries may be seen with each grave marked by a small mound. Closeness among relatives, mutual assistance, respect for elders (associated with ancestor worship), and a patriarchal organization of the family proper remain the dominant values of the Chinese social group. The celebration of the Chinese New Year is a major event in Thailand. The streets resound with exploding firecrackers and gifts are exchanged.

FROM THE CRESCENT TO THE GUN

The Songkhla fisherman has forgotten to pin the king's portrait to the wall of his house. A small Japanese transistor, bought with much sacrifice, is sputtering out the news from Radio Kuala Lumpur. Bangkok is more than 600 mi/1000 km to the north. Like 800,000 other Thai Muslims, mostly ethnic Malays, he looks steadfastly to the south, which he sees as the natural direction of his daily existence. He goes to the mosque, sends his son to the Koranic school, observes Ramadan, celebrates the prophet's birthday, and dreams of making a pilgrimage to Mecca. He is Thai, they tell him, but he refuses to believe it.

Some peoples of Southern Thailand were converted to Islam in the 15th century and their natural allies are the people of the Indonesian archipelago, where the tenets of the Muslim Koran and Hindu Ramayana co-exist in peace. The great majority of Thailand's Muslim population (85%) is concentrated in the provinces of Yala, Narathiwat, Pattani, Trang, Krabi, and Songkhla, and it has never accepted Thai domination.

Although the Koran reigns supreme in the south, this is Islam with a gentle face. Women, for example, are not subjugated to the submissive, secondary role they occupy in orthodox Islamic societies. In fact, one of the revolts of Thai Muslims (in 1636) was led by a woman, the queen of Pattani.

Life is organized around three main activities: fishing, rice-growing, and work in the *hevea* (rubber) plantations. Since they possessed neither the economic power of the Chinese nor political muscle of the Thais, the Malay minority was progressively impoverished. By the early 1950s, a number of oppressive measures aimed at destroying Malay cultural identity had been introduced, provoking violent resistance and the creation of a communist guerilla force. Finally, in 1965, Bangkok signed an agreement with Kuala Lumpur whereby Malaysia agreed to withhold support for the secessionist ambitions of the Thai Malays. In exchange, Thailand pledged to assist Malaysia in the struggle against its own communist insurgents. The Thais then set about grouping the villages of the southern region together, with a view to tightening their grip on the area; this application of the stick was followed by the offer of a large carrot in the form of a withdrawal of all discriminatory measures against Thai Malays. The government even presented the largest mosque ever built in Thailand to the city of Pattani! Nevertheless, the basic problem remains and there is little doubt that the Thais will have trouble for years to come with their adopted southern cousins.

THE PEOPLES OF THE MIST

The Montagnard or hilltribe minorities of Thailand live far away in the northern forests of Thailand in a world apart.

All are recent arrivals in Thailand and some have only been in the country for ten years or less. Originating in the mountain valleys of Yunnan (China) from where they were driven by Chinese forces and by the need for new land, the hilltribes moved gradually southward over the various borders that lay across their path.

China, Laos, Thailand, Burma — none of these names held any meaning for people whose only desire was to find a land where they could live in peace. The Meo, Karen, Akha, Lahu, Yao, and Lisu, along with many other hilltribes, tried their luck in the various states along the Chinese frontier. Their only requirement was to live at high altitudes (over 3300 ft/1000 m) beyond the range of malaria. Maintaining contact with one another, even across borders, presented no problem. Thus the Karens of Thailand have cousins in Burma, while the Meos live in Laos, Thailand, China, and Vietnam. Their group awareness and sense of belonging to an extended family is very strong, yet some villages live in such extreme isolation that they are unaware of the existence of Chiang Mai, the capital of Northern Thailand, or of Bangkok.

Most Montagnards burn off the land before cultivating it. The land is rapidly exhausted, which obliges them to move on at frequent intervals. Some villages change their site every five or six years, which in no way facilitates the task of the census taker.

Apart from rice (a non-irrigated variety) and a few vegetables, the Montagnard villagers' main crop is the poppy. Hence the strong emotions that are inspired by a handful of these people, not only in the countries in which they live, but also in the international community. The area known as the Golden Triangle, which produces between 50% and 70% of the world's heroin, is in the heart of the territory occupied by the Montagnards, astride the three frontiers of Thailand, Laos, and Burma.

Local consumption of opium is insignificant; as one proverb says, 'who is the madman who will eat his own money?'

While the individual character of these groups is a delight to tourists, the Thai government views them in a different manner. One fifth of its territory is inhabited by people who do not speak the national language, live in closed economies that are frequently outside the law, and do not even respect frontiers. One day, perhaps, they will simply vanish into the mountain mists, as suddenly as they came. For the moment there are no fewer than 20 ethnic sub-groups in the northern provinces and differences exist even within each ethnic group, such as the Meo group (see below).

At present, a drive to educate the Montagnards is under way, administered by the border police force which supervises the region. Some results have been recorded in literacy and improvement of sanitary conditions. Though these efforts are at best perfunctory, they are small improvements.

Lords of the mountain: the Meos

A meeting with a family of Meos at the Chiang Mai market is not the least of the surprises in store for you in Northern Thailand. With their bulky silver necklaces, their indigo-fronted jackets and their embroidered aprons partially covering full trousers or a little girl's pleated skirt, the Meo women dress in a style worthy of Western high fashion. Their beauty and elegance are sometimes breathtaking, with their rounded foreheads, ample chignons, and black or white turbans.

Also known as the H'mong, the Meos constitute Thailand's largest Montagnard minority. They belong to an ethnic group of about six million individuals, originally from the Chinese provinces of Yunnan, Hunan, Kweichow, and Kwangsi, whose history stretches back over 4000 years. They first arrived in Thailand at the close of the 19th century. The 1975 revolution in Laos led to a massive exodus of Meos from that country, with the result that the present Meo population of Thailand is between 100,000 and 150,000. They are concentrated in the provinces of Chiang Mai and Chiang Rai, as well as in the Tak, Phrae, and Petchabun regions.

There are also several sub-groups belonging to different linguistic families, whose names echo the costumes of their women: you will hear Meos referred to as 'Blue', 'White', 'Striped', or 'Flowered'. Apart from such minor distinguishing features, however, the Meo group appears to be highly cohesive in terms of economic and social behaviour. Proud, independent, resourceful, sociable, but also lazy and imbued with precepts of male superiority, the Meo man is lord of his mountain home. The Meo woman is canny enough to accept this situation; her lot is to work in the fields with the children, fulfilling menial tasks which the menfolk reject in favour of hunting and building.

'Fish rule the water, birds rule the air, and Meos rule the mountains', says the Thai proverb. Meo villages are built on slopes, so that water can easily be channeled down to them in bamboo aqueducts. They usually include some 20 to 30 slightly raised dwellings, with the chief's house occupying a central position. The fields are often some distance from the village. Because of the Meo habit of burning off the land and then working it to death, their migratory cycles have become drastically shorter; nowadays, it is rare for them to exploit the same plot for 15 or 20 years. Nevertheless, the Meos are among the more privileged of the region's hill peoples. Apart from the 'sticky rice' which is their basic diet, they grow a plentiful supply of vegetables (marrows, beans, maize, sugar cane, yams, potatoes) as well as tobacco and flax. They are capable of making all their own tools (axes, knives, grindstones) and they have no equals in the art of embroidery. They also raise chickens, pigs, and goats, along with the occasional buffalo or mule. The Meos are open-minded toward new techniques and often come down to the lowland market towns to buy medical supplies or ammunition, as well as other more sophisticated products.

Their lives are divided between fieldwork, building chores, commerce, and celebration. The Meos are great bons vivants, rarely missing an opportunity to down a bottle of rice wine. The new year, the birth of a baby, a marriage or a funeral are all taken as occasions for drinking and good cheer. Care is taken when celebrating to honour and mollify the local spirits, in case the revelers should wake up the next day transformed into werewolves. Meo animism is blended with a belief in a creator god who is the wellspring of all knowledge, especially concerning the cultivation of the opium poppy. Each individual is thought to possess three souls whose ways part after death: one goes to a kind of paradise, another remains with the corpse, and the third is reincarnated. Otherwise, Meo funeral rites are akin to Chinese ancestor worship. Because of their numbers and their stage of development, the Meo tribes form a significant political force at the core of the struggle between the Thai government and the procommunist guerilla forces. Because of the political implications of the situation, the Meos have excellent reasons for mistrusting outsiders, whoever they may be. Recently, efforts by the government to integrate the Meos, who have proven themselves to be gifted students, have begun to yield results. There are already numerous Meos in Thai universities.

The Yaos

If a young Yao woman is asked to marry, her father will demand a payment of several thousand baht, or the equivalent value in black pigs. Should an unmarried woman become pregnant, her lover may refuse to marry her; but if he does so, he must pay a 'fine' to the woman's parents (far less, as it happens, than it would cost for him to marry her). Whatever happens, Yaos always manage to settle their disputes in a climate of courtesy.

The Yao nation numbers about four million people, living variously in Southern China, Burma, Laos, Vietnam, and Thailand. Of these, 20,000 to 25,000 inhabit the Thai provinces of Nan and Chiang Rai, having come there in successive waves of immigration since the early 19th century. Most Yao villages are located above an altitude of 3300 ft/1000 m, but the Yaos (unlike the Meos) would welcome a chance to move to the plains. They are hardworking farmers, self-sufficient in growing rice and vegetables, who sometimes use irrigation methods even in the high altitudes. Their domestic and farm animals are well cared for. Nevertheless, the bulk of their income is derived from opium poppies. They are frequent visitors to neighbouring towns where they shop for supplies and maintain cordial relations with the plains folk. The Yaos have a natural gift for languages and are often capable of speaking Yunnan Chinese, Lao-

Monk from Wat Mahathat.

Thai, and Lahu. They even try to communicate with the Meos, whose language is very different.

Although the Yaos live in very simple surroundings, their women dress sophisticatedly. Their traditional dress consists of trousers embroidered with cross-stitched red, white, and yellow geometrical motifs against an indigo background. The ample tunic, which is belted and slashed from the waist downward, is embellished with a kind of red boa. The scalp is usually shaven, under a voluminous and elegant turban. The Yao women, like the Meos, wear heavy one-piece silver necklaces, along with bracelets, pendants, and earrings and their embroidery work is of a high quality. By contrast, the men's costume consists of a jacket buttoned at the side and broad dark blue trousers, with the occasional small fancy hat to lend charm to a rather sober ensemble.

Although they are by no means puritanical, the Yaos tend to be reserved. They are poor singers and indifferent dancers; they make up for this by being indefatigable storytellers. Tea flows freely in Yao villages but alcohol is reserved for rare and special occasions.

The animist beliefs of the Yaos are accompanied by rites borrowed from the Chinese tradition, notably ancestor worship. Domestic spirits regularly receive offerings of joss sticks and, from time to time, a pig or chicken is called upon to 'banish devils'.

The Akhas

You find yourself facing a short, round-faced woman with a mouth stained red from chewing betel nut. She has a roguish twinkle in her eye and is smoking a pipe. Her indigo-blue linen jacket is intricately studded with pearls and brightly coloured patchwork. On her head she wears a curious bonnet, tied under the chin, which is adorned with silver coins, pearls, buttons, and monkey fur or dog tail pompoms. This is an Akha woman and you will be glad to see her because you will have had to walk for several hours on a difficult uphill path to find her mountain retreat.

The Akhas are one of the most interesting ethnic groups in Thailand. Their original home was in Burma but now there are about 30,000 of them living to the north of the Mae Kok River in Thailand's Chiang Rai province (mainly around Mae Sai and Mae Chan). They are commonly believed to be descended from the Lo-Los, a tribe whose existence has been traced back some 4000 years. Akhas are the poorest of the hilltribes and resist assimilation more than other ethnic minorities.

Though austere in their material existence, the Akhas are rich in music, dancing, and poetry. Akha men wear a long pigtail at the centre of their shaven scalps; they believe it contains their strength and natural superiority over the female gender. If a man commits a crime against society, this pigtail is shorn, which for the Akha is a punishment worse than death. Naturally, everything possible is done in this society to avoid offending spirits, since animism is at the core of all Akha attitudes. They especially mistrust strangers, whom they suspect of introducing evil spirits into the village. Water, too, is viewed with deep antipathy: who can say what might be hiding in this mysterious element? From time to time, the Akhas sacrifice a well-fattened pig, or hang a dead dog at the entrance to their village, as a tribute to evil spirits.

Women's rights do not figure in Akha customs. In this traditional agricultural community where wealth is measured in crops and livestock, a marriageable woman is often exchanged for no more than one small black pig, which is why the Akha male frequently has several wives who supply him with cheap labour for his fields of poppies and maize.

The Karens

Should you come across an elephant working in the teak forests around Mae Sariang, there is a good chance that the driver will be a Karen. The men of this ethnic group are specialists in the art of making elephants understand how to manipulate a ton of timber as if it were a matchstick.

There are about two million Karens in Burma, where they have had their own state within the Federation ever since 1848. In Thailand, their numbers vary between 75,000 and 150,000, according to different estimates. Census-taking is rendered all the more difficult because there are several distinct subgroups. Of these, the most numerous are the Skaw (or Sgaw) Karens who are dispersed over 800 villages, while the Pwo (or Po) Karens occupy about 500 villages. Another much smaller group is that of the Kayah Karens, whose 20 villages are concentrated in the Mae Hong Son region along the Burmese frontier. The latter are poorer than their cousins and live at a higher altitude.

A special characteristic of Karen society is that it is matrilineal, with property transferring down the female line. As a result, it is common practice for a newly married couple to set up house with the mother-in-law. In Karen religious ceremonies, the person officiating is always a woman. The Karen moral code is extremely strict; most marriages are arranged and tend to take place relatively late, at 25 to 30 years of age.

These puritanical tendencies have worked greatly to the advantage of missionary Baptists in Thailand, who have made some 25,000 'conversions' in the group. Since they believe in the existence of a supreme being, the Karens have little trouble with the idea of a single god. But true conversions are rare: animism remains the dominant religious factor here, as elsewhere, with its propitiatory rites and ceremonial sacrifices. When a child is born, Karen parents traditionally invite a spirit to enter its body and then close him in by knotting strings around the baby's wrists.

The Karens' economic activities are changing rapidly. Although they still cultivate poppy in the higher mountain areas, their priority today is rice, especially when the land permits irrigation. To increase the family income, the men hire themselves out as agricultural labourers or elephant drivers (*mahouts*) in the teak forests. The women sell their woven fabrics, embroideries, and traditional tunics.

The Karens of Thailand are by no means indifferent to the struggles of their Burmese cousins, who have been in revolt for over 30 years against the central government in Rangoon. The clandestine Karen army is assured of sympathy and assistance on the Thai side of the border and the agreement between Bangkok and Rangoon allowing the Burmese army to pursue insurgents across the frontier has merely strengthened the bonds of brotherhood. Moreover, much of the Burma-Thailand border is effectively controlled by the Karens.

The Lisu

The Lisu know how to celebrate and New Year is their biggest feast. For up to six days, they sing, dance, and make merry, consuming much rice brandy. Beautiful women are heavily laden with jewels. Over broad trousers, they wear their prettiest embroidered tunics and their spangled leggings shimmer to the rhythm of the dance. The men look magnificent in white turbans with traditional daggers carelessly thrust into their belts. Their jackets, which are closed at the side, Chinese-fashion, glitter with silver buttons. Everyone enjoys these festivities to the utmost.

The Lisu (also called Lishaw or Lissaw) are of Burmese-Tibetan origin. They live mainly around Chiang Mai (Chiang Dao, Fang) Chiang Rai, Tak, and Mae Hong Son. About 20,000 of them live in Thailand and 400,000 in Burma. Their villages, which may include up to 100 houses, are situated in the highest hill areas. The Lisu have a marked preference for defensible spots because they are extremely reluctant to abandon the poppy fields which are their principal source of revenue. As a result they burn off the forest in ever more inaccessible areas, and are quite content to live a day's journey from the nearest water source. Essential supplies are brought up on the backs of ponies or mules.

Visitors who avail themselves of Lisu hospitality should expect to spend a sleepless night: assorted dogs, pigs, chickens, goats, and mules roam around outside their houses, which are not raised off the ground. The family gets up at dawn and, at an hour when other children are heading for school, the little Lisu set out for the fields of maize, millet, and melons. Meanwhile, the men string their crossbows and sharpen their poisoned arrows in preparation for the hunt. If the opium harvest is good, they may buy themselves a gun. The women use their share of the profits to purchase new silver bangles, even though they have no need to augment their personal worth: a marriageable girl is worth a small fortune. Lisu men have been known to languish for years before they could assemble enough money to pay for their brides. For example, a good opium harvest may bring in 4000 ฿ for the work of an entire family, but a young man must assemble 10,000 ฿ for a wife. One can understand why he may end up courting farther afield — among the Lahu women, for instance.

Although, with their gift for languages, the Lisu maintain excellent relations with other minority groups, they do not care very much for strangers. Moreover, they tend to be quarrelsome and their system of justice is nothing if not harsh; their death sentence, though rarely used, entails beheading with a sabre.

Like other hilltribe groups, the Lisu practice ancestor worship and certain forms of exorcism which seem to be designed to make the spirits forget the Lisu's existence, rather than to placate them with repeated offerings.

The Lahu

'When a Lahu leaves the mountains, he misses his hunting more than his family.' This saying justifies another name by which the Lahu are known: *moussuh* (a Thai term meaning hunter). But the Lahus are not to be defined quite so easily, since they are divided into several sub-groups which differ not only in costume but also in language and traditions. The two most closely allied groups are the Lahu Nyi (or Moussuh Daeng) with 98 villages, and the Lahu Nah (or Moussuh Na) with 15. The Sheleh constitute another group with 25 villages, while the Lahu Shi (or Moussuh Kwi) are the smallest of all, occupying only three villages. All are of Burmese-Tibetan origin and their arrival in Thailand dates from the mid-19th century. Today, they represent a total population of 20,000 people, concentrated in the provinces of Mae Hong Son, Chiang Mai, and Chiang Rai.

Love of the chase is an essential characteristic of the Lahu. They spend days on end polishing their crossbows, in hopes of winning the title of 'supreme hunter', an honour as much prized in the mountains of Thailand as a diploma in the West. The Thais buy cured game from the Lahu, along with the antlers of deer as ingredients for magic potions (usually aphrodisiacs). As poor farmers, the Lahu rely chiefly on opium to improve their economic lot. The forest-burning cycle usually lasts only three years, and poppies, rice, maize, and sunflowers are their principal crops. Their few animals are alternately used as nourishment for men and spirits.

The biggest Lahu celebration takes place during the Chinese New Year. This is also a prime period for courting. In this, the women take the initiative: the morning after the young men return exhausted from the hunt, they are woken with songs about 'having plenty of time to sleep when they're married'. Once he has taken a wife, the young man has to work for his in-laws for three years to pay for her, unless he can put up the fabulous sum of 500 ฿ or 600 ฿. This custom does not exist among the Lahu Sheleh, who are polygamous: their first wives are the same age as their husbands, but the others are usually between 13 and 15 years old.

The Lahu believe in the existence of a creator god surrounded by a pantheon of lesser divinities. Lahu have been converted to Christianity, but their most singular religious characteristic is a longing for a messiah. Consequently, on several occasions, they have been exploited by false prophets. Knowing what awaits them after death, the Lahu watch their step; if they behave themselves, they will reap their heavenly reward, but if they don't, they will stew in the seven cauldrons of hell.

OPIUM OF THE GOLDEN TRIANGLE

At the beginning of the 1970s, Thailand was the largest exporter of opium, morphine, and heroin in South-east Asia. Although the cultivation of poppies had been illegal since 1958, Thailand at that time was still producing 1000 tons per year of illegal opium (according to American estimates), i.e., six times more than Afghanistan and 20 times more than Turkey. Thai opium was assumed to include the crops harvested on Burmese and Laotian territory, since both geography and politics conspired to make Bangkok the main focus of the traffic. Today, the golden age of opium traffic is far from over.

The flowering opium poppy is delicately beautiful, but the people directly concerned with its cultivation are liable to be more interested in dollars than in botany. The cycle commences between January and March, when the wind ruffles the ocean of white, mauve, and purple poppy blossoms. As soon as the petals fall, an oblong capsule appears at the top of the stalk; this is the moment the Montagnards have been waiting for. The whole family goes to work to bring in the harvest. Every evening, they make a tiny incision in each pod; a droplet of sap quickly forms and goes brown in contact with the air. This droplet is left to grow all night, and in the early morning a little pea-sized lump of dried sap is harvested. Later, these lumps will be boiled in water to eliminate impurities, then dried in the sun in bricks of about one kilo each. Soon after, the buyers come: Haw Chinese, who live in the foothills and serve as intermediaries between the mountain villagers and the Thais down in the plains. The Chinese bring salt, tea, sugar, candles, matches, and other small consumer articles to sell in exchange for 50% to 100% profit, added to the 100% profit they will make on the opium they buy. The bricks of opium are loaded onto mules; when the rounds have been completed, an average caravan will bring back between seven and eight tons of opium worth more than US $100,000. To increase profits, part of this consignment may be diverted to a clandestine refinery, a simple hut built of boards in which amateur chemists will set about producing heroin.

This seemingly improvised system masks a deadly efficient organization of considerable power, which exploits corruption, poverty, and political interests and rivalries. The last remnants of the anti-communist Chinese forces under General Li Mai took refuge in the Golden Triangle area in 1949. After various attempts between 1950 and 1952 to recapture power in China, they finally settled down to a less hazardous occupation. Unable to survive on meagre subsidies from Taiwan, they cast about for other means. Committed, well-armed soldiers were needed to escort the opium caravans; and all parties settled on this solution.

Because of the expanding drug problem worldwide, the Thai government has frequently been exhorted to put an end to a traffic of which Thailand itself is one of the main victims. Experts have given much thought to eliminating the trouble at its source, namely the cultivation of the poppy, but what else can possibly replace this plant which grows like a weed, brings in fabulous profits, can be stored indefinitely without losing its value, and caters to an ever-increasing demand? The World Bank assists the Thai government in resettlement programs for minorities in the provinces of Mae Hong Son, Chiang Mai, Chiang Rai, Nan, and Lampang. The goal is to relocate 200 villages to eight centres where the government will assume responsibility for training villagers in methods of agriculture and stock-rearing. But it is quite clear that the Montagnard minorities will not readily accept being placed on the public payroll and will do whatever they can to preserve the opium trade which guarantees their freedom. As a result, opium stocks are on the increase to such a degree that police checkpoints have been set up in the villages and identity cards issued. Villagers under surveillance no longer have the right to leave their homes without special permission — otherwise they risk arrest.

THAI WOMANHOOD: THE MIRAGE OF EMANCIPATION

To a Westerner, the Thai woman seems fragile and delicate. In reality the truth is somewhat different: Thai women in influential circles are involved in the national economy to a

> **Buddhism and feminism**
>
> Thus spoke the Buddha in regard to the preparation of young girls for marriage: 'To this end, oh young women, you should apply yourselves in the following manner: whomsoever your parents may choose for you as a husband, — wishing the best for you, in compassionate hope for your happiness, and altogether motivated by compassion — for him you should rise early, and retire to bed after he has retired; for him you should work with diligence, order everything with gentleness and speak always in dulcet tones. Prepare yourselves in this fashion, oh young women.'

degree that Western women are not. They frequently hold posts of very high responsibility in banks and hotels: The largest department store in Bangkok today is managed by a woman, and there are more female students at Bangkok University than male.

Still, Thailand is not a model of equal rights and opportunities for women. On the contrary, the situation is more complex. Thais consider the two noblest professions to be the civil service and the priesthood and commerce is, therefore, left to women and the Chinese.

In many respects, Thai women are much freer than their Western counterparts. Since marriages are still frequently arranged by the family, their emotional attachment to their homes is less profound and allows them to devote themselves entirely to their profession. They often earn more money than their husbands and their economic independence is absolute. Moreover, Thais readily accept the principle of one member of the family working to feed the rest. The masseuses of Bangkok, along with the streetwalkers and nightclub singers, send most of the money they earn back to their families in the country, or else use it to pay for their younger siblings' education. No one worries about these girls; the general feeling is that they can take good care of themselves.

Thai women stand no nonsense from anyone: when we read in the newspapers of family disputes ending in murder, as often as not the husband is the victim. Recently, it became known that a woman had sold her husband to another woman. The case came to public attention purely by chance: the purchaser had paid with a bad check!

Such excessive behaviour is rare but the anecdote illustrates the power of Thai women.

RICE FARMERS AND SKYSCRAPERS

Thailand is a country in which 75% of the active population works in the fields. While a swollen agricultural sector is characteristic of developing countries, Thailand is better off than most other South-east Asian countries (with the exception of Malaysia and Singapore).

With the exception of tourism, rice is Thailand's greatest source of wealth. In all, over 3.6 million acres/9 million ha, or 70% of the country's arable land, is occupied by high-yielding rice paddies. When one considers that rice is Thailand's number one agricultural export (17% of the annual yield is sold abroad), there are good grounds for the claim that it is the peasants with their feet in the water who provided the funds for raising the skyscrapers of Bangkok. In any event, rice is the livelihood of three quarters of Thailand's population and, notwithstanding its primitive farming methods and low yields (barely 20% of those of Taiwan), Thailand is currently the world's sixth most important rice-producing nation.

The other main agricultural exports are manioc, sugar, wood, rubber, and jute. The Thai peasant, however, especially in the eastern provinces, is perpetually on the brink of poverty. He continues to be exploited by moneylenders and mystified by the unpredictable foreign demand for his product.

The country's forests remain another important economic asset. Teak (also known as ironwood because iron will not rust in contact with it) is the king of water-resistant timbers. Constant burning-off of virgin forest has greatly reduced Thailand's reserves of forest land (forest covered 53% of the country's land surface in 1964, falling to 43% in 1974). The forest police impose heavy penalties for illegal felling: 10- to 20-year prison sentences are common. Meanwhile, three- to five-year concessions are habitually accorded to large timber companies and land-owners. Over 20,000 highly trained elephants are used by the timber concessions; without subscribing to any union, these beasts have obtained a statutory working day of five hours maximum, due to their inability to tolerate long exposure to heat. The timber is floated down from the jungles to the port of Bangkok, a journey that can take four or five years. All felled teak trees are immediately replaced.

Fish, the indispensable accompaniment to rice, is omnipresent in Thailand: most farmers are fishermen, and vice-versa. Two out of every three peasants fish regularly in canals, irrigation ditches, ponds, and even water-logged rice fields. The country also specializes in raising crayfish: Thailand is the world's largest exporter of the *Macrobachium rosengergii* species.

Thailand's economic development is hampered by a lack of raw materials with the exception of tin, which is the major resource of Southern Thailand, the third-largest tin-producing

---

Tourism and rice

In 1987, tourism replaced rice production as Thailand's largest source of revenue. Thai tourism is a fabulous success story; the number of visitors to the country has tripled in the last decade. The basic conditions for tourism in Thailand are of course quite exceptional and facilities have kept pace with the industry's growth. Thai hotel capacity is constantly increasing (at the moment there are nearly 50,000 first-class rooms available across the nation), provisions are of a very high quality, service is remarkable, and a systematic policy has been carried out in the exploitation of the country's potential for tourism.

Thanks to over 40 airlines which operate in and out of Thailand, Bangkok is no longer so remote. Over three million visitors arrived in 1986. Of these, 60% came from South-east Asia and the Pacific zone, mostly from Malaysia and Singapore, and 20% from Europe. Curiously enough, American tourists account for less than 8% of the total.

Akha tribeswoman.

area in the world. The mineral ore is processed in Singapore or Penang. The bulk of industry is concentrated on converting agricultural products (sugar refineries, rice processing factories, distilleries, textile factories). However, the discovery of huge gas deposits in the Gulf of Thailand has raised hopes of reducing the country's massive energy deficit.

THE WONDERFUL TALE OF PRINCE SIDDHARTHA

Pilgrims in search of the absolute have often been drawn to the Himalayas, and Buddhism itself originated in Nepal in the 6th century BC.

There was once a prince named Siddhartha, for whom an extraordinary destiny was prophesied by the soothsayers. In his youth, Siddhartha lived in luxury and surrounded by beauty, far from the sufferings of the ordinary world, but for all his good fortune, he was discontented. At the age of 17, he was married to a beautiful princess. Then, one day, while walking outside the precinct of his palace, Siddhartha discovered the four scourges of existence: Sickness, Old Age, Poverty, and Death. This discovery led him to convert to the life of an ascetic. At the age of 29, after the birth of his son, the prince slipped out of his palace alone at night, exchanged his rich clothes for the bark of a tree, cut off his long hair, and went into the jungle in search of truth. For seven years, Siddhartha lived a life of wandering and privation but still he found no satisfaction. A last, while sitting under a banyan tree, he discovered the four noble truths, namely 'Pain', the 'Origin of Pain', the 'Cessation of Pain', and the 'Way that leads to the Cessation of Pain'. After this enlightenment, he went to Benares (modern-day Varanasi in India), where he preached his first sermon ('the setting in motion of the wheel of the Law') at Sarnath, a few miles away from Benares. Subsequently he founded the first Buddhist monastic community and spent the remainder of his life teaching his doctrine. In short, Siddhartha was Buddha, he who has known enlightenment and who, at his death, attains Nirvana, the Supreme Illumination which enables him to break out of the cycle of reincarnation.

In the 3rd century BC, the Emperor Asoka spread Buddhist doctrine from Kashmir to Ceylon (present-day Sri Lanka). The southern regions developed a preference for the Theravâda tradition, while the north turned to the Mahâyâna school of thought, which was later propagated throughout Central Asia and China. Theravâda Buddhism, which had emerged directly from Brahmin philosophy, took root in South-east Asia from the 10th century onwards.

THERAVÂDA BUDDHISM AND THE SPIRIT WORLD

Officially, 90% of the Thai population are followers of Theravâda ('teaching of the elders') Buddhism. This doctrine, which is based on a strict interpretation of Buddha's teachings, is also qualified as Hînayâna (The Lesser Vehicle). It originally came from Ceylon and is firmly established in Thailand, Laos, Kampuchea, and Burma. It rejects the speculative aspects of Mahâyâna Buddhism (The Greater Vehicle), so called because it 'expanded' upon the basic Buddhist doctrines by adding new concepts. In Theravâda Buddhism, religion is integrated with life in the sense that the Buddhist is obliged to behave as a disciple in order to attain sainthood *(arahant)*.

Buddhism, in general, is distinguished by tolerance, moderation, and restraint.

Thai Buddhism is a rich blend of paradoxes. This union is all the more easily accomplished because Buddhism is not, strictly speaking, a religion. There is no miracle recipe for attaining Nirvana. The individual faces his own choices and destiny. The numerous rules help him make his way through life and give him a sense of security. In formal terms, Buddhism can co-exist with other forms of belief. Of these, the dominant ones are various types of animism and astrology. The king himself is said never to make an important decision without consulting his astrologer and the same is true for most other Thai leaders.

Nearly all Thai households have their own miniature temples, placed on a post not far from the main building. This represents the abode of the earth spirit, displaced during the construction of the house. The spirit receives regular offerings, and the householder customarily places himself under its protection. Whenever a new house is built, the temple is carefully placed where it will never be in the house's shadow.

In Bangkok, large modern hotels, gas stations, and even banks all have their 'spirit houses'. During the construction of the new Chiang Mai University there was a lively debate among the distinguished professors about whether or not a spirit house should be set up. In the end they decided to build one rather than to risk giving offence.

Harvests in the countryside are thought to depend on the goodwill of the spirit world. The forces of good must defeat a host of werewolves and other demons. Everywhere in the fields, you will see altars raised to the rice goddess.

THE MONASTIC LIFE

The Buddhist clergy usually share the animistic beliefs of the lay people. At some point during their lifetimes, all Buddhist males are temporarily ordained. Thus, in addition to professional priests, there is a large corps of part-time ones. At any given time, about 10% of Thai males live in monasteries. The abbé of Choisy, who visited Thailand in 1686, drew the following dubious conclusion: 'The reason for this plethora of monks is not hard to find. All the people of the realm are obliged to work for the king whenever he wishes them to do so — and he so wishes frequently. Only the monks are exempt'.

The religious orders also accept those who desire to withdraw from the world for a while. The reasons for such a retreat are not always mystical: well-known personalities have found it a way of purging themselves. Temporary ordination is generally considered a valuable acquisition of merit for a man's future life as well as that of his family. Except for a few women *(maichis)* with shaven heads and white tunics who do domestic chores, the Buddhist temple is an exclusively male institution.

Monastic life is regulated by 227 rules of which the following are the most important: all forms of life must be respected,

Spirit houses are decorated according to the simplicity or luxury of the owner's home.

absolute chastity must be observed, and it is forbidden not only to lie and steal but also to possess money. The monk must not smell flowers, perfume himself, burn wood, whistle, sing, sleep in a soft bed, touch money, sit down with his legs stretched out, etc. Monks take vows of poverty and theoretically their possessions are limited to three robes, a begging bowl, a needle, a belt, and a sieve through which everything is strained to avoid swallowing some living creature by mistake.

The monks are fed by the entire population. In every town and village, they may be seen roaming the streets in silence between six and seven in the morning, perpetuating the rite of humility as taught by Buddha. The monastic rule forbids them to eat in the afternoon. They do not have the right to beg, but they must accept everything that is offered to them. Their diet, however, is usually quite wholesome.

The monk's lot is not a bad one. It can even turn out to be a professional alternative, given that the monk earns social pres-

> **Observations on pain**
>
> 'This, oh monks, is the sacred truth with regard to pain. Birth is pain, old age is pain, sickness is pain, death is pain, union with those we hate is pain, separation from those we love is pain, not receiving that which we desire is pain, in short, the five elements of appropriation are all pain.'
>
> Sayings of Buddha ('Sarnath Sermon')

tige while living at the expense of the monastic and village communities. The people themselves take as good care of their clergy as possible in the awareness that they acquire 'merit' by so doing (this system is not unlike the Catholic 'indulgences' of the Middle Ages).

Young people traditionally take advantage of the rainy season to don the orange robe for a least three months, during which time they avoid excursions into the countryside. As Buddha himself remarked, it takes only one monk in the rice field to ruin the harvest!

ROBOTS AND LOTUS BLOSSOMS

The Thailand of 'peasants with their feet in the water' is also the Thailand of the computer age. Young Thais are torn between modernity and tradition. According to the Children's Foundation, thousands of the nation's school-age children work ten hours a day, seven days a week, in appalling conditions. In 1978, the National Bureau of Statistics calculated that 1.4 million Thai children lived in such conditions. Since then, this figure has increased by 6% per year.

Town-bred children are liable to have more modern problems. The Anti-Drug Coordination Centre and the Social Welfare Council of Thailand report that heroin addiction has become a major scourge in Bangkok's schools. The most frequently cited causes for this are teacher negligence, parents too involved in their work to take proper care of their children, and a huge increase in children's pocket money. These are the symptomatic excesses of a society which is both extravagantly rich and miserably poor and which is desperately trying to enter the 21st century.

While elephants transport timber out of the northern mountains, there is talk of using nuclear energy to blast a passage through the Kra isthmus in Southern Thailand. Thousands of young Thais study abroad, in America, Australia, New Zealand, and Europe, with the idea of returning to participate in the transformation of their country. At the same time, Thailand's separatist movements, communist insurrections, and dramatic economic problems, along with the changing policies of the US, expansionist Vietnam, and the evolution of relations with China, all contribute to make the country's future uncertain.

The West's image of Thailand tends to be one of a country of smiles and garlands of flowers. Thailand's true nature is very much more complex — and very much worth investigating.

BANGKOK

During the Ayutthaya epoch, Bangkok was no more than a fishing village surrounded by orchards on the east bank of the Chao Phraya River. At the fall of Ayutthaya (see p. 39), a new capital, Thonburi, was founded on the west bank of the river. Then in 1782, Rama I abandoned the new capital for Bangkok; from that moment, Bangkok began its irresistible rise. Two years later, the town's first road was built, still called New Road although it is the oldest in the city.

Change came quickly: the traditional houses, built in the river on stilts, gave way to banks, stores, hotels, and the headquarters of international organizations. The country was opened to foreigners and, today, the Chinese inhabitants of Bangkok make up over half of the city's population. Their quarter teems with activity; their shops are stacked with products and, along the last *klongs* (canals), Chinese soup flows freely in the little market booths and stalls. Shades of Hong Kong, Manila, Jakarta, and Taipei can all be found in Bangkok, with just the same mixture of dirt and opulence as their originals. Over six million people, rich and poor, make their living in Thailand's capital. The rich live in tall modern buildings or in beautiful villas set in the dense greenery of the back lanes *(sois)*. The poor reside in decrepit alleys and tumbledown shanties washed by the black water of the *klongs*.

Bangkok (known to the Thais as Krung Thep, the city of the gods) wears many contrasting faces. Beyond the seductive exoticism of the temples and the brightly coloured markets, and the easy pleasures of Bangkok at night, the tourist must accept the hard reality of a city in the midst of significant changes.

Every year, after the floods that drown entire districts of the capital, causing destruction, deterioration, traffic jams, and fever, the Metropolitan Administration submits a series of grandiose projects for the architectural and urban renewal of Bangkok. At present, a 3 million ฿ plan to protect 35 sq mi/89 sq km of the urban area is under consideration. This would be financed partly by the World Bank and partly by various Japanese and Dutch firms (the latter being masters of the art of flood control). The project hinges on the construction of a canal parallel to the Chao Phraya River to absorb the floodwaters and balance their levels. During the catastrophic floods of 1983, no less than 170 sq mi/450 sq km of suburban Bangkok disappeared under water; since that time, insurance companies have refused to pay flood claims.

The state, which is acutely aware of these problems, favours the construction of large architectural and administrative complexes outside the capital. Thus the Petroleum Authority, the Rajavithee Hospital and the new finance ministry are to be built outside Bangkok. The Royal Military Academy has already been moved to Nakhon Nayok.

Recently, a project advocated by the ex-ruler Phibul Songgram has re-emerged. Phibul's contention was that Bangkok was too difficult to defend militarily and the capital should be moved to Phetchabun. With the advance of the Vietnamese army to within 125 mi/200 km east of Bangkok, the old marshal's project has begun to attract new attention, though the difficulties involved in making such a move would be formidable.

The charm of Bangkok

In spite of many drawbacks, modern Bangkok is still full of charm. The temples open the way to a world of timeless enchantment and artistry. The streets and markets provide a spectacle which changes with every day that passes. Bangkok is a city to experience: temples and old Thai residences, bowls of soup in the markets, treasure hunts through the city's countless shops, the equivocal delights of Patpong (Bangkok's red-light district), wild escapades in *tuk-tuks* (three-wheeled vehicles), or even a Thai boxing-match. And if, after all that, you still thirst for adventure, turning down the first *soi* (lane) to the right or left of the thoroughfare will lead you into a different world altogether. Behind the concrete walls is another Bangkok, untouched by the turmoil of progress.

GETTING THE MOST OUT OF BANGKOK

Most tourists spend about four days in Bangkok: they usually find this to be either too long or too short. Bangkok is not easily accessible, like Rome or Paris. It is complex city that makes few concessions to the casual visitor and cannot be summed up in terms of spectacular monuments.

First of all, you will waste a great deal of time getting around. At peak traffic hours, it is not uncommon for a trip of 2-3 mi/3-4 km to take over one hour. The first thing to do is to buy a street map of Bangkok at the TAT office (see p. 32) or at any news-stand. These maps are excellent, with all the city's centres of interest clearly marked. Work out your program according to the time at your disposal, without trying to see everything.

It's no easy matter to find your way around Bangkok. The names of streets are not always marked, and the way in which houses and buildings have been numbered is baffling. The main traffic arteries *(thanons)* are intersected by *sois,* smaller streets which frequently turn out to be cul-de-sacs. When a *soi* is unnamed, it has a number (one side of the *thanon* is even, the other odd). This is a thoroughly practical system when it comes to giving an address to a taxi driver. Since streets and avenues are often very long, you find the closest *soi* to the place you wish to get to, and say, for example, 'Sukhumvit, Soi 20'. For this you will have to learn to count in Thai, which presents no special difficulty (see 'Useful Vocabulary' p. 178).

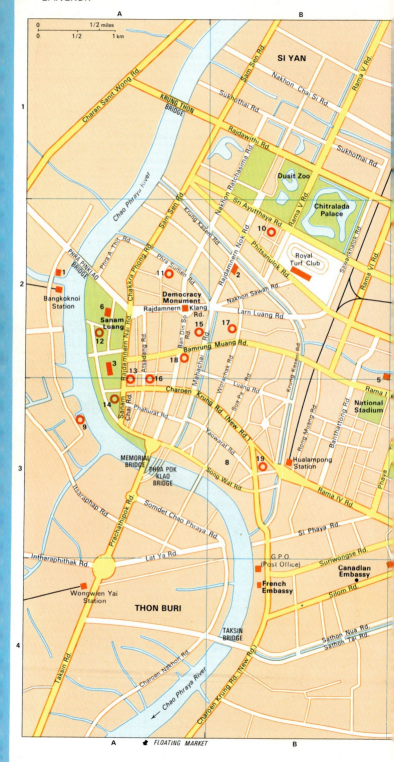

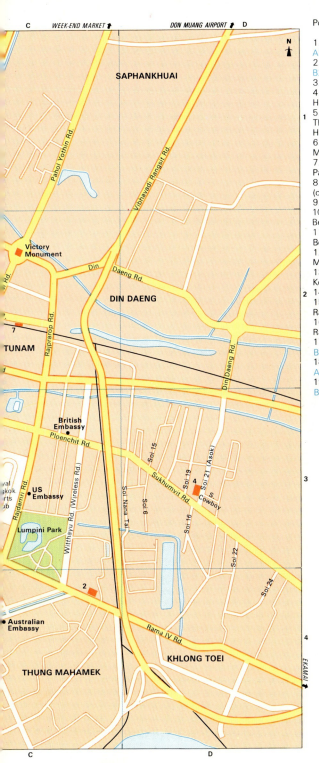

Points of interest:

1. Royal barges A2
2. Thai boxing B2, C4
3. Palace A2
4. Kamtieng House D3
5. Jim Thompson's House B2-3
6. National Museum A2
7. Suan Pakkard Palace C2
8. Chinatown (centre) B3
9. Wat Arun A3
10. Wat Benchamabopit B2
11. Wat Bovornives A2
12. Wat Mahathat A2
13. Wat Phra Keo A3
14. Wat Po A3
15. Wat Rachanada A2
16. Wat Rajabopitr A2-3
17. Wat Sakhet B2
18. Wat Suthat A2
19. Wat Traymit B3

Bangkok taxi drivers generally make little effort to understand foreigners. Nor is it worthwhile mastering a complicated name such as Wat Benchamabophit if you then pronounce it in the wrong tone. Thai is above all a tonal language and you will have great difficulty in making yourself understood. The best policy is to give the name of a neighbouring hotel, preferably a big one; you will find them all marked on the street map. This works about 90% of the time, except in the case of *tuk-tuks* that are less accustomed to carrying tourists than are taxis. As a last resort, you can always have your destination written out in Thai by the hall porter of your hotel.

PRACTICAL INFORMATION

Telephone area code for Bangkok and the surrounding area: 02.

Access

Bangkok's Don Muang Airport is about 15 mi/25 km from the capital. The drive into town takes a good hour because of the traffic. If you are not being met by a tour organizer, you have several options.

Limousines and taxis

Tickets for the air-conditioned limousines are sold at the 'Limousine' counter at the airport: 300 ฿ from the international terminal, 200 ฿ from the domestic terminal.

There are also licensed taxis, which charge approximately the same price as limousines, and pirate taxis that can be identified by their white license plates with black lettering. Airport authorities warn against using the latter.

Minibus

Thai Airways International offers a minibus service to the main hotels that costs 80 ฿. Buses leave the airport only when full.

Public buses

Lines n° 4 and n° 10 are air-conditioned; line n° 19 is not. Slow and uncomfortable, public bus transportation is not recommended for first-time visitors but, at 15 ฿, it is by far the cheapest way of getting into the city.

Getting around Bangkok

On foot

It is a hopeless task to try to go everywhere in Bangkok on foot because the distances are too great. You should take time to walk around at least one area and explore the market, perhaps visit a local temple, or wander down some of the smaller streets. As in all large cities, be sure to keep a careful eye on your bag and camera.

While strolling or crossing the street, beware of holes and open manhole covers. Thais drive on the left, but keep alert as they frequently flaunt the rules. Crosswalks exist but they are frequently ornamental and red lights are so seldom respected away from the main thoroughfares that it is best to forget about them altogether.

In spite of the precautions you must take and however time-consuming it may be, you will find that the best way to see the beauty and poetry of Bangkok is by moving around on foot as much as possible.

Taxis

There are over 10,000 working taxis in the capital. Despite a general improvement in the quality of the vehicles, many of which are now air-conditioned, there is still a fair proportion of patched-up old jalopies. The Bangkok taxi meter, like the Bangkok traffic light, is often purely decorative. You must bargain over the fare before you enter the taxi, following this rule of thumb: offer half the fare the driver proposes, then reluctantly agree to pay three quarters of it.

Allow about 60 ฿ for an average ride within the city (Silom - Sukhumvit or Silom - Chinatown). At peak traffic hours (8am-10am and 4pm-5pm), the rates rise because drivers are slowed down by the jams and can take fewer fares. If you have to pay with a large bank note, which should generally be avoided if at all possible, don't get out of the taxi until the driver has given you your change.

Taxis parked in front of hotels are usually more expensive but, on the other hand, they are often air-conditioned. Pay for them in advance at the hotel reception desk. Even though the driver may ask for a supplement, remember that the price is fixed and bears no relation to the number of passengers.

Tuk-tuks

Tuk-tuk is the Thai name for the *samlor,* a rackety, polluting three-wheeled vehicle. The *samlor* will carry no more than two passengers at a time because the rear seat is very small. Open on two sides, but secure in the protection of the charms and blessings attached to its dashboard, the *samlor* weaves in and out of the traffic. On arrival at your destination, decisively tell the driver to stop immediately or else he will take the initiative and carry on regardless of your protests. Finally, take care to determine the price in advance: the driver will understand that two fingers mean 20 ฿, three fingers mean 30 ฿, etc. 20 ฿ is the minimum, with 40 ฿ covering the cost of an average ride.

Most of the city's 8000 *samlors* are rented to the drivers for 100 ฿ to 210 ฿ per day. Add 50 ฿ per day for gasoline and you will readily understand that the life of a *samlor* driver is not a bed of roses.

The Thai authorities are rightly concerned about the pollution caused by *tuk-tuks* and have stopped issuing new vehicle licenses for them, but Bangkok mechanics use the chassis of old *tuk-tuks* to build new ones, thereby circumventing the law.

At one point there was a proposal to replace all the *samlors* with taxis, to which the *tuk-tuk* drivers responded with a petition to the king. They obtained satisfaction and, to mark their gratitude, they voted to give blood once a year.

Buses

If you aim to take a bus, the first thing to do is buy a map of the Bangkok bus network (from a postcard and tobacco vendor in Silom or New Roads, or from the TAT, see p. 32).

The bus system can carry you just about anywhere in the capital, but Bangkok's hundreds of bus drivers love to race one another. There are two categories of buses: air-conditioned and ordinary (much cheaper and much more crowded). Notice that some buses have blue plates and others red, even though they may share the same number. A red plate means a bus is operating on partial service only.

A few major bus routes

Bus nº 1: New Road, Central Post Office. Crosses Chinatown via Yaowarat to Sanam Louang (temples, palace, museum).

Bus nº 2: Phra Khanong, Sukhumvit, and Ploenchit. Goes past the Rajprasong Commercial Centre and the Pratu Nam Market and takes in a section of Phetchaburi and Rajdamnern Avenue.

Bus nº 4: Leaves the docks on the Klong Toey (*klongs* are canals, most of which were paved over as roads), passing the Lumpini Stadium, the Dusit Thani Hotel, the Pasteur Institute, and Hualampong Station, before crossing the river at Memorial Bridge and continuing on to Thonburi. Practical for reaching Wat Arun.

Bus nº 17: Goes the whole length of Sathorn Road, then down Wireless Road (Vitthayu), Ploenchit and Pratu Nam Market via Rajprasong and Sri Ayutthaya to Banglampoo (standing Buddha) and Sanam Louang.

Bus nº 25: Leaves from near Sanam Louang, crosses some of Bangkok's most lively districts (Yaowarat, Hualampong and Patumwan), passes by

Rajprasong and continues down Sukhumvit to Pak Nam on the riverside (excellent seafood in local restaurants here).

Bus nº 29: Goes out to Don Muang Airport. You can catch this bus at the station at Samyan on Phya Thai Road, by the Victory Monument, or at Saphan Kwai.

Boats

Some small boats cross the river, others stop at various jetties. You can go up river to Sanam Louang from the Oriental Hotel or else take a taxi boat. This craft is usually a *hang yao* (pirogue), one of many that operate along the little *klongs* (canals).

Accommodation

(Map coordinates refer to the map p. 80.)

The city has excellent accommodation in all categories from the plainest to the most luxurious. The list below is far from exhaustive but will give you an idea of what is available. It has been categorized according to the general quality of services rather than solely by reference to price levels (for a detailed description of each category see p. 17).

▲▲▲▲ **Ambassador:** Soi 11, Sukhumvit Rd. (D3). Tel: 251 0404 or 251 5141-70. 1000 rooms and 1400 staff. Conveniently situated in a lively quarter of Bangkok, the hotel boasts a dizzying list of services including 24 restaurants, full business facilities and an aviary of exotic birds.

▲▲▲▲ **Dusit Thani:** Rama IV Rd., Saladeeng Circle (C3). Tel: 233 1130-9. 525 rooms. Easily identifiable by its towering spire, the Dusit Thani stands opposite Lumpini Park in Bangkok's business and shopping centre. A ten-minute walk from Patpong, the hotel has seven restaurants, of which the **Bassaracum** is the best. Pleasant atmosphere, efficient management.

▲▲▲▲ **Erawan:** 494 Rajdamri Rd. (C3). Tel: 252 9100-29. The Erawan, one of Bangkok's oldest hotels, stands on the corner of Ploenchit in a lively quarter. Alas, its site is said to be cursed. An attempt was made to remedy this problem by building a large spirit house but apparently this was insufficient. A Brahmin priest was called in and he recommended the erection of the small Hindu temple which now adjoins the hotel, where ceremonies and sacred dances are performed around the clock. This is something worth seeing, but superstitious travelers may feel happier in another hotel. More's the pity because the Erawan takes excellent care of its guests. At the time of publication, this hotel was closed for repairs. It is expected to open in several seasons.

▲▲▲▲ **Hilton:** 2 Wireless Rd. (C3). Tel: 253 0123. 389 rooms. Situated in a residential quarter, close to most of the foreign embassies and only a few minutes by taxi from the liveliest area of Sukhumvit. Up-to-date luxury with everything to restore the tired traveler.

▲▲▲▲ **Indra Regent:** Rajprarop Rd. (C2). Tel: 252 1111. 436 rooms. Well-situated, close to the Pratu Nam Market and the Daimaru department store, but in an area which is frequently choked with traffic.

▲▲▲▲ **Meridien-President:** 135/26 Keson Rd. (C3). Tel: 253 0444 or 252 2151-7. 381 rooms. Formerly the Hotel President, now part of the French Meridien Hotel chain, this hotel will please anyone who likes nightlife. Situated in the liveliest section of Gaysorn.

Pirogues are still the most widely used means of transporting merchandise.

▲▲▲▲ **Montien:** 54 Suriwongse Rd. (B3). Tel: 234 8060 or 233 7060. 535 rooms. Another hotel for nightbirds. Newlyweds may care to try the special romantic honeymoon suite at 15,000 ฿ a night.

▲▲▲▲ **Narai:** 222 Silom Rd. (B4). Tel: 233 3350. 519 rooms. At the centre of Silom, between Patpong, with its restaurants and nightclubs, and New Road, with its antique and souvenir shops. A practical hotel for shopping.

▲▲▲▲ **The Oriental;** 48 Oriental Ave. (B4). Tel: 236 0400. 403 rooms. At the bottom of New Road, beside the river, the most elegant hotel in Bangkok. The original building, dating from 1876, has been enlarged but the two modern wings lack the charm of the original. Attractions include four restaurants, two swimming pools and trips along the river aboard the *Oriental Queen* as well as interesting evenings at the **Chitr Podhana,** an elegant Thai restaurant on the other side of the river. Former guests at the Oriental include Somerset Maugham, Joseph Conrad and Graham Greene. This hotel gives off an aura of old Bangkok and is extremely charming.

▲▲▲▲ **Royal Orchid:** 2 Captain Bush Lane, Siphya Rd. (B3). Tel: 234 5599. 780 rooms. Situated close to the Oriental Hotel, on the riverbank. Beautiful view from bedrooms and access to all the Oriental Hotel's restaurants.

▲▲▲▲ **Shangri-La:** 89 Soi Wat Suan Plu, New Rd. (C3). Tel: 236 7777. Close to the Oriental, it rivals its neighbour for refinement and style. Thanks to the star-shaped design, most of its 700 rooms look out over the river. Its superb Thai restaurant, **The Salathip,** is recommended.

▲▲▲▲ **Siam Intercontinental:** 967 Rama I Rd. (C3). Tel: 253 0355-7. 411 rooms. At the heart of a 'new tourist district', 220 yds/200 m from Jim Thompson's House (see p. 112), another palace-type hotel, daringly designed in the traditional Thai manner. Huge gardens, with private zoo and craftsmen's workshops. A sparkling oasis hidden from the roar of the city, but only a step away from the excitement of Siam Square. Very chic and very expensive.

Several other hotels in Bangkok offer much the same services at similar prices. Among them are the **Hyatt Central Plaza,** 1695 Paholyothin Rd. Tel: 270 1820-35; the **Bangkok Peninsula,** 155 Rajdamri Rd. Tel: 251 6127 or 251 6370; and the **Menam,** by the river on 2074 New Rd., Yannawa. Tel: 289 1148-9.

▲▲▲ **Asia:** 296 Phya Thai Rd. (D3). Tel: 215 0780. 166 rooms. This is an excellently situated hotel, close to Siam Square and Jim Thompson's House (see p. 112). Solid comfort for reasonable prices.

▲▲▲ **Impala:** Soi 24, Sukhumvit Rd. (D4). Tel: 258 8612-6. 220 rooms. Situated between Soi 24 and Soi 26, this hotel is a little farther from the centre of Bangkok than most hotels but the area is very animated in the evenings.

▲▲▲ **Imperial:** Wireless Rd. (C3). Tel: 252 8070-9. 400 rooms. The Imperial is in the embassy section of town and has its own garden. A garden party is held three times weekly with charcoal-grilled *(satay)* Thai food of the kind you can buy in the street, only more refined and more expensive and served in a wonderful atmosphere.

▲▲▲ **Mandarin:** 662 Rama IV Rd., near Suriwongse. (B3). Tel: 233 4980 or 233 5370-9. 420 rooms. Not to be confused with its Hong Kong namesake. Not outstanding but good value for money.

▲▲▲ **Monohra:** 412 Suriwongse Rd. (B4). Tel: 234 5070 or 234 5086-9. 250 rooms. Not far from the Suriwongse-New Road intersection, an excellent base with several centres of interest

Practical information

close by (Silom and Suriwongse, the Oriental Hotel and the river, the antique shops of New Road).

▲▲ **Park:** Soi 7, 6 Sukhumvit Rd. (D3). Tel: 252 5110-3. 132 rooms. In Sukhumvit's best shopping area with a large garden and a pleasant swimming pool.

▲▲ **Royal:** 2 Rajdamnern Ave. (A2). Tel: 222 9111. 140 rooms. Probably the best-situated hotel in this category. Very close to Sanam Louang, the Bangkok central square (Royal Palace, Wat Phra Keo, Wat Po, museum, national theatre). Slightly antiquated, with huge bedrooms and good food.

▲▲ **Viengtai:** 42 Thanee Rd. (A2). Tel: 282 8672-4. 300 rooms. Well-situated near Sanam Louang and the Wat Bovornives. Easy access to Chinatown.

The following hotels are particularly recommended for night owls:

▲▲ **Grace,** 12 Nana Rd. (D3). Tel: 253 0671. With a discotheque full of young people.
▲▲ **Nana,** 4 Sukhumvit Rd. (D3). Tel: 252 4101-5.
▲▲ **Rajah,** 18 Sukhumvit Rd. (D3). Tel: 252 5102. Close to a number of nightclubs.
▲▲ **Rose,** 118 Suriwongse Rd. (B4). Tel: 233 7695.

For people who wish to spend less on accommodation, dozens of other reasonably comfortable hotels are regularly listed by the TAT and the weekly *Where*. Our recommendations:

▲ **Atlanta,** Soi 2, Sukhumvit Rd. (D3). Tel: 252 6069 or 252 1650.
▲ **Federal,** Soi 11, 27 Sukhumvit Rd. (D3). Tel: 252 5143.
▲ **Florida,** 43 Phaya Thai Sq. (B3). Tel: 252 4141.
▲ **Malaysia,** 54 Ngam Duplee Rd. (C4). Tel: 286 3542.
▲ **Prince,** 1537/1 New Phetchaburi Rd. (D2). Tel: 251 3318.
▲ **Star,** 36/1 Soi Kasemsan. (B2). Tel: 215 0020.

Food

(Map coordinates refer to the map p. 80.)

Mealtimes are less formal in Thailand than in the West and quick meals (not to be confused with fast food) are available at all times in tiny open-air restaurants and even on street corners. Fritters, soups, fried noodles, brochettes, and pastries can all be had at a moment's notice. Traditional Thai cooking is a mixture of styles but always tasty and appetizing.

There were 24,235 officially registered restaurants in the Bangkok-Thonburi area at the last count but this figure is probably too low. The range of choices is especially wide, extending from fried snake to French *coq-au-vin,* and from lacquered duck to Swiss fondue.

The lists of restaurants that follow always begin with those offering Thai cuisine. In reality, it is not always easy to dissociate Thai from Chinese because many Bangkok restaurants belong to Chinese people (as does much of the food supply trade). Given this and the large Chinese population of Bangkok, chopsticks are often placed on the table as a matter of course, even though the Thais do not customarily use them. Restaurants offering a type of cuisine other than Thai are listed under the appropriate heading.

The areas of town which have the best selection of restaurants are the new tourist sections (Sukhumvit, New Phetchaburi) and the traditional business areas (Silom, Suriwongse). Because of Bangkok's circuitous roads and traffic, you should always try to lunch in the quarter where you happen to be, even going into the first restaurant that comes to hand. For dinner you can choose a restaurant and take your time getting there.

The restaurants listed below are classed as follows (prices don't include drinks):
Expensive (E), at least 500 ฿; Moderate (M), 300 ฿ to 400 ฿; Inexpensive (I), 60 ฿ to 200 ฿.

Sukhumvit — New Phetchaburi (D3)

Baan Thai (E), 7 Sukhumvit Soi 32. Tel: 258 5403 or 258 9517. Dinner only. A beautiful wooden Thai house. Slightly sweetened Thai food. Dance show.
Bangkeo Ruenkwan (M), 212 Sukhumvit Soi 12. Tel: 251 8229. Excellent seafood Thai-style, amid old-fashioned decor.
Bua Thong, Soi Asoke/Din Daeng Rd. An enormous collection of open-air restaurants (the largest seats 3000 people) with more than 100 dishes at all prices. Thai, Cantonese, and Shanghai cuisine. Definitely a must, for lunch or dinner. All taxi drivers know Bua Thong.
Chitr Pochana (M), 60 Sukhumvit Soi 20. Tel: 391 6401 or 391 8346. Excellent Thai cuisine in a pleasant environment. Careful presentation, translated menu.
Koom Luang (I), Soi Asoke/Din Daeng Rd. (Part of the Bua Thong complex mentioned above.) Tel: 246 3273. Excellent value; fish in coconut milk, seafood. Menu in Thai only.
Lai Cram (M), Sukhumvit Soi 49, 11/1 Soi Akkrapad. Closes at 9pm (8pm Sun.). Authentic Thai cooking.
Royal Kitchen (M), 754 Sukhumvit Soi 31. Excellent cooking.
Toll Gate (M), 245/2 Sukhumvit Soi 31. Tel: 391 3947. Thai *nouvelle cuisine* of exceptional quality in understated decor.

American

Cheesecake House (M), 7/1 Sukhumvit Soi 49. Tel: 258 8344. Grandmother's cookies and other pastries.

French

Jean la Grenouille (M), 220/4 Sukhumvit Soi 1. Tel: 252 0311. A charming restaurant with a growing reputation.
Le Petit Moulin (M), 2/33 Sukhumvit Soi 22. Tel: 258 2852. Family cooking (*steak au poivre,* homemade *rillettes*).
Le Vendôme (E), Hotel Ambassador, Sukhumvit Soi 22. Tel: 252 6753. Excellent cooking, Thai chefs trained by Madame Belleuvre.

Steak and grill

Chokechai Steakhouse (M), Sukhumvit. Tel: 258 6872. Chokechai Building. Filipino orchestra and Western ambience.

Ploenchit - Phetchaburi - Siam Square (C2-C3)

There are far fewer restaurants in this quarter than big hotels.
Green House (M), 41 Soi Lang Suan, Ploenchit. Tel: 579 6273. Mainly Thai cooking with one or two Chinese and Western dishes.
Pratu Nam (I), an open market at the intersection of Phetchaburi and Rajprarob. Many open-air restaurants. Thai Chinese dishes, seafood.
Talay Thong (E), Siam Intercontinental Hotel (see p. 86). Seafood.

Chinese

Ming Palace (E), Indra Regent Hotel (see p. 85).
Tien Long (M), 50 Soi Lang Suan, Ploendhit. Tel: 251 3048. More than 50 different dishes. *Dim-sum* meals (steamed food).

French
Fireplace Grill (E), Meridien-President Hotel (see p. 85).
Ma Maison (E), Hilton Hotel (see p. 85).
Siam Grill (E), Siam Intercontinental Hotel (see p. 86).

Silom Suriwongse (C3-B4)

Good selection of international restaurants in the old tourist and business quarter.
Banana House (I), 66 Silom Rd. Tel: 234 9967. Braised shrimp soups, curries, Thai snails, and other delicious dishes.
D'Jit Pochana (E), Oriental Hotel (see p. 86).
Laksmi (E), Narai Hotel (see p. 86).
Silom Village Trade Center (M), 286 Silom Rd. Tel: 233 9447 or 234 4448. Restaurant and craft shops in wooden houses. Original atmosphere and remarkable cooking.
Sukothai (E), Dusit Thani Hotel (see p. 85). With Thai dance show.

Chinese
Jade Garden (M), Montien Hotel (see p. 86).
Mayflower (M), Dusit Thani Hotel (see p. 85).
New Shangri-La (M), 154/4-5 Silom Red. Tel: 234 5588. A festival of Chinese cooking, at the sign of the Dragon.

French
Le Gourmet (E), Montien Hotel (see p. 86).
Normandie Grill (E), Oriental Hotel (see p. 86).
La Rotonde (E), Narai Hotel (see p. 86).

Indian
Café India (M), 460/8 Suriwongse (in front of Trocadero Hotel). Tel: 234 1720. Good Indian cooking, vegetarian and non-vegetarian; Rajput decor.

Korean
Arirang (M), 106 Silom Rd. Tel: 234 7869 or 233 0419. Korean barbecue and other dishes, accompanied by birdsong.

Vietnamese
Vietnam (I), 82-4 Silom Rd. Tel: 234 6174. North Vietnamese specialties and Malay brochettes *(satay)*.

Seafood
Lord Jim's (E), Oriental Hotel (see p. 86).

Sanam Louang-Old Bangkok (A2)

There is only a narrow choice of restaurants in this quarter, which, paradoxically, is one of the areas most frequented by tourists. From Sanam Louang, therefore, it's best to make your way back to Chinatown or cross Pinklao Bridge to Thonburi, where there are many more places to eat. In the Sanam Louang area, we would nevertheless recommend:

Sorn Daeng (I), 70 Rajdamnern Ave., in front of the Monument to Democracy. Tel: 224 3088. Relaxed, lively atmosphere, unpretentious cooking.

Chinese

Hoi Tien Lao (E), 308 Suapha Rd., in Chinatown. Tel: 221 1685 or 222 7191-3. One of Bangkok's most famous restaurants. Excellent menu.

On the other side of the river, at Thonburi (A2-A3)

Chao Phya Paradise (M), 451/3 Arunamarin Rd. Tel: 424 2389. People who like to eat in quiet intimacy should abstain: this is the biggest restaurant in Thailand (seating for more than 3000). In fact, the Chao Phya Paradise consists of several establishments side by side, featuring both Cantonese *dim sum* and chic dinners with Thai floorshows.

Kaloang Home Kitchen (M), 127-141 Thanon Lieb Menam, Chong Nonethee. Close to the royal barges. Excellent traditional Thai cuisine, pleasant decor; open-air tables. A popular family restaurant.

Rimnam (M), below the Pinklao Bridge. Tel: 424 1112. Fantastic aquarium from which you order your meal: prawns, shellfish, crayfish, crabs.

Shopping

(Map coordinates refer to the map p. 80.)

Shopping in Bangkok is as exciting as it is exhausting. Don't be in a hurry to buy; take enough time to compare prices and quality. The shopkeepers compete frantically and are usually willing to cut their prices to make a sale. Crocodile and snakeskin bags and accessories are readily available in the shopping malls of big Bangkok hotels. Their prices are low but sometimes so are the standards of craftsmanship.

The principal shopping areas of Bangkok
Banglampoo, Phrasumane Rd. Chakraphonse Rd. (A2).
Chinatown, Yaowarat. (A2-A3).
Gaysorn, Ploenchit-Rajprasong intersection. (C3).
Oriental Plaza Shopping Centre, near the Oriental Hotel, access via Custom Lane. Luxury shopping. About 50 boutiques on three levels. (B4).
Ploenchit Arcade, Ploenchit Rd., at the level crossing. (C3).
Pratu Nam, Phetchaburi-Rajdamri and Rajprarob Rd. (C2).
Rajprasong, at the crossroads of Ploenchit, Rajdamri, and Rama I Rds. (C3).
Siam Center, Rama I Rd., near the Siam Intercontinental. (C3).
Silom and Suriwongse, and the lower half of New Rd. (B4).

Department stores

Bangkok department stores are usually open every day from 10am to 10pm and offer a wide choice of craftwork at reasonable prices as well as clothing, luggage and toys.

Big Bell, Ploenchit Arcade. (C3).
Central Department Store, 306 Silom Rd. (B4).
Chidlom Department Store, Ploenchit Arcade. (C3).
Robinson, on the corner of Silom and Rama IV Rd. (C3), with a branch near the Bangkok Bazaar, behind Thai Daimaru.
Sogo, Ploenchit Arcade. (C3), a completely new commercial centre (also Japanese).
Thai Daimaru, Rajadamri Arcade. (C2). Japanese department store.

There are many other department stores to choose from on Phetchaburi Road.

There are no 'special addresses' in Bangkok, only cautious buyers. You may drive an exceptional bargain in the same shop that royally swindled a friend of yours only the day before. Everything depends on your skill at haggling, your shrewdness, and your good luck. The addresses that follow are general indicators but on no account are they guaranteed. Beware of buying false gems, or so-called antiques of recent manufacture.

Handcraft and gift shops

You will gain a general impression of Thai handcrafts in most souvenir and gift shops.

Golden Bo Tree, 8-A Soi Chitlom. Contemporary jewelry, handcrafts, antiques.
House of Jute, 20 Soi Chitlom (the *soi* linking Phetchaburi to Ploenchit, C3). Batiks, bags, belts, scarves, ties, jute mats, etc.
House of Siam, 8 Sathorn Nua Rd. (B4). Silks, jewelry, bronzes, antiques, etc.
Naraipan, 275/2 Larn Luang Rd. (B2). Huge shop run by the government, offering a broad selection of Thai handcrafts.
Silom Village, Silom Rd. (close to the Narai Hotel — B4). A must for its atmosphere and choice.
Sirie's Gallery, 215 Sukhumvit, Soi 20. (D3).
Thai Family Handicrafts, 1268 Chartered Bank La., New Rd. (B4).
Thai Home Industries, 14 New Rd. (A3).

Antiques

The traditional antique dealers' district is Nakhon Kasem, (B3), the 'Thieves Market' in Chinatown. Sadly, real Thai antiques have become exceedingly rare and expensive and the market in fakes has become highly profitable. As the export of antiques is strictly forbidden, you will need to get an export certificate from the seller or the government Fine Arts Department if you do buy anything. If you don't feel confident enough to tangle with the antique dealers of the Chinese quarter, you'll find shops that are more traditional (and also more expensive) on Rajprasong Road and Sukhumvit Road, as well as at the following addresses:

Art and Antique, 421/4 Siam Square 6. (C3).
Asian Antiques, 16-19 Henry Dunant St. (C3) in Siam Square.
Capital Antique Shop, 975/9 Ploenchit Rd. (C3).
Erawan Antiques, 90-82 Radjamri Rd. (C3).
Monogram, Erawan Hotel Arcade, Rajdamri Rd. (C3).

Bronze

Handcraft shops often display objects in bronze but there isn't always much of a choice. If you want matching sets of bowls or plates, you should go to one of the following specialized shops:

Anan's Bronze, 157/11 Phetchaburi Rd. (C2).
House of Siam, 8 Sathorn Nua Rd. (B4).
Siam Bronze, 1250 New Rd. (B4).
Thompson's Jewelry, 6/30-31 Sukhumvit Rd., Soi Nana. (D3).

Celadon and porcelain

Old celadon can be found in antique shops (see Antiques). Reasonably priced, attractive modern celadon is sold at the small shops around the Rajtewi roundabout on Phetchaburi Road. One shop particularly worth a visit:

Celadon House, 278 Silom Rd. (B4).

Fabrics

Thai silk is sold everywhere but the quality is uncertain. If you want good fabric that is made to last, buy it in one of the larger shops and pay a little more. Silk, like everything else, must be bargained for. Most fabric shops have their own tailors and cutters and their prices are often higher than those of the small tailoring establishments. The shops below also sell Thai cotton.

Alexandra Thai Silk, 1297 New Rd. (B4), (near the New Rd.-Silom intersection).
Anita Thai Silk, 294/4-5 Silom Rd. (B4).
Chinawatra Thai Silk, Soi 23, 94 Sukhumvit Rd. (D3).
Choisy, 1 Patpong, 2 Suriwongse Rd. (B3), around the corner from Jim Thompson's House. A pleasant shop run by a Frenchwoman, where your clothes will be cut in the latest Paris styles.
Irene Thai Silk, 248/3-4 Silom (B4 — Narai Hotel).
Kanitha, Oriental Plaza Shopping Centre or 1086/7 Indra Arcade. (B4).
President Thai Silk, 135/21-2 Gaysorn Rd., (C3 — near the President Hotel).
Star of Siam, Rajprasong (C3 — opposite the Erawan Hotel).
The Thai Silk Co. Ltd., 9 Suriwongse Rd. (B3), close to the Rama IV-Rajdamri intersection. This shop was founded by Jim Thompson (see p. 112). The fabrics, which are expensive, are very fine and the staff are superb.

Flowers

More than 1000 different types of orchids grow in Thailand, both wild and under glass. The orchid is used as the emblem of Thai Airways International and as a favourite ornament by Thai women. Orchids travel well; when carefully packaged, they can survive for several weeks after being flown overseas. Visitors from the US should be aware, though, that entry of plants to the US is restricted, and many are banned altogether. During your stay in Thailand, try decorating your hotel room with the delicate garlands of jasmine and orchids sold by children as temple offerings.

Lacquerware

There is only one shop in Bangkok that specializes in lacquerware alone: **Chiang Mai Lacquerware Shop,** 276 Silom Rd. (B4). Practically all handcraft and souvenir shops have lacquerware objects of one kind or another but it is more interesting to buy these things at Chiang Mai, where they are made.

Precious stones and jewelry

Bangkok jewelry shops are like Ali Baba's caves, offering beautiful gems at very reasonable prices. Most come from Burma, notably the fabulous Mogok rubies. However, there are no spectacular bargains to be had: a low-priced stone may only be fake or imperfect (blemished or spoiled in cutting). 'Jade' sold for very little will be 'jadeite': real jade is very clear and extremely expensive.

There are also many sapphires to be found; from the cheaper, dark blue variety to the more expensive clear blue and the curious round-cut star sapphire.

Some useful addresses:
Alex and Co., 14-14/1 Soy Oriental, New Rd. (B4). Branches at the Dusit Thani and Intercontinental Hotel shopping centres.
Anita International, 240/3 Siam Square Soi 2, Rama I Rd. (C3).
Beng Hua Jewelers, 1233 New Rd. (B4).
Diamond Head, 252 Silom Rd. (B4 — close to the Narai Hotel).
Exotic Siam, 204 Siam Centre (C3 — 2nd floor).
Linson's Jewelry, 316/3 Silom Rd. (B4).
Rusami Jewelry Co. Ltd., 246-250 Mahaesak Rd.
Sammy's Gems, 595 Sukhumvit Rd. (D3).
S.B. Jewelry Co. Ltd., 176/1-2 Silom Rd. (B4).
Thailand Jewelry, 2-4 Oriental La. (B4).

Wickerwork

Traditional basketwork can be bought in the markets (weekend markets especially). If you are interested in larger, more intricate pieces (such as rattan furniture) you should go to Sukhumvit, on the odd-numbered side between *sois* 45 and 63. Here you will find armchairs, shelving, trunks, tables, etc. Demand for these items is huge, quality is declining, and prices are going up. So be forceful when bargaining for them.

With its pirogues and taxi-boats, Bangkok's river is a major transportation route.

Entertainment

Entertainment of a specifically Thai nature takes place during festivals and fairs, especially in the provinces. They tend to be more frequent during the dry season (kite contests, cockfights) but the Thai love of gambling is apparent everywhere. The National Lottery even gives rise to 'parallel' bets. Here is some entertainment you shouldn't miss.

Thai boxing

This is a unique sport, in which no holds are barred (except those of judo): blows with the knees, feet, elbows, and head are freely exchanged. If the sport seems ferocious today, it is worth remembering that, until the advent of the boxing glove, the fighters wore bandages studded with crushed glass. A percussion orchestra accompanies the match, modulating its rhythms according to the various phases of the struggle. The spectators seem to vibrate in unison, yelling their approval or otherwise. In the tradition of Thai courtesy, the two fighters open hostilities with a polite *wai* (bow).

Thai boxing matches are scheduled every evening:
at the **Lumpini Stadium** (C4), near the Dusit Thani Hotel. Tel: 251 4303 or 252 8765. On Tue., Fri., and Sat.

at the **Rajdamnern Stadium** (B2), near the Parliament. Tel: 281 4205. On Mon., Wed., Thur., and Sun.
Price: 350-800 ฿, according to the quality of your seat and the reputation of the performers.

Classical dance and traditional theatre

Classical dance is one of the best-known aspects of Thai artistic expression. Its themes are borrowed from the Hindu mythology of the *Ramayana* (*Ramakien* in Thai) and the *Mahabharata*. Complicity between dancers and spectators is established by rigorous coded gestures: the direction of the gaze, the movement of the neck, the curve of the fingers, and the tension of the ankles are all carefully controlled. Thai dance originated as a court art and evokes the sentiments of special individuals such as gods, kings, princes, or princesses.

One of the most important choreographic styles in the classical repertoire is the *Lakhon*, which inextricably mixes theatre and dance. Here women can play a number of separate roles, since the code of gesture eliminates any ambiguity as to the sex of the character at issue.

Another form of Thai theatre is the masked play, or *Khon*. Westerners find this very difficult to understand, since the good characters look just as terrifying as the bad ones, though lately, these fearsome masks have begun to disappear. Performances usually last between four and five hours, demanding almost as much effort from the audience as from the actors.

The Shadow Theatre, or *nang taloung* is still very much alive in Indonesia and the east coast of Malaysia, but has practically disappeared in Thailand.

Most of the big hotels have dance shows. The best of them is unquestionably at the **Oriental,** where the performance takes place in the gardens beside the river. If you feel like treating yourself to a dinner with floor show, try the **Baan Thai**, 7 Soi, 32 Sukhumvit Rd. (D3); the **Maneeya Lotus Room,** 518/4 Ploenchit Rd. (C3); or the **Sala Novasingh,** Soi 4 South Nana Rd. (D3).

The best plays are at the **National Theatre** Sanam Louang, near the museum (A2). You can also go to the **National Drama Hall** on Rachinee Rd. (A2). The TAT will supply you with information about timetables, which vary according to the season (see p. 32).

Sabre fencing

Once used as a lethal weapon in duels to the death, the sabre has now become the accessory for a matchless demonstration of virtuosity, along the same lines as *kung-fu*. The Thais know how to handle a sabre (or an *épée*) with an elegance which verges on dance.

Exhibition fencing may be viewed at the **Rose-Garden** (see 'Outside Bangkok' p. 124) or at the **Oriental Hotel** (Thur. and Sun. at 11am — see p. 86).

Cock, fish and mongoose fights

Although officially banned, cockfights are still an institution in Thailand, where the emphasis is more on gambling than on blood. Thais are willing to wager considerable sums on a cockfight.

Fish fights are also staged. Two fish about 3 in/7 cm long are placed together in the same bowl and the spectators gamble on the outcome of their confrontation. While they wait to fight, the two creatures are kept in separate containers, hidden from each other by a sheet of paper, because the very sight of their opponents would drive them to frenzy.

Snakes and mongooses are another diversion. One trembles at first for the sweet little mongoose but, in fact, the animal is such an accomplished snake-killer that it invariably wins. Cock, fish, and mongoose fights take place at the weekend market.

Chinese opera

An odious warlord, a sweet, persecuted girl, a courageous hero, and a happy ending; the plot is invariably the same and surprisingly unimportant

Practical information 95

in Chinese opera. What really counts is the atmosphere in which you will find the ancient myths of China told in the purest tradition of the Peking Opera: **Sin Fah Theater,** 309 Yaowarat Rd. (B3). Daily, 12:30pm to 7:30pm.

You may also be lucky enough to see impromptu performances (at funerals, weddings, and parties) in the narrow streets of Chinatown as well as near the Erawan Hotel and Sanam Louang, especially during Chinese New Year celebrations.

Cinema

Locally made films provide visitors with an insight into the mainstream Thai entertainment and culture. The principal themes are long and complicated love stories punctuated with bitter family feuds. Thai films are obviously not subtitled but nobody will force you to sit through them from beginning to end: the first 20 minutes will probably provide an ample return for your money.

If you have not yet discovered the frantic world of the Soy Western (epic movies made in Hong Kong), you should definitely treat yourself to one. You won't need an interpreter; within a few minutes you'll grasp that the plot turns on the rivalry between two karate schools. Audience reaction is an essential part of the spectacle: watch when the man in the next seat laughs or applauds; you'll be surprised. Seeing a Western film in Bangkok will also make the true nature of Thai humour clearer.

Bangkok by night

Bangkok by night has an appalling reputation. 'Sex tours' to Bangkok have become basic fare in many countries and the vacuum left by the withdrawal of American GIs from South-east Asia has quickly been filled.

The focus of Bangkok's nightlife is prostitution. Exhibitions, propositions, and shows are there on all sides: some blatant, some discreet. Once the initial novelty has worn off, the atmosphere quickly becomes oppressive. The pimps always have something to sell (boys, girls, opium, cocaine) and there's no vice that can't be found at Patpong.

The sex industry exploits tourists for every penny they are worth. The passerby is constantly harassed by eager salesmen who are masters of misleading publicity. Bars will charge from 100 ฿ - 200 ฿ for drinks that they advertise as costing 50 ฿, and if there is a show the customer will be expected to pay extra again.

The authorities are by no means indifferent to these goings-on. Many attempts have been made to clean up Bangkok's nightlife. In June 1985, the police and provincial governors were ordered to severely crack down on establishments operating nude shows.

Although the prostitutes themselves are not considered condemnable, the sex trade is widely viewed as a scandal by the Thai population. Most Thais are prudish, even puritanical, by nature; you will never see older Thais kissing in public under normal circumstances.

Yet the sexiest street in Bangkok, which lies between Silom and Suriwongse, is known all over the world. Patpong (C3) contains about 40 bars, a dozen massage parlours, and as many restaurants, over the 100 yd/90m of two parallel axes, Patpong 1 and Patpong 2. It is considered good form to start the evening in a quiet pub (**Alley Cat Pub,** on Silom, or **Bobby's Arms,** on Soi Charuwan) before moving on to the next stage. The show at the **Pink Panther,** on the corner of Suriwongese and Patpong 2, starts at 11pm on Tue., Wed., Fri., and Sat. Beware of the ravishing creatures floating through the smoke at the **Rome,** in front of **Bobby's Arms.** They may have pretty calves and tiny feet but they're men. The **Rome** is the headquarters of gay life in Bangkok.

Other districts of Bangkok provide equally high-voltage nightlife; the **Sukhumvit** (D3 — between Soi 21 and Soi 23), **Cowboy Soi** (D3), Rajdamnern Klong, Silom and **Siam Square** (C3).

Bars and discotheques

All the big hotels have at least one discotheque and a bar. In general, you can expect to spend a minimum of 80 ฿ on drink, even in a more modest, independent establishment. The centres of Bangkok's nightlife are always deafening, with Filipino bands churning out American pop tunes. Every bar offers its own attraction, from the innocent little show with aesthetic pretensions to the pornographic exhibition.

Massage parlors

These establishments usually operate from 4pm till midnight. The expensive ones have carpets and piped music, the cheap ones resemble municipal bath houses. As the Wat Po School of Massage attests, Thai massage is an old and respectable art; but many Bangkok massage parlors are no better than brothels. Others remain firmly within the bounds of decency. In reality, what takes place between the masseuse and her client is strictly between the two of them.

Massage parlors are essentially frequented by men, but in the larger establishments women are also welcome. They are usually allotted a female masseuse, like the men. A traditional massage costs about 333 ฿ for one hour. Supplements have to be negotiated on the spot.

Atami, 1573 New Phetchaburi Rd. (D3).
Cesar's Palace, Soi Ekamai, Sukhumvit Rd. (D3).
La Cherie, 25-35 Suriwongse Rd. (B4).
La Costa, 105/1 Patpong Rd. (C3).
Plaza Onsen, 7 Carpak Building, Patpong Rd. (C3).
La Sacia, 46/27 New Phetchaburi Rd. (D3).
Takara, Soï 2 Patpong Rd. (C3).

For further information on Bangkok nightlife, ask at your hotel reception desk for the free publication entitled *Bangkok After Dark*, which contains all the addresses, street maps, and photos you will need.

Useful addresses and information

Airlines

Most of the airline offices are in Rama IV Road (in the new Charn Issara Tower) and Silom.

British Airways, Charn Issara Tower (2nd floor), 942/81 Rama IV Rd. (C3). Tel: 236 8655-8.
Thai Airways, 6 Larnluang Road. (B2). Tel: 280 0080-110. Reservations: 280 0070-80. Airport office: 523 8271-3.
Thai Airways International, Vipavadi-Rangsit 485, Silom. (B4). Tel: 511 0121. Reservations: 511 0821. All destinations in Asia. Student reductions.
United Airlines, Regent House (16th floor), Rajdamri Rd. (C3). Tel: 233 5900.

Banks

Visa cards are accepted at all **Thai Farmer's Banks** throughout Thailand and at the **Indosuez Bank,** Kiang Guang Bldg., 142 Vithayou Rd., PO Box 303, Bangkok. Tel: 252 2111-19. They are also accepted at the **BNP,** Dusit Thani Bldg., Suite 506, Bangkok. Tel: 233 1655 or 233 4310. American Express cardholders may draw out extra money in traveler's checks in the American Express offices at the **Siam Center,** 4th floor (Rama I Rd.).

Bookshops

Bangkok has two bookshops that offer an excellent choice of books: **Duang Kamol Bookshop,** 244/246 Siam Square, Soi 2 (C3); and **The Bookseller,** 81 Patpong 1 Rd. (B4). A large number of interesting books on Thailand, in English, may be found at the **Asia Bookstore,** 221 Sukhumvit Rd. (C3 — near the Chavalit Hotel) or at the **Calermnit Bookshop** (C3 — near the Erawan Hotel).

Diplomatic missions

Australian Embassy, 37 Sathorn Tai Rd. (B4). Tel: 286 0411.

Bangkok at night.

British Embassy, 1031 Wireless Rd. (C3). Tel: 253 0191-9.
Canadian Embassy, Bunmitr Bldg. (11th and 12th Floors), 138 Silom Rd. (B4). Tel: 234 1561-8.
Consulate of Ireland, Thaniya Bldg. (11th floor), 62 Silom Rd. (B4). Tel: 223 0876.
New Zealand Embassy, 93 Wireless Rd. (C3). Tel: 251 8165.
US Embassy, 95 Wireless Rd. (C3), Tel: 252 5040-9 or 252 5171-9.

Emergency phone numbers
Ambulance: 246 0159 or 252 2171-5.
Fire: 109 or 246 0099.
Police assistance: 123, 191 or 246 1338-42.
Directory inquiries: 13 (the operator speaks English).
Airport information: 523 7410.
Weather information: 258 2056.

Hospitals
Thailand's larger cities have high-quality health facilities with many US-trained, English-speaking doctors.
Bangkok Nursing Home, 9 Convent Rd. (C4). Tel: 233 2610. A surgical clinic.
Chulalongkorn Hospital, Rama I Rd. (C3). Tel: 252 8181.
PSE Clinic, 3/4 Nares Rd. (B3). Tel: 236 1389 and 236 1489.
Saowapha Institute, Rama IV Rd. (C3 — near Lumpini Park). Tel: 252 0161-4. Essential facility for all cases of snakebite or dogbite.
St Louis Hospital, 215 Sathorn Tai Rd., Soi St Louis (B4). Tel: 211 2769.

Post office and telephone
The Bangkok Central Post Office is on New Road, near the Oriental Hotel. (B4). *Open Mon. to Fri. 7:30am-5:30pm; Sat., Sun., and holidays 9am-1pm.* Telegrams accepted 24 hours a day.
To reach the Central Post Office by taxi, tell the driver: 'Praisani

Klong'. There are about 20 other post offices in Bangkok, but they are hard to find.

The contents of packages sent abroad must be checked and stamped by the customs section at the Central Post Office. Often the shops where you make purchases can take care of sending packages for you. In general, however, try to avoid sending packages from Thailand.

Telephone area code for Bangkok and the surrounding area: 02.

Tourist information and assistance

Tourism Authority. The TAT Bangkok is at 4 Rajdamnern Nok, near the boxing stadium on the wide avenue leading from the Wat Phra Keo to the National Assembly. Tel: 282 1143-7 or 282 0073.

Tourist Police. Don't panic if you lose your papers or even your passport, or have your air ticket, credit card and camera stolen. Call the Tourist Police (Tourist Assistance Center) at 221 6206-9. Their clearly marked offices can be found in various parts of town. The staff, most of whom speak English, will do their best to help you and provide accurate information on how to recover visas and passports.

VISITING BANGKOK

Most tourists underestimate the time it takes to get around Bangkok, the fatigue brought on by the heat, and their own capacity to endure successive visits to temples. It is essential to have a coherent idea of what you intend to do before you start, so that you can rationalize your movements. As there are no clearly identifiable and demarcated districts apart from Chinatown, we have tried to make planning easier by presenting a theme-by-theme Bangkok itinerary.

ORGANIZING YOUR TIME

A week in Bangkok

When you map out your itinerary, try to leave yourself a free day to relax and laze around the pool at your hotel. Here is a suggested program for a full week in Bangkok.

Important: Be sure to reserve half a day on Sat. or Sun. for the weekend market, and check the opening times of temples and museums before you set out to see them.

Day 1 Drop your pretensions to being an independent, adventurous tourist and book a city tour at your hotel agency. This is the best possible way to get a general idea of how Bangkok is laid out. Take along your street map and familiarize yourself with the various landmarks. In the afternoon, take a boat tour around the *klongs* (canals) for a sight of the 'other' Bangkok.

Day 2 Concentrate on Sanam Louang, the area on the east bank of the river. With temples such as Wat Po and Wat Phra Keo, the Royal Palace, and the National Museum there is plenty to choose from. If you have time, spend an hour or two wandering around in nearby Chinatown.

Day 3 Leave early in the morning to visit the floating market of Damnoen Sadhak (see 'Outside Bangkok' p. 117). You should be back at your hotel by early afternoon, and if you're too tired to go window-shopping, why not relax with a good massage.

Day 4 Rise late and visit Jim Thompson's House (see p. 112). In the afternoon, tour the 'marble temple' or else wander around the Siam Centre.

Day 5 Make an excursion by boat to Ayutthaya and Bang Pa In (see 'Outside Bangkok' p. 117). By the time you get back, you'll only want one thing — a long swim in the hotel pool.

The temples of Bangkok 99

Day 6 You should now be sufficiently confident to embark on an adventure. Take a boat along the Chao Phraya River, visit Wat Arun and follow the waterways.

Day 7 Visit the antique dealers of Nakhon Kasem (Chinatown). Alternatively, go and see the Crocodile Farm (see 'Outside Bangkok' p. 124) or explore some more of Bangkok's temples.

THE PRINCIPAL SECTIONS OF BANGKOK

The old royal centre (A2)
Sanam Louang (the main square) is the heart of Bangkok. Around it stand the Palace, Wat Po, Wat Phra Keo, and the National Museum. The city's foundation stone is on the broad esplanade (Lak Muang), and the kings of Thailand are cremated here. Allow a day.

The new royal city district (B2)
North of Phitsanulok Rd. This district includes the king's residence (Chitralada Palace), the racecourse, the National Assembly, and other government buildings. There is little for visitors to see, except the Marble Temple.

Chinatown (A2-A3)
Lively streets and alleys radiating off Yaowarat, the area's principal street. Good for at least half a day.

The old tourist quarter (B4)
At the lower end of New Rd, Silom and Suriwongse (near the Oriental Hotel). There are many hotels, tourist shops and money-changers in this area.

The new tourist quarters
These consist of avenues, streets, and *sois* (lanes) where businesses such as restaurants, shops, bars, and massage parlors congregate close to the major hotels. Three new tourist sections represent the changing face of Bangkok.

Patpong, upper Silom and Surinwongse (C3-B4)
Although the name of Patpong is all too often associated with sleazy nightlife, it is also the business and finance area of Bangkok, where the banks, airlines, insurance companies, and import-export firms have their offices.

Siam (Rama I), Rajdamri, Pratu Nam, Ploenchit (C3)
These streets now form the heart of the commercial tourist trade in antiques, precious stones, fabrics, and souvenirs of all kinds. Bangkok's biggest stores are here, along with innumerable shopping malls where you will search in vain for the authentic odours of an Oriental market. Siam Square is a favourite rendez-vous for young people because of the nearby cinemas. The Pratu Nam Market has managed to retain its cachet but, in general, this zone is in the throes of change.

Sukhumvit, New Phetchaburi (D3)
The liveliest part of Sukhumvit lies between Wireless Rd and Soi 23. It is vital to have a clear idea of where you are in relation to the *sois*, which are numerous off this avenue. Their original residential use has changed to accommodate other attractions: restaurants (Soi 55, but also around the hotels), bars, shows, nightclubs (Cowboy Soi, between Soi 21, also known as Asok Soi, and Soi 23). New Phetchaburi is also a nightclub area, usually frequented by local men.

THE TEMPLES OF BANGKOK

Thai architecture finds its most perfect expression in the thousands of temples around the country. There are about 400 in Bangkok alone, some lavish, some less so. These temples are centres of religious and social life, not monuments. They are never dull or tedious; in fact, they offer an atmosphere of relaxation which is in strong contrast to the city's turmoil. The *wat* is a perfect place to stop for a rest when you are moving around on foot and you should never hesitate to enter one, even if it is not mentioned in a guidebook. The temples listed below have been chosen for their fame and their architectural qualities.

N.B. For a glossary of technical terms used, see p. 47.

Wat Phra Keo*** (Temple of the Emerald Buddha) (A3)

Open daily 8:30am-11:30am and 1pm-3:30pm. No entrance fee on Sun. and Buddhist holidays.

This temple, built by Rama I at the end of the 18th century, is the most venerated in all Thailand. Situated on Sanam Louang, it shelters the celebrated Emerald Buddha — the story of which dates back to the beginning of the 15th century when lightning struck a small, insignificant pagoda at Chiang Rai, leaving the building in ruins.

Among the objects retrieved from the wreckage was a statue of Buddha covered in stucco which the abbot placed in his own cell. After a while, the stucco began to flake away, revealing a beautiful deep green statue covered in pure jasper. It quickly became known as the Emerald Buddha. When the King of Chiang Mai learned of this, he sent one of the royal elephants to collect the Buddha and carry it back but the elephant refused to move in the direction of Chiang Mai and, instead, set out towards Lampang. No one dared defy this sign from heaven until, towards the middle of the 15th century, King Tiloka installed the Emerald Buddha in the Wat Chedi Luang at Chiang Mai. It remained there for over a century, until a young prince of Chiang Mai was called to assume the throne of Luang Prabang, in the kingdom of Laos, and took it with him as protection against the perils of destiny. Subsequently, the Emerald Buddha was moved to Vientiane when that town emerged as the new capital of Laos. The Thais never accepted its loss and when the future Rama I (then a general in the army of a king at Thonburi) conquered Viangchan (Vientiane) at the close of the 18th century, one of his first acts was to recover the statue for Thailand. The Chakri dynasty installed it in the most beautiful temple, Wat Phra Keo, at Bangkok.

Visit

As a royal temple, Wat Phra Keo is used for special ceremonies only and no monks live within its precincts. The ensemble of buildings is very impressive, with tall-roofed pavilions, *chedis,* and statues of mythical creatures. One entrance is on the palace side, and the other is on Sanam Chai Road.

The bot***, or royal chapel

The Emerald Buddha is kept here. The Buddha is only 26 in/65 cm tall but is placed under a huge parasol. It also has a wardrobe of three sets of garments: blue spangles for the rainy season, gold and diamonds for the hot and cold seasons.

The cloister***

The cloister surrounds the royal chapel; here the galleries are adorned with murals illustrating the *Ramakien* and the exploits of Hanuman, the monkey-god. The frescos, which date from the beginning of the reign of Rama I, have been restored six times, most recently in 1987 for the king's 60th birthday celebration.

The Royal Pantheon**

Only open to the public on April 6 (the day when the foundation of the Chakri dynasty is commemorated). Built in 1855, it contains life-size statues of all the Chakri kings.

Wat Phra Keo, jewel of the ancient royal centre.

The Mondop**

Sacred library containing the canonical texts. In each corner of this room stands a Javanese-style (Borobudur) Buddha.

A scale model*** of Wat Angkor

Built at the time when Kampuchea was still under Thai control.

The golden chedi** (Ayutthaya)

By popular repute contains relics of Buddha himself. Built by King Mongkut, it is notable for its quantities of mythical creatures: demons, bird-women (kinari), bird-men.

Wat Po*** (Temple of the Reclining Buddha) (A3)

Open daily 8am-5pm. Entrance fee.

This temple, which is close to Wat Phra Keo, is Bangkok's largest and oldest. Also known as Wat Phra Chetupon, it was founded in the 16th century at the time of Ayutthaya ascendancy. Rama I and Rama II embellished it and the latter built its *viharn*, which houses a colossal reclining Buddha. The two traditional occupations of Wat Po are teaching and medicine. In the past it was an institution known for its promotion of knowledge, operating as a kind of cathedral-university. Inside you will find teachers' slates dealing with astrology, literature, the arts of war, morality, and medicine, and geological samples from all over Thailand.

The buildings are arranged around two courtyards separated by Soi Chetupon. There are 16 entrances, of which only two are open to the general public: each entrance is guarded by a menacing stone figure wearing what appears to be a top hat. These statues, which are probably meant to represent Europeans, were cut from the blocks of stone which served as ballast on the old ships used for the China trade route.

The bot*** (eastern courtyard)

The *wat's* principal building, surrounded by two galleries containing 394 seated Buddhas. The inner walls are decorated with (damaged) frescos. The four chapels leading to the outer galleries mark the four cardinal points of the compass and the entire design is considered to be one of the finest pieces of architecture in Bangkok.

The four chedis

Decorated in porcelain, they symbolize the first four kings of the Chakri dynasty.

The medical hall***

Not to be missed. The hall is at the foot of the south *chedi*, and contains a collection of marble engravings of the human anatomy. Consultations take place between 4pm and 6pm daily and the physicians authorized to practice here all belong to the Association of the Old Medical School of Thailand. Wat Po is also the home of traditional Thai massage.

The European Pavilion and the Chinese Pavilion

On either side of the library.

The Reclining Buddha***

This immense statue is said to be 145 ft/44 m long and 50 ft/15 m high though argument about these measurements continues. The colossal Buddha barely fits the room it's in. Visitors, who are often disappointed because they cannot stand back to look at it, can see very little except the soles of the feet (which are encrusted with mother-of-pearl and illustrate the 108 marks and qualities of Buddha). Recently, the colossus has been rejuvenated by a new coating of gilt.

The south part of the *wat* (on the far side of the *soi*) is a veritable **monastic township*****. It houses some 300 monks, with their own schools, little chapels, and Thai houses. You will have no trouble finding a monk to guide you round.

Wat Arun*** (Temple of Dawn) (A3)

Open daily 9am-4:30pm. Entrance fee.

The temple stands beside the Chao Phraya River on the Thonburi side (easy access from the Tha Thien quay on the Bangkok side). Most of the tour circuits organized for the floating market stop here. If possible, try to visit Wat Arun at dawn when the millions of fragments of porcelain set into the stone sparkle in the rays of the sun (the architects had to appeal to the people for smashed china when they were completing this gigantic project). The *wat* is on the site of the former royal temple of Taksin, which stood here when Thonburi was the capital of Thailand. It was begun by Rama II at the beginning of the 19th century and finished by Rama III.

Visit
The central prang

260 feet high, with its terraces supported by gods and demons, and the

four niches containing statues of Indra (the Hindu god of rain and thunder) riding Erawan (the three-headed elephant). The construction of this prang presented considerable difficulties because the ground beneath it was found to be unstable.

The four prangs
Situated around the central one, they are decorated in the same spirit (their niches contain images of the moon god riding a white horse).

The four pavilions
At the foot of the main *prang*, they describe the four principal phases in the life of Buddha; birth, illumination, appearance of the first disciples, and death. Take advantage of your visit to Wat Arun to see the **royal barges**** (A2), slightly farther up river in the Bangkok Noy *klong*. In former times these barges were used by the king during the Thot Kathin festival. His Majesty's private barge, with its sacred swan figurehead, needed 54 oarsmen, officers, and a singer to cry the rhythm of the oars.

Wat Benchamabophit*** (The Marble Temple) (B2)

Open daily 9am-5pm. No entrance fee.

Built on the instigation of King Chulalongkorn in 1899, this is the most recent of Bangkok's great temples and perhaps the most charming. It is on Sri Ayutthaya Rd., on the corner of Nakhon Pathom Rd., with surrounding gardens where monks still stroll.

Benchamabophit is elegantly proportioned, with building materials of the highest quality (Carrara marble and varnished Chinese tiling).

The bot
Its main staircase is guarded by two marble lions. The interior houses a copy of Phitsanulok Buddha; Chulalongkorn's ashes are kept in its base.

The cloister***
With 52 Buddhas representing the main periods of Buddhist art. These were collected by King Chulalongkorn with a view to assembling a complete history of Thai Buddhist iconography. Many are reproductions, since some of the authentic pieces could not be moved. It is relatively simple, even for a beginner, to tell the real statues from the false ones, especially since the former have been placed behind bars for security.

The two pavilions
Situated on either side of the courtyard. These show Javanese influence; one contains a Burmese Buddha, the other a Buddha from Southern Thailand with a 12th-century Khmer inscription.

The monk's quarters and the former residence of King Chulalongkorn
Brought en bloc from the monastery to which he retired.

The gardens
With sacred turtles paddling in a pool that reflects the surrounding spires. These turtles are presented to the temple by the faithful, who thereby acquire merit.

Wat Sakhet** (Temple of the Golden Mount) (B2)

Situated to the north of Chinatown, not far from Wat Suthat, this temple's *chedi* dominates the whole of Bangkok. The 'Golden Mount', 260 ft/80 m tall, is the highest point in Bangkok. It was built by Rama III, in imitation of another artificial hill at Ayutthaya. The new skyscrapers with their elevators have detracted somewhat from the 'mount's' former reputation as a place from which to view the panorama of Bangkok. Wat Sakhet stands at the foot of it and dates from the Ayutthaya epoch. Every November, there is a splendid festival to honour the temple.

Wat Suthat** (Temple of the Giant Swing) (A2)

Bamrung Muang Rd., a street of shops selling religious articles.

Begun in the reign of Rama I, its construction was not completed until Rama III's time. Wat Suthat is one of the largest in Bangkok, with a particularly grandiose *bot*. Its standing Buddha, which is in the Sukhothai style, is surrounded by the images of 80 kneeling disciples, each one painted in vivid colours. There are also some fine early 19th-century wall frescos illustrating the *jataka*. The temple is the only one in Bangkok which contains neither a *chedi* nor a *stupa*.

Bamrung Muang Road leads through a very high portal to the Square of the Giant Swing, a long beam lying across two tall red poles. The 'swing' was used as a kind of springboard by young Brahmin priests in a ritual honoring the god Phra Isman. Purses were hung 80 ft/25 m in the air and the Brahmins tried to seize them in their teeth. This ritual is no longer performed.

Wat Traymit** (Temple of the Golden Buddha) (B3)

Open daily 9am-5pm. No entrance fee.
This temple stands in Chinatown, near the Odeon Cinema (Charoen Krung Rd.); it has the singular good fortune to possess a solid gold statue 10 ft/3 m tall and weighing 5.5 tons, which has been valued at US $14 million. This statue is a fine example of Sukhothai art and was discovered completely by chance during construction work. It had been carefully concealed under a layer of stucco, doubtless to foil the greed of the Burmese enemy prior to the sacking of Ayutthaya (from where the statue originally came).

Other temples well worth a visit are:

Wat Rajabopitr** (A2-3)

Close to the Ministry of the Interior on Atsadang Rd. Small but full of charm, this temple was built in 1863 in the reign of Chulalongkorn and contains a Lopburi Buddha. An interesting detail on its sculpted doors is the presence of soldiers dressed in European clothes. This temple is considered to be the finest example of Ratanokosin art (Bangkok period).

Wat Mahathat* (A2)

Between the National Museum and Wat Phra Keo. This temple is known as the 'Temple of the Great Relic'; it dates from the reign of Rama I, and specializes in teaching meditation techniques. Wat Mahathat also houses a famous school of Buddhist studies, the Maha Chulalongkorn Ratchawitayalai.

Wat Bovornives (A2)

Phra Sumen Rd. Where King Mongkut went into retreat for 27 years. There are two bronze Sukhothai-style statues, both of which come from Wat Mahathat in Phitsanulok.

Wat Rachanada (A2)

Facing the Golden Mount. It has a market devoted to the sale of amulets***. Here you can buy charms to insure against virtually every possible disaster from plane crashes to gunshot wounds, adultery and sickness or sterility. These objects are by no means intended to be ornamental. In fact the most effective among them are often the ugliest.

■ THE PALACE (A2)

Open daily 8:30am to 11:30am and 1pm to 4pm, excluding holidays. No entrance fee on Sat. and Sun. (exterior visit only). Proper clothing must be worn, i.e., no shorts or any other attire that could be considered disrespectful to the king.

The Palace is part of the same ensemble as Wat Phra Keo, so it is advisable to try and combine the two visits; unfortunately, many of the buildings are frequently closed to the public.

The Palace was completed about 100 years ago, in the reign of

Millions of pieces of porcelain embellish Wat Arun.

Rama IV. Its style is a mixture of Oriental and Western. It is no longer occupied, since the present king resides in Chitralada Palace near Rama V Road.

As you enter the Palace, you will notice on the left a gate leading to Wat Phra Keo, the temple used by the monarch for his private devotions. The doors of the second portal leading to the Royal Palace have escaped damage by lightning no less than seven times, hence their sacred character.

Chakri Maha Prasad

This is the main building and is a haphazard marriage of Victorian and Thai styles. It houses the throne room (closed to the public). The lower half of the building was designed by a British architect but the roofing is traditional Thai. Visitors are only authorized to enter the reception rooms, which are adorned with sundry art objects, royal portraits, and busts of foreign monarchs and dignitaries who met Rama IV on state visits.

Dusit Maha Prasad

Built on the right-hand side of Chakri Maha Prasad at the end of the 18th century when Rama I reigned in Thailand, this shows a much more elegant side to Thai architecture. This building was last used in 1911 for the investiture of Rama VI. Its mirrors are intended to dispel evil spirits. The small Amporn Phimok Prasad pavilion, decorated with mosaics, is one of the purest pieces of Thai design in existence. It was formerly used by the king when changing from ordinary town clothes into formal court costume. A reproduction of this pavilion was exhibited in 1958 at the Brussels International Exhibition, and another replica exists at the Summer Palace of Bang Pa In, 38 mi/60 km from Bangkok.

Amarin Vinachai Hall

To the left is the old High Court of Justice, Amarin Vinachai Hall, built under Rama I, where the coronation ceremony traditionally takes place. You will note the royal elephant's parking place in front of two red posts, to which it would be tethered while the king took his place on its back.

The Old Royal Harem

Closed to the public, it is now dilapidated. A pity: it would be delightful to catch a glimpse of the pavilions and gardens where the king's young mistresses once lived. Dignitaries of the royal court and foreign diplomats are permitted to visit the grounds once a year for a garden party that takes place on the king's birthday.

Borompiman Hall

This backs on to the Temple of the Emerald Buddha and was the scene of King Ananda's murder in 1946. It remains closed to the public.

THE NATIONAL MUSEUM*** (A2)

Open daily 9am-4pm. Closed Mon. and Fri.
Na Phra That Rd. (north-east side of Sanam Louang). Tel: 224 1396. Guided tours in English Wed., Thurs., starting 9:30am. Rendez-vous at main door (map:1), duration: 2 hours.

A visit to the National Museum is essential if you wish to acquaint yourself with the history of Thai art. Two visits are better than one, if you have the time: one quick tour as soon as you arrive in Bangkok, and another, more leisurely, after you have traveled around the country. In this way you will be able to gain a deeper knowledge of the subjects which interest you. For assistance in your choices, refer to the map and the room-by-room description of the museum.

The National Museum is a juxtaposition of old buildings and two modern wings which are more functional than elegant. The old buildings (1 to 22 on the map) were originally part of a palace dating from Bangkok's construction (1782). This was the residence of the surrogate monarch, an office which was abolished by King Chulalongkorn, who created the museum in 1874. The original park extended over the northern area of Sanam Louang and the space occupied today by Thammasat University, the School of Dramatic Arts, the Fine Arts School and the National Theatre. Today, the buildings of the former palace house collections which refer to court life (precious objects, palanquins, musical instruments, etc.). Also in the park is a *wat* for the use of the surrogate monarch, and various small pavilions, most of which have been moved to other sites.

The modern buildings were added to the complex in 1966 to house collections of Thai art. They are divided into two wings, each on two levels. The south wing (map S1 to S9) deals mainly with antecedents, while the north wing (map N1 to N10) is devoted to the nation's artistic heritage.

For a quick visit

It is essential to determine your priorities if you only have a couple of hours to spare for the museum.

The National Museum

Court life collections (old buildings)
Precious objects (room 5)
Palanquins (room 6)
Shadow theatre and entertainment (room 7)
Antique weaponry (room 10)
Costumes, fabrics, religious articles (room 14)
Cremation hall (room 17)
Tamnak Daeng (room 22)

Thai art (new buildings)
Lopburi (rooms S3-S5)
Dvaravati (rooms S6-S7)
Srivijaya (room S9)
Sukhothai (rooms N7-N8)
Ayutthaya (rooms N9-N10)

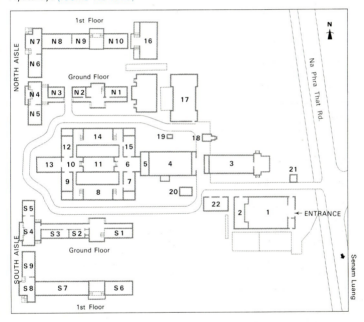

National Museum

1. Gallery of Thai history
2. Gallery of prehistory
3. Wat Buddhaisawan
4. Audience hall
5. Precious objects
6. Palanquins
7. Shadow theatre and entertainment
8. Ceramics and mother-of-pearl
9. Ivory
10. Antique weaponry
11. Royal regalia
12. Steles
13. Wood-carvings
14. Costumes, fabrics, religious articles
15. Musical instruments
16. Residence of King Pin Klao
17. Cremation hall
18, 19, 20, 21. Pavilions
22. Tamnak Daeng (red pavilion)
S1. Asian art
S2. Director's office
S3. Lopburi
S4. Hindu divinities
S5. Lopburi
S6, S7. Dvaravati
S8. Java
S9. Srivijaya
N1. Ratanakosin
N2. Minor arts
N3. Coins
N4, N5. Buddha images
N6. Lan Na
N7, N8. Sukhothai
N9, N10. Ayutthaya

The National Museum room by room
(Figures refer to the museum map.)

1. Thai history

This gallery was opened to mark the bicentenary of Bangkok in 1982. It recounts the main events in the history of Thailand, from Sukhothai to our own time, by way of photographs, manuscripts, art, and everyday objects. Wandering around the collection, you can see numerous models depicting battles and historic events as well as the miniature train King Mongkut presented to Queen Victoria. In the entrance hall, a prize exhibit is the famous *stele* of Rama Khamheng, describing the happy life of the people of Sukhothai. It begins as follows: 'In the [Thai] year 1205, the [Chinese] Year of the Goat 1283, King Rama Khamheng applied himself with great zeal to the composition of written characters for the Thai language and these characters now exist because the king composed them...'.

2. Prehistory

This section exhibits the early mastery of bronze achieved in South-east Asia (3500 BC). The greatest discoveries were made in the 1960s; some of the objects found at Ban Kao are 10,000 years old. Note also the superb pottery from Ban Chieng (300 BC) which is decorated with brick-coloured arabesques.

3. Wat Buddhaisawan

Built at the close of the 18th century for the royal devotions, this structure houses a fine gilded bronze Buddha, the Phra Buddha Sihing, from the mid-15th century. The interior is decorated with mural paintings illustrating the life of Buddha.

4. Audience hall

The king's former audience room (Issarawinitchai Hall) is used for various temporary exhibitions.

5. Precious objects

This is the 'treasure room', filled with exquisite gems and gold ornaments. Along with the breathtaking Ayutthaya jewelry, there are a number of superb older pieces from U Thong and Nakhon Pathom.

6. Palanquins

The display of palanquins and howdahs (howdahs are boxed seats for riding on the backs of elephants) gives an idea of the lavishness of royal procession during the 18th century. Sculptures and encrusted gems are used profusely (see the Rajenthrayan royal palanquin of Rama I). Perhaps the most astonishing piece is the ivory howdah given to King Chulalongkorn by a Chiang Mai prince.

7. Shadow theatre and entertainments

The main exhibits in this intriguing room are *khon* masks (traditional theatre); shadow theatre figurines *(nang taloung);* and head-dresses used in classical dance. The *khon* masks were worn by dignitaries of the court of Rama VI for the plays they performed for the king. See also the ivory chessboards, Thai polo mallets, and various table games from China.

8. Ceramics and mother-of-pearl

The most precious tableware is displayed on the ground floor. In addition to the Chinese and Japanese porcelain, admire the Sino-Thai ceramics of the 19th century and the earthenware from various other epochs (Lopburi, Lan Na, Sukhothai). A few European pieces are also shown. The mother-of-pearl objects are exhibited in another room on the floor above this one; they are beautifully crafted and their themes are like those of *wat* frescos (the life of Buddha).

9. Ivory

The elephant has played an important part in the history of Thailand. It served as a weapon and transport in wars and a parade animal; the fact that it belonged to the king gave it a sacred character. Elephant armour sculpted with religious motifs is displayed in this room.

10. Antique weaponry

Many types of weapons (including firearms) are exhibited here. The centrepiece is a warrior who is mounted on a life-size elephant and is using a standard of peacock feathers to give the signal to charge.

11. Royal regalia
Five traditional emblems of royalty are exhibited here: the *chatra* (tiered umbrella), the crown, the gilded sword, the fly whisk, and the golden shoes. This room also contains a display of thrones and howdahs, along with a small royal pavilion which at one time sheltered the relics of the princes of Wang Na.

12. Steles
The main interest of this room is historical and archaeological. The stones exhibited carry inscriptions in Sanskrit, in Pali, in Khmer, and in Thai, covering the years from the 8th to 18th century.

13. Wood-carvings
The skill of the artists in this department (if not the aesthetic quality of the somewhat fussy pieces displayed) is impressive. The wood is usually teak, which is densely-textured and rot-resistant. Mythical creatures (such as *kinarees*, or bird-women) stand alongside religious objects. Particularly fine are the doors of the Wat Suthat (late 19th century) which were brought to the museum after the temple was burned down in 1959. Certain sections of these doors were carved by the royal hand of Rama II himself.

14. Costumes, fabrics, religious articles
The fabrics and costumes exhibited on the ground floor deserve close attention. For sumptuousness of material, wealth of subject matter, and beauty of execution, they are hard to beat. Besides the more precious fabrics, such as silks and brocades, note the special style of the woven cotton, with its geometrical motifs. The section devoted to religious articles (in another room on the floor above) displays a monk's possessions: three robes, a begging bowl, razor, sieve, belt, and small sewing kit.

15. Musical instruments
Thai music, which has five keys, bears no relationship whatever to Western music. Its instruments include xylophones, metallophones, gongs, cymbals, drums, string instruments, and flutes, all of which are exhibited along with a Javanese *gamelan* (an ensemble of percussion instruments) presented as a gift to Rama VII.

16. The residence of the surrogate king, Pin Klao
This building, which dates from the late 19th century, has a lived-in atmosphere thanks to the furniture that remains in place.

17. Cremation hall
Palanquins and royal funerary carriages from the Chakri dynasty, some of which are still in use. Royal cremations take place on Sanam Louang (the esplanade in front of the museum). A golden funeral urn containing the ashes of the dead king is hoisted on top of the funerary carriage, which then proceeds to the centre of Bangkok drawn by several hundred men. The carriages on display are impressively huge and sumptuous; there is also a replica of the pavilion used for the cremation of Rama VI.

18, 19, 20, 21. Pavilions
Three of the four little pavilions within the museum precincts have been moved here from other places; the exception is the Mangkhalaphisek pavilion (18) which was part of the old palace. The most graceful Samaranmukhamat (20) comes from Dusit Palace. Numbers 19 and 21 were part of Rama VII's palace at Nakhon Pathom.

22. Tamnak Daeng
This pretty wooden house, known as the Red Pavilion, began as the home of Rama I's sister, and was subsequently used by the wife of Rama II. It was moved twice before finally coming to rest in the park of the National Museum. This pavilion is a pleasant place to linger; it contains fine late

19th-century furnishings (chests and windows) as well as a number of objects which once belonged to Queen Si Suryen (wife of Rama II).

South buildings (S1 to S9 on map) — ground floor

S1. Asian art
This room shows the Indian origins of Siamese art. Indian influences on literature, theatre, and dance; also the effect of Indian religious thought as communicated in Pali, the official language of Buddhism. Objects discovered in Thailand would seem to place the process of Indianization as beginning around the first century AD. Apart from Gandhara Buddhas, note the bronze Roman lamp that dates from the 1st-2nd century (on your right as you enter) and the graceful 5th-6th-century Gupta which prefigures the Sukhothai style. Other exhibits include pieces from Ceylon, Burma, China, Tibet, and Japan.

S3. Lopburi
This covers the Khmer period (7th-14th centuries), principally illustrated in Thailand by the sites of Pimai, Pnom Rong, Muang Tham (to the east), and Prasat Muang Singh (Kanchanaburi region). Note especially the huge stone Buddha's head which typifies the 13th-century Bayon period, an exquisite meditating Buddha from Lopburi, and a collection of bronzes. Sculptured lintels, like those that can still be seen on temples today, are also shown.

S4. Hindu divinities
A collection of statuettes dating from the early period of the Indianization process (3rd-7th centuries), found at Si Thep (Phetchaburi province), Dhaya, and Wiang Sa (Surat Thani province). The most precious piece here is a monumental stone statue of Vishnu (the Preserver in the Hindu trinity) discovered at Takna Pa in the south and dating from the 6th century. The most extraordinary are a collection of gigantic phallic sculptures from Mukhalinga.

S5. Lopburi
Small Lopburi-style bronzes, along with earthenware and zoomorphic vases (a pot in the form of a monkey which resembles an Egyptian canopic jar and an urn with the head of an elephant). The outer gallery houses a display of demons, deities and *nagas* (snakes).

South buildings — 1st floor

S6, S7. Dvaravati
Corresponds to the pre-Thai artistic period, the Mon culture (6th-11th centuries). This period is distinguished by the quality of its Buddhist sculpture. The post-Gupta Indian influence is strong. Room S6 exhibits a small number of stone statues and heads of Buddha. In S7 are stone wheels of the law, one of which (6.5 ft/3 m high) was found at Nakhon Pathom; it describes Buddha's first sermon at Sarnath (India). The most remarkable piece is a terra-cotta head of Buddha, whose closed eyes and ecstatic smile poetically evoke in stone the attainment of Nirvana. Also displayed in this section are a number of archaeological finds including coins and fragments of temple decorations.

S8. Java
Most of the pieces here are Javanese art objects which belonged to King Chulalongkorn. At the beginning of this century, the Thai government was tactful enough to restore to Indonesia a number of objects from Borobudur. The kingdoms represented are those of Central Java (7th-10th centuries) and Eastern Java (10th-11th centuries). Note the enormous *Ganesh* 5.5 ft/1.7 m high; this is the Hindu elephant divinity, which is particularly associated with the arts in the Thai pantheon.

S9. Srivijaya
Corresponds to the pre-Thai artistic period when Indonesian culture was predominant (8th-13th centuries). The Indonesian kingdom spread from

Sumatra to the Thai peninsula and the region of Nakhon Si Thammarat. It produced innumerable representations of *boddhisattvas* (disciples of Buddha on the threshold of Nirvana), of which the most famous is that of Avalokitesvara, found at Chaya. There is also a superb bronze Buddha, 5 ft/1.6 m tall and protected by a *naga* (snake) which dates from 1183. A 14th-century piece shows one of Buddha's disciples.

North buildings (N1 to N10 on map) — ground floor

N1. Ratanakosin

Also called the Bangkok period, covering Thai art from the Chakri dynasty (since 1782). In sculpture as in architecture, the period emphasizes the mannerism of Ayutthaya. Its Buddhas tend to be richly ornamented and not very expressive. More interesting is a series of small bronzes depicting episodes in the life of Buddha. These date from the reign of Rama III.

N2. Minor arts

This room has a fascinating display of Thai decorative arts from the 19th and early 20th centuries: lacquerware, porcelain, silver, enamel, mother-of-pearl, palm-leaf manuscripts, ivories, and everyday objects that attest to the refinement of life at court and among the richer Thai families.

N3. Coins

A display of the many different types of coins used in Thailand over the ages. Apart from the rarer pieces, which are primarily of interest to numismatists, there is a collection of Chinese porcelain counters and blocks of beaten metal, which were used as currency until the 19th century.

N4, N5. Buddha images

This collection includes outstanding statues from many different epochs. Especially noteworthy are a colossal quartzite Buddha in the Dvaravati style and the various bronze heads that have been recovered from Sukhothai and Ayutthaya.

North buildings — 1st floor

N6. Lan Na

This style was exclusive to Northern Thailand; it was also known as Chiang Saen, and blossomed from the 13th century onwards. Lan Na was much influenced by Sukhothai in the second half of the 15th century, although from the beginning of the 16th century Burmese influence was predominant. The quality of Lan Na statuary is somewhat disappointing, especially when you consider that the artists often worked with precious and semi-precious materials such as rock crystal or the jasper of the Emerald Buddha of Wat Phra Keo. The room also contains some porcelain and a few fine examples of the goldsmith's craft.

N7, N8. Sukhothai

The greatest period of Thai art begins with the kingdom of Sukhothai (late 13th-15th centuries), which is exemplified by the cities of Sukhothai, Si Satchanalai, and Kamphaeng Phet. Apart from its architecture, the Sukhothai style impresses most with its monumental statuary and mastery of ceramics. The Sukhothai Buddha has characteristic facial traits (hook nose, elongated earlobes) which forcefully express the Buddhist ideal.

Sukhothai was also responsible for a new attitude — the Walking Buddha, of which the museum possesses a fine example in black bronze. Also in this section are a number of Hindu divinities, such as a colossal Vishnu and an image of the goddess Harihara. Sukhothai earthenware, known as *Sawankhalok*, is remarkable: see the ochre or white monochrome ceramics, pale green celadons, and the painted and varnished pottery on display in N8.

N9, N10. Ayutthaya

The Ayutthaya era was a period that qualified as 'national', spanning four centuries (15th-18th centuries). Various influences (Mon, Khmer, and Sukhothai) were channeled by an increasing demand for artistic refinement. Increasing numbers of decorated Buddha statues began to appear from the 16th century onwards; note the splendid examples from the Thai border kingdom of U Thong in room N9, especially a 14th-century head and a seated Buddha 3 ft/1 m high, from the late 13th century. The Ayutthaya epoch produced works of art in every field; see also the very fine lacquered and painted furniture (N10).

▬ OLD THAI HOUSES

These old Thai residences combine the wealth of detail normally reserved for museums with the intimacy of private houses. You should try to visit at least one of them.

Jim Thompson's House*** (B2-3)

Soi Kasemsan 2 (in front of the National Stadium). *Open Mon. to Fri. 9:30am-4pm.* Entrance fee (all proceeds are given to charity).

This building is also known as the house beside the *klong* because it stands alongside the Saen Saep Klong (canal). Jim Thompson, the American who single-handedly revived the Thai silk industry, had excellent taste and his home is very much out of the ordinary. It consists of six houses made of teak assembled in so harmonious a fashion that they seem to have been originally constructed as an ensemble. The interior is decorated with hundreds of works of art: statuettes, Chinese porcelain, paintings, and Thai furniture fittingly piled with silk cushions.

But don't imagine this is a museum: the people who live in Jim Thompson's House today still eat off Ming plates. Jim Thompson is a legend in Thailand. Originally trained as an architect in New York, he arrived in Asia for the first time during the war, while working for the American OSS. When he came to Bangkok after the end of the war, he fell in love with Thailand and swore to make the country his permanent home. From 1946 onwards he became interested in the silk industry, which at that time had dwindled to almost nothing; only a few families living beside a *klong* at Bang Krua, a district in old Bangkok, still carried on the trade. Thompson founded the Thai Silk Company, which quickly became enormously prosperous; later, he became intrigued with Thai architecture. Having installed himself in Bangkok, he assembled a number of wooden Thai houses in a spectacular garden. He dismantled these houses, each between 50 and 180 years old, piece by piece at their original sites all over Thailand, then reassembled them exactly as before in his chosen setting. Even the tiles were fired in old-fashioned kilns at Ayutthaya, and Jim Thompson finally moved into his house in 1959, after the omens had been pronounced favourable by Thai astrologers.

In 1967, Jim Thompson vanished mysteriously in the Cameron Highlands of Malaysia, where he had apparently gone for a quiet holiday. He has never been seen or heard of since.

The story of Jim Thompson later inspired Gerard de Villiers, a French writer, in his spy story entitled *Gold on the River Kwai*. For a more prosaic account of his life and disappearance, see William Warren's *The Legendary American* (Houghton Mifflin, Boston), now out of print but available in libraries.

Suan Pakkard Palace*** (C2)

352 Sri Ayutthaya Rd. (on the left as you go down Phaya Thai Rd.). *Open Mon. to Sat. 9am-4pm.* Entrance fee.

This palace is the residence of Princess Chumbot, who combines the functions of businesswoman, art patron, and gardener. It consists of five traditional wooden buildings in a beautiful garden, which is full of plants collected by the princess in Thailand and abroad. A visit to this palace will satisfy even the most eclectic taste, for it not only possesses a rare collection of botanical marvels, but also a trove of minerals, shells, and valuable antiques.

The collections of Prince Chumbot, who died in 1959, testify to his extraordinary taste. The princess has arranged them in such a way that the overall impression bears no resemblance to a museum. Thus, all the old furniture is in exactly the right place, and it is not a shock to see a bronze Dvaravati or a Khmer stone head here and there. Similarly, bronze drums, musical instruments, sabres, and porcelains of museum quality may be seen all over the house. The centrepiece of the collection is a lacquerwork pavilion, brought from a *wat* near Ayutthaya and restored by the prince. The inside of this pavilion has remained virtually intact: the lacquer paneling, covered in gold leaf, illustrates scenes from the life of Buddha along with an extraordinary chronicle from the Ayutthaya era. Look in these illustrations for the envoys sent by Louis XIV, as seen by the court artists. For those interested in archaeology, one pavilion offers a selection of Ban Chiang earthenware, bronzes, and primitive jewelry. Princess Chumbot's collection of stones and minerals is also worth a detour.

Siam Society** (D3)

In the Kamthieng House, 131 Soi Asoke (Sukhumvit Soi 21). *Open Mon. to Sat. 9am-5pm.* Entrance fee.

The Siam Society is a cultural association, founded in 1904. It is based in a teak house which remains one of the rare survivals of Northern Thai 'Lannathai' architecture. The house was built towards the middle of the 19th century and formerly belonged to a rich Chiang Mai family, with plenty of blue blood on the Thai side and plenty of money on the Chinese. The building remained on the banks of the Ping River until 1969, when the family's heirs decided to donate it to the Siam Society. The process of dismantling and reconstructing the three component structures we see today in Bangkok took nearly three years. Originally conceived as an ethnographic museum, this house has retained its functional aspect as a living area for the larger pavilion, a storehouse and kitchen for the two smaller ones.

Objects of all kinds are exhibited: furniture, cooking utensils, tools for fishing and agriculture, wickerwork, wagons, gongs, and ewers. Note the carved teak panels above each of the doors leading into the living and sleeping area; these panels, which have now become extremely rare, have a magical function in that they are supposed to protect the virility of the male occupants of the house.

The Siam Society, 131 Soi Asoke, Sukhumvit 21, publishes a regular cultural review along with scientific papers on Thailand. Many of its publications may be consulted on the spot, in the library; some are for sale.

▬ THE MARKETS

The Thai markets *(talat)* offer a whole new register of sensations, ranging from ecstasy (the scent of jasmine) to abhorrence (the stench of *durians* and dried fish).

There are all kinds of markets in Bangkok, from the small local ones you will come across by chance to huge nationally known ones like the Sunday Market. The steady disappearance of the *klongs* (canals) has reduced the floating markets to the rank of tourist curiosities. Not so long ago, all market activity took place on the water; but this feature of Bangkok is changing, just like everything else, and even the Sunday Market has now abandoned Sanam Louang for an out-of-town area (see p. 114).

The Floating Market (A4)

Little remains of this hallowed institution. The famous Wat Sai Talat on Thonburi hardly floats at all any more, having been invaded by the boutiques that now flourish all along the *klong*. All the same, if you get up early, the area is well worth a visit. You can be there to see the boat stalls that sell provisions to local residents — the taxi-boat, the postman, the charcoal merchant, the soup-seller, and the ladies who still wear their famous straw hats and blue smocks. If your timetable permits, try to visit the **Damnoen Saduak*** floating market (see 'Outside Bangkok', p. 123), which is still a real marketplace though heavily infiltrated by tourists. You can embark on your excursion to Wat Sai from the pier by the Oriental Hotel, or have it arranged for you by a local travel agency.

Other floating markets

Less frequented by tourists, they still possess an authentic flavour of the past.

Pak Klong Talat** (A3)

Near Memorial Bridge. The produce sold here is brought in by water from the Thai provinces. Again, if you go early in the morning, you will discover a variety of flowers, fruits, and vegetables.

Saparn Pla Talat** (A4)

Chan Rd. (on the Chao Phraya side). This is the largest fish market in Bangkok.

The Sunday Market** (C1 off map)

Sat. and Sun. 7am-6pm at Suan Chatuchak in front of the North Bus Station in Pahoi Yothin Rd. Until 1982, this market was held on Sanam Luang against the majestic backdrops of Wat Phra Keo and the Palace. To coincide with the Bangkok bicentenary, the Sunday Market was exiled to a dreary site outside town. Despite this change, the people of Bangkok show no sign of giving up their weekly fête. The market is enormous: everything under the sun can be bought there. Baskets, radios, fabrics, exotic fish, orchids, soups, German shepherd dogs, pens, photographs of the king and queen, fruits, vegetables, and parrots. The crowd is huge and varied, ranging from school children in uniform to saffron-robed monks and whole families from distant suburbs. During the dry season, children hold kite-flying matches and all summer there are fighting fish contests which enthrall large groups of men for hours at a time. Although the goods at the Sunday Market are intended for Thai consumption, there is plenty there to interest the tourist. Wickerwork, for example, is sold at very low prices. One can also find fabrics, bronze tableware, jewelry, and even antiques (more or less authentic). But take care as you bargain for these items. Be careful of pickpockets as well.

Other markets

These are held at frequent intervals in the vicinity of the canals and are especially lively at night. In Chinatown, there are Chinese opera performances in the marketplace.

Pratu Nam*** (C2)

At the intersection of Phetchaburi and Rajprarop Rd. This is a particularly pleasant night market. The inhabitants of Bangkok meet here for dinner after the theatre or cinema; you will see women in evening dresses happily sipping bowls of Chinese soup. The cooking is varied and the prices very reasonable. You can also eat here during the day or rent a boat for a ride along the Saen Sap Klong.

Din Daeng** (C2)

Another night market, close to the Century Hotel on Din Daeng Rd. Here you can stuff yourself with seafood and wash it down with Mekhong, all for a handful of *satang*.

Bangrak (B4)

On New Rd., between Silom and Sathorn: a fascinating food market where you can work out your menu for the day.

Theves (B3)
On the banks of the Krung Kasem Klong (close to Hualampong Station). A beautiful flower market which operates round the clock. See also the coconut market, close by on the other side of Krung Kasem Klong. Baskets of special shapes are used to transport and calibrate the coconuts, many of which are picked by monkeys on Samin Island.

Banglampoo (A2)
North of Sanam Louang. Specializes in cotton, silk, and other craftwork from the provinces.

Charoenphon (B2)
On the corner of Rama I and Rama IV, close to the National Stadium (go at night).

Nakhon Kasem** (A3) (the thieves market)
In Mahachai Rd., Yaowarat and Charoen Krung, for antiques. Remember that the antiques for sale here are usually either authentic and expensive or else cheap and fake.

■ CHINATOWN: RED AND GOLD (B3)

Bangkok's Chinatown is one of the oldest districts in the capital. It clusters around Yaowarat, its main thoroughfare, and three other roads running parallel: Charoen Krung (New Road), Samphaeng Road and Songwat Road. For a long time Chinatown was the most prosperous section of Bangkok and it was here that the city's first 'skyscrapers' were built: 'Nine Storey Building' and 'Six Storey Building'. Since that time, progress has accelerated and new buildings and shopping centres have sprung up on the sites of the old markets. The shops which used to be the principal homes of many Chinese families are gradually vanishing. Yet this district retains its individuality, with red and gold as the predominant colours and ideogram shop signs and oilpaper lanterns to set the tone.

Yaowarat** (B3)
The jewelers' street. Here you can see impressive mountains of gold (the price is fixed by the government). Jewelry may be bartered for other pieces, more or less valuable in real terms depending on the luck of the draw. See also the **'Fabric souk'*** (B3), run by Indians (mostly Sikhs) on Soi Samphaeng and Pahurat (access via Soi Wanit, parallel to Yaowarat, then cross Chakrawat Rd. and Chakrapet Rd.). Afterwards, pay a visit to **Nakhon Kasem,** where good quality Chinese objects are still to be found (porcelains, stone statuettes, small bronzes) amid stacks of undefined bits and pieces.

Take advantage of your stroll through Chinatown to snatch a meal at the **Ho Tien Lao** restaurant (308 Suapha Rd., B3), a famous Bangkok establishment. **Wat Traymit** is also in the district (see 'Temples' p. 104). Above all, don't miss seeing the Chinese temples, which have an atmosphere very different from that of the *wats* (**Leng Nei Yi**** is the largest of them). Traditional Chinese opera is still performed in the open air on feast days and the Chinese funeral ceremonies you may see have remained unaltered for centuries.

■ BANGKOK SEEN FROM THE KLONGS

To travel around Bangkok's *klongs* (canals) is to enter a time warp. How is it that islands of countryside still remain in the heart of this great city? It's a mystery. The one thing that's certain is that you should prepare yourself for surprises. Under the Soi Ekamai Bridge (n° 63 on Sukhumvit), the *hang yao* boatmen are waiting to show you Bangkok's canals. *Hang yaos*, or 'long-tailed boats' (see 'Transportation' p. 33), can carry from one to six passengers, and the price of the ride is open to negotiation.

An even better idea is to take one of the regular *hang yaos* on the Chao Phraya River. There are five piers right in the centre of Bangkok, between

Memorial Bridge and Pin Klao Bridge. These are: **Saphan Phut** (Chakraphet Rd.), **Rachini** (Rachini Rd. perpendicular to New Rd.), **Tha Thian** (Thai Wang Rd., between Wat Po and the Palace), **Tha Chang** (Na Phralan Rd., behind Wat Phra Keo), and **Mahathat** (near the Trapachan Market, behind Wat Mahathat). Embarking from any of these various points, you can skim along the *klongs* of Thonburi, stopping wherever you like and taking the next boat at your leisure.

Fast motor launches leave the pier at **Thanon Tok** at the southern extremity of Charoen Krung Rd. and travel up the Chao Phraya as far as Nonthaburi (28 stops over 3 mi/4.8 km, a route which is covered in under an hour).

OUTSIDE BANGKOK

Lovers of ancient monuments, beaches, and local colour will find plenty to interest them in the areas around Bangkok. Local tourist agencies offer a variety of one- to three-day excursions. Here are some examples:
— Ayutthaya and Bang Pa In (one day).
— The Floating Market at Damoen Saduak, Nakhon Pathom, and the Rose Garden (one day).
— The River Kwai and Kanchanaburi (one day).
— Pattaya (two days).

ANCIENT CITIES AND MONUMENTS

AYUTTHAYA

53 mi/86 km north of Bangkok.
Ayutthaya, built on an island in the Chao Phraya River, became the capital of Siam in 1350. From then until it was sacked by the Burmese in 1767 (see p. 39), it was ruled by 33 kings. The city boasted close to one million inhabitants at the beginning of the 18th century; in the shadow of the temples, palaces, and churches, the populace lived in wooden houses on stilts, similar to those that can still be seen in the countryside today.

Thanks to careful renovation, Ayutthaya has become a foremost archaeological site where crumbling buildings and Buddhas have been restored to their former glory. Try to spend a night here if you plan to travel north. This will give you the chance to see an unforgettable sunrise. A word of warning about the 'Ayutthaya bronzes' that are offered for sale: they are copies — excellent to be sure — but copies nevertheless.

Access
If you join an organized excursion, choose one that takes you there by bus and brings you back by boat.
Train: Departures every half hour from Bangkok's Hualampong Station between 4:45am and 8pm.
Bus: Departures every ten minutes from Bangkok's North Bus Station on Pahol Yothin Rd. between 6:30am and 5pm; or every 20 minutes from the Victoria Monument between 6am and 8pm (2 hours).
Boat: Regular departures from Tha Thian pier. Tel: 221 2296. Allow about three hours to reach Bang Phaeng; from there take a *hang yao* to Ayutthaya.

Outside Bangkok

Accommodation and food

If you want a spectacular view of the sunrise, stay at the U Thong Inn (▲), 210 Rojana Rd., 1.5 mi/2 km from the town on the Bangkok Rd. Tel: 242 2369.

Other hotels in town include:
▲ Cathay Hotel, U Thong Rd. (across from the boat landing). Tel: 25 1562.
▲ U Thong Hotel, U Thong Rd. (also across from the landing). Tel: 25 1505.

There are several restaurants on Rojana Rd. leading into Ayutthaya from Bangkok, and the large market across from the boat landing has wonderful things to sample. For a particularly pleasant meal, however, you might want to try one of the two floating restaurants located on either side of the Pridi Damrong Bridge.

Visit

(Monuments and temples are indicated on the map below)

Old Ayutthaya is built on an artificial island at the confluence of three rivers: the Chao Phraya, the Lopburi, and the Pasak. To gain some idea of the area, hire a *hang yao* in front of the Chandrakasem Palace (tour of the island: 1 hour, including stops).

During the reigns of the kings of Ayutthaya, an impressive number of temples and palaces were constructed. Their ruins are scattered over 6 sq mi/15 sq km and it is a good idea to hire a taxi to visit them. We suggest that you begin your visit at the museum.

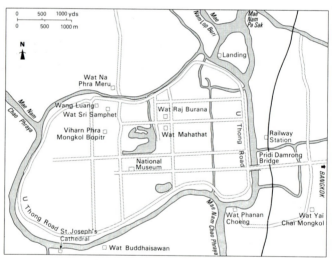

AYUTTHAYA - *location of principal temples.*

On the island

Chao Phraya National Museum***

Open daily 9am-noon and 1pm-4pm. Closed Mon. and Tues.

This is a particularly interesting museum, as all styles of Siamese art are represented. The 'Ayutthaya' style itself was a blend of several earlier traditions. Don't miss the exquisite gold and silver work exhibited on the first floor.

Viharn Phra Mongkol Bopitr**

This sanctuary, which was rebuilt in 1951, houses the largest Buddha in Thailand. It is a bronze statue that apparently dates from the end of the 15th century and incorporates both U Thong and Sukhothai influences.

Wat Raj Burana**
Built in 1421, this temple is dominated by a *prang* (tower) which miraculously escaped demolition by Burmese armies. It contains a number of mural paintings in poor condition on the inside of the principal *chedi* (access to the paintings is by way of an outside stairway which leads to a flight of steep, narrow, and badly ventilated steps on the inside).

Wat Sri Samphet**
This was the royal temple, with three *chedis* representing the first three kings of Ayutthaya, and was originally a part of the Wang Luang ensemble. Founded in the 15th century, it was Ayutthaya's largest *wat* and once housed a gold-covered statue of Buddha. This *wat* was so thoroughly looted by the Burmese that what little remained is now walled up in a small *chedi* at the Wat Po.

Wang Luang
Plenty of imagination is needed to visualize the splendour of the former royal palace amid the ruins of Wang Luang, which was razed by the Burmese. From this site, however, you can clearly see the way in which the ancient capital city was laid out.

Wat Mahathat
This imposing ensemble, now in ruins, was once dominated by a *chedi* 135 ft/40 m high, of which only the base remains. Twenty years ago, the gold and silver work now exhibited in the museum was unearthed here. At the entrance of the Wat Mahathat, a scale model of Ayutthaya before its destruction will give you an idea of the capital's former expanse.

Outside the island

Wat Na Phra Meru**
Across the river to the north of the island, restored during the Bangkok period (19th century). A small pavilion with finely carved wooden doors houses a stone Dvaravati Buddha, seated European-style. This is considered to be a very remarkable piece.

Wat Yai Chai Mongkol**
Boasts one of the tallest *chedis* in Ayutthaya, built by King Naresuan to commemorate a victory over the Burmese. The temple itself dates from 1360. It was entirely rebuilt in 1982 and restored as a tribute to Ayutthaya architecture. The result is striking although it still looks a little too new.

Elephant Kraal (3 mi/5 km north of Ayutthaya)
This was a fenced area where wild elephants were once herded and trained for both domestic use and warfare.

Saint Joseph's Cathedral
At the south end of the island. This cathedral was built during the reign of King Narai, for French and Portuguese Catholics living in Ayutthaya.

Wat Buddhaisawan
Also in the southern part of the island. This temple, which is very badly damaged, dates from 1353.

Wat Phanan Choeng
In the south-east part of the island. This temple was founded in 1324, before Ayutthaya gained prominence, by one of the U Thong kings. It contains a seated Buddha 45 ft/13 m tall.

BANG PA IN
38 mi/61 km north of Bangkok.

Access
See access to Ayutthaya (p. 117) for trains, buses, and boats, which all stop at Bang Pa In.

Car
Take the road leading to Ayutthaya but, about 12 mi/20 km before reaching that town, take the left fork marked for Nathon Sawan; the first left turn off that road will take you to Bang Pa In.

Visit
Bang Pa In, the site of the summer residence of the kings of Ayutthaya, was destroyed by the Burmese at the same time as the capital. The present buildings date from the Bangkok period (late 19th century).

The Park
Open daily 8:30am-3:30pm. Closed Sun. Entrance fee.
The **Aisawan Thi Paya,** which stands on an island in the middle of the lake, is the finest pavilion here and shows Thai architecture at its best. This building is the only one outside the palace grounds that could be visited at the time of writing (the others were either closed to the public or under repair). The Aisawan Thi Paya contains a statue of King Chulalongkorn, who came here regularly during the dry season. His wife died at Bang Pa In: she drowned under the very eyes of her servants, all of whom were paralyzed by a rule which forbade them to touch the royal person.

The **royal palace** itself consists of five large buildings. Except for an observatory on one of the islands in the lake, they are all royal or court apartments. The mixture of styles here is intriguing: it seems to meld quite naturally from classical Chinese to Victorian by way of Italian Baroque. This is because Rama V, the first Siamese sovereign to discover Europe, wanted to express his admiration of Western architecture in the construction of his palace.

The **Chinese Pavilion (Wehat Chamrun)** that stands at the centre of the grounds was presented to the monarch by the Chinese community of Thailand in gratitude for the welcome accorded them by his government. This sumptuously furnished pavilion is the only palace building open to the public.

If you go up the river by way of the palace grounds, you can visit the **Wat Nivet Dharmaprawat** as well as a small neo-Gothic church that has been converted into a Buddhist temple on the island opposite. (You reach the island in a cabin on a ropeway operated by one of the monks.)

■ NAKHON PATHOM
35 mi/56 km west of Bangkok.

Access
Train
Irregular departures from Bangkok's Hoi and Hualampong Stations: check the train schedules (1-hour journey).

Bus
Departures every ten minutes from Bangkok's South Bus Station on Charan Sanitwong Rd., between 6:30am and 8pm (1 to 2 hours, depending on traffic).

Visit
This little Thai town owes its fame to the **Phra Pathom chedi***** which is 415 ft/127 m tall, the highest in the Buddhist world and completely covered with gilded tiling. The *chedi* was begun under Rama IV and completed under Rama V. The sanctuary consists of several terraces, of which the highest has 24 towers. A circular cloister surrounds the *chedi* and a chapel marks each of the four points of the compass. In the *bot* is a Dvaravati Buddha, seated Western style.

During September and October, Nakhon Pathom is the site of a popular festival featuring a variety of restaurants and shops set up for the occasion as well as games and a beauty contest.

Pattaya at night.

▰▰ *ANCIENT CITY*
20 mi/33 km south-west of Bangkok.

Access

Buses daily at 8am and 1pm, from the Democracy Monument. Tel: 221 4495.

Visit

'Ancient City' is a huge open-air museum, conceived and created by a millionaire who was fascinated by Siamese civilization. Over 60 replicas of ancient buildings (life-size and one-thrid-scale models) are scattered over the 200-acre/80-ha park. Some are copies of existing buildings; others, such as the Great Palace of Ayutthaya and its royal chapel, give an idea of the splendours of the vanished monuments. As a concession to folklore, traditional houses have been built for modern artisans to work in. The resident elephant will carry you around the park if you wish. The interesting Crocodile Farm (see p. 124) can also be visited because it is only a few miles away.

THE BEACHES

From Bangkok, the most easily accessible beaches are those of the east coast. For the beaches of the south, see the section entitled 'Southern Itinerary: the Eastern Seaboard' (p. 155).

BANG SAEN**

65 mi/106 km east of Bangkok. For access, see Pattaya, below.

Accommodation

For those who enjoy local colour, there is a small 19-room motel with a pool and 18-hole golf course. **Bangphra Motel:** Tel (038) 31 1149.

There are also 150 TAT-run bungalows, all with modern conveniences. Information and reservations can be obtained in Bangkok. Tel: 221 8151.

Visit

The closest resort to Bangkok, Bang Saen is extremely popular with the Thais. The beach is very fine and water-skiing facilities are readily available. Excursions by boat and visits to neighbouring fishing villages **(Monkey Cliff)** are also popular. There is a pleasant provincial tone to Bang Saen which is in stark contrast to Pattaya's international atmosphere.

PATTAYA**

86 mi/138 km west of Bangkok.

Access

Pattaya is most easily reached by bus. Allow about three hours for the journey.

Special tourist bus

Several companies do this trip three times daily (morning, noon, and mid-afternoon). Pick-up points at all the larger Bangkok hotels. Ask for information at your hotel reception desk.
Asian Pearl Travel Service. Tel : 282 0121-9.
Diamond Coach. Tel : 252 6045.

Regular bus

Air-conditioned buses leave Bangkok's Eastern Bus Station (Soi Ekamai) every hour from 7:30am to 8:30pm and leave Pattaya for Bangkok from the front of the Yacht Club from 6:30am to 7:45pm. Other buses run from 5:40am to 9pm to Pattaya and run from 4am to 7:30pm to Bangkok. On arrival at Pattaya take the minibus to the beach.

Accommodation

Telephone area code: 038

Pattaya has an impressive selection of accommodation and large hotels have extensive gardens, swimming pools, and attentive staff. They also occupy the best seafront locations.

- ▲▲▲ **Asia Pattaya,** Cliff Rd. Tel : 418608-2. 314 rooms.
- ▲▲▲ **Grand Palace,** Beach Rd. Tel : 418541. 420 rooms.
- ▲▲▲ **Merlin,** Beach Rd. Tel : 418755-9. 360 rooms.
- ▲▲▲ **Montien,** Beach Rd. Tel : 418155-6. 320 rooms.
- ▲▲ **Nipa Lodge,** Beach Rd. Tel : 418321. 139 rooms.
- ▲▲ **Novotel Tropicana,** Beach Rd. Tel : 418645-8. 200 rooms.
- ▲▲ **Orchid Lodge,** Beach Rd. Tel : 418175. 236 rooms.
- ▲▲ **Siam Bayview,** Beach Rd. Tel : 418728. 302 rooms.

Those with limited budgets can always fall back on the Sophon (▲), or play Robinson Crusoe in a cabin at the Nipa Hut (▲).

Food

Pattaya is a great place for seafood. Crab is the star seafood item and the rock lobster is excellent but extremely expensive. The hotel restaurants are better than average and offer a great variety of cuisines including Polynesian, French and Italian.

The most famous restaurant in Pattaya is the **Nang Nual** in south Pattaya which offers some 200 different seafood dishes. In general, most of the seafood places are in south Pattaya, while other types of restaurants are concentrated on Pattaya n° 2 Rd., back from the beach. The best plan is to wander around these areas and choose a restaurant according to the type of cuisine you feel like having and the price you are willing to pay (the seafood restaurants in south Pattaya are perhaps the most spectacular but they are also the most expensive). Our recommendations would include **Barbo's**, the **Thai Restaurant**, the **Villa Seafood Restaurant**, **Dolf Riks** (Indonesian cuisine) and, for classic Thai cuisine, the **Choonruechai**, **Charinda**, **Plathon**, and **Kron**.

Visit

Pattaya is the most fashionable beach resort on the Gulf of Thailand. It also offers a wide range — from the best to the worst — depending on when you go there. At the height of the season (Nov. to Mar.), it is packed with tourists and the attendant industry is determined to take maximum advantage of them. Apart from this inconvenience, Pattaya is a pleasant place to rest for a weekend after your trip around Thailand. Pattaya, which at one time suffered from the popularity of Phuket, has regained favour with a new clientele of wealthy Arabs in recent years. With water-skiing, sea-scooters, parachute gliding, horse-back riding, sailing, and sunbathing on the beach, there is no shortage of things to do. Also, the bay is studded with islands, all of which are accessible.

Ko Phai*** (2 hours by boat): a paradise of multicoloured fish and coral.

Ko Khrok** (served by the Ocean View Hotel's launch): A pleasant guesthouse here offers a day's relief from the bustle of Pattaya. Otherwise, you can rent bicycles or motorbikes to explore the resort and its environs. If you want to see elephants, try the Pattaya Elephant Kraal (1 mi/1.6 km from the beach). Demonstrations every day from 3pm to 5pm.

Ko Larn** (1 hour by boat): many small open-air restaurants where you can gorge yourself on crabs and lobsters. Also called the 'coral island'.

Pattaya by night

By night, Pattaya is like Bangkok's wayward sister, sinister and depressing. The more fashionable nightclubs are the most cheery, if a little unoriginal: try the **Royal Cliff** and **Siam Bayshore** discotheques. Beware of wandering out alone at night: people with money in Pattaya are a tempting target for those who have none.

OTHER ATTRACTIONS

DAMNOEN SADUAK FLOATING MARKET***

One hour by road south-west of Bangkok.

Access

If you shrink from the idea of joining a guided tour, you can always take an early local bus to Samut Songkram and catch the connection to Damnoen Saduak from there. Purists may prefer to make the trip memorable by doing it all by boat from Bangkok.
Organized excursions, however, will also take in Nakhon Pathom and the Rose Garden (for information, contact TAT, see p. 32).

Visit

The market at Damnoen Saduak will give you a vivid idea of what Bangkok itself was like less than a century ago. This market is held every day until noon on Damnoen Saduak Klong, in the province of Ratchaburi. You should try to arrive before 10am when the boats disperse along the *klong* (canal) to sell their produce from house to house. The road skirts a stretch of salt pan as it approaches the village; the excursion bus will drop you just outside Damnoen Saduak, and from this point a *hang yao* (boat) will carry you at breakneck speed to the market proper. Damnoen Saduak is slowly going the way of Bangkok's nearly defunct floating market but, in the meantime, you can still take photographs that include only the local people. This is because all visitors are kept on the side of the *klong* where the stalls are and are not allowed into the market proper. The spectacle is a very charming one.

CROCODILE FARM**
Samut Prakan (Pak Nam) 18 mi/30 km south-east of Bangkok.

Access

By car, take route 3 to Samut Prakan at the mouth of the Chao Phraya River. For organized excursions, telephone 395 1477. A trip to the Crocodile Farm can easily be combined with a visit to Ancient City, which is close by (see p. 121).

Visit

This highly original 'farm' on the road to Pattaya contains some 8000 crocodiles and crocodile cousins. Here you will discover that these fearsome creatures have a mortal dread of mosquitos and that they are capable of dying of heart failure if frightened by some sudden noise. A wide variety of goods made of crocodile skin are on sale, and crocodile meat is prepared by a battery of imaginative cooks in the Samut Prakan restaurants.

ROSE GARDEN**
20 mi/32 km west of Bangkok on the Nakhon Pathom Rd.

Visit

The Rose Garden is a huge park beside the Kachin River, named for its 20,000 rose bushes. It also contains a number of traditional Thai houses, fully modernized on the inside. Every afternoon at 2:15pm and 3:15pm there is a brief presentation of Thai cultural activities, including arts and crafts, sabre fencing, traditional dance *(Lakhon)*, traditional theatre *(khon)*, and fighting animals.

The park possesses five hotels, two swimming pools, boats, water-skiing facilities, children's playgrounds, among other attractions. Everything is too clean and the peasants are made up like music-hall dancers but the result is nevertheless very appealing. Pleasant bungalows can be rented for the weekend. Information and reservations from Bangkok can be obtained from the **Rose Garden booking office**, 264/4 Siam Square. Tel: 251 1935-6.

THE BRIDGE OVER THE RIVER KWAI***
75 mi/120 km west of Bangkok. For access, see Nam Tok p. 125.

Visit

The Bridge over the River Kwai near Kanchanaburi was the scene of an inspiring incident during the Second World War. A famous novel and film were made from the story. The bridge itself is a most ordinary metal bridge that only has merit as a historical monument. The centre of the bridge was destroyed during the Second World War and rebuilt, which explains why there is a difference in architectural style between sections.

An impressive cemetery on the site contains some of the graves of over 50,000 prisoners of war who died during the Japanese occupation of Thailand while building the 'Death Railway' that led over the bridge on the way to Burma. It is gloomy and depressing, like any other military cemetery.

Near the bridge, a steam locomotive from the war era is displayed, and, during the first week of December every year, there is a spectacular sound-and-light show commemorating the destruction of the bridge by the Allied forces in 1945. The surrounding area is worth discovering (see below).

NAM TOK AND THE RIVER KWAI***

125 mi/200 km west of Bangkok.

Access

If you decide against an organized excursion from Bangkok, make your own way to Nam Tok (4.5 hours by train from Bangkok Noi Station in Thonburi, via Kanchanaburi). Take a taxi to the Sai Yok Yai boat landing and wait for a pirogue to take you to the hotel. You can also make the trip by boat from Kanchanaburi (8 hours) or from Nam Tok (2 hours) but you will find it very hard to agree on a price with your boatman. If you decide on this option, you should know in advance that Kwai is pronounced 'Kwey' in Thai.

Accommodation

The River Kwai Village, beside the river a few miles above Nam Tok, is excellent value for the money. With its swimming pool fed by a natural waterfall and its treetop bar, this hotel offers a fine setting for rest or exploration (excursions by jeep or boat in the vicinity). Information in Bangkok: **River Kwai Village**, 923 Silom Rd. Tel: 234 4568 or 234 6840.

If you like the idea of spending a few hours, or even a few days, far from the city bustle in a most unusual place, go up the River Kwai valley as far as Sai Yok Yai some 60 mi/100 km above Kanchanaburi. Here you can leave your bags and enjoy a drink in a most unusual hotel — **palm-and-bamboo houseboat** — before settling down to a delicious Thai or French meal. Jacques Bes, the friendly French proprietor, built this jungle hideout (40 rooms) complete with singing gibbons to wake you in the morning and a tribe of Mons (an ethnic minority) as staff. A stay here on the River Kwai will definitely be a high point of your trip to Thailand. It will include a comfortable country atmosphere and good entertainment (beautiful Burmese dances in which the dancers enjoy themselves just as much as the spectators). Information in Bangkok: **Flotel**, Hotel Narai, Suite 307. Tel: 233 3350.

Visit

If you like the taste of adventure, go to **Pilok***, a mining village close to the Burmese frontier. Thais, Mon, Burmese, Karen, Chinese and even Nepalese come here on foot to prospect for tin. You can also go up the river by boat, swim below the Erawan waterfall, walk through the jungle along the old railroad, or ride around on the back of an elephant. Best of all, perhaps, is the thrilling **Three Pagodas Pass*** on the Burmese frontier, which you can reach on foot, by boat, truck, bus or taxi. Otherwise, you can simply go butterfly- or orchid-hunting in the woods. All these delights can easily be organized on the spot. Information in Bangkok: Thai International Tours. Tel: 235 4100-4.

BANGKOK TO CHIANG MAI VIA THE FALLEN CITIES

There is certainly a striking contrast between the fast pace of Bangkok and the bucolic charm of the Thai ricelands. Nothing has changed in the Chao Phraya River basin; neither the mirror-like paddies, nor the rich villages clustered round their pagodas. Added to this is the mysterious spectacle of Thailand's ancient, fallen cities: Ayutthaya, Lopburi, Sukhothai, Si Satchanalai, and Kamphaeng Phet, which still embody Thailand's greatest artistic achievements.

On the road to the north

Chiang Mai province remains little known and exciting, despite the recent influx of visitors. Here, the heroin of the Golden Triangle is all too real an influence and the 'Peoples of the Mist' — the Sino-Tibetan and Sino-Burmese minorities (see pp. 62-69) — continue to live their lives as if Bangkok did not exist. For these people, and even for the inhabitants of the region's larger townships, Bangkok is viewed as the distant, inaccessible, intimidating capital.

▬▬ PRACTICAL INFORMATION

Access

Northern Thailand has the best transportation in the country. All forms of transportation are available and you can take your pick according to the time and money at your disposal (always allowing for imponderables such as flooded roads during the rainy season and flight delays).

Plane

Thai Airways serves several northern cities from Bangkok including Phitsanulok (p. 128) and Lampang (p. 134) which are on this itinerary (three flights daily). For information, contact **Thai Airways**, 6 Larn Luang Rd., Bangkok. Tel: 282 7640 or 282 7151 from 8:30am to 4:30pm, Mon. to Fri. and 281 1787 or 281 1989 from 9am to noon and 1pm to 4pm, Sat., Sun., and holidays.

Train

Ayutthaya, Lopburi, Nakhon Sawan, Phicit, Phitsanulok (access to Sukhothai), Uttaradit, Mae Mo, Lampang, and Lamphun are all served by the Bangkok-Chiang Mai trains. You can obtain detailed timetables at Hualampong Station in Bangkok. Tel: 223 7010 or 223 7020 from 5am to 10pm.

Bus

Buses leave from the Northern Bus Station on Pahol Yothin Rd. Tel: 279 4484-7, from 5:25am to 10pm (11 services per day).

EXPLORING THE FALLEN CITIES

AYUTTHAYA***
You can allow a whole day to visit the site, spend the night there, and take the bus or train to your next destination the following morning. For access information, see 'Outside Bangkok' p. 117.

LOPBURI**
95 mi/154 km from Bangkok.

Access

Train
Departures from Bangkok at 9:30am, 3:45pm, 6pm, and 8pm (2.5-3 hours).

Bus
Departures from Bangkok every 20 min., from 5:20am to 8:20pm (three hours).

Accommodation
Telephone area code: 036
- ▲ **Asia**, Amphoe Muang. Tel: 41 1892. 111 rooms.
- ▲ **Taipei**, Surasongkhram Rd. Tel: 41 1524. 104 rooms.
- ▲ **Viboonsri**, Naraimajaraj Rd. Tel: 41 1009. 54 rooms.

Visit

Lopburi was at the height of its glory during the Dvaravati epoch (6th-11th centuries) but archaeological evidence shows that the site was already inhabited during the Neolithic and Bronze Ages. In the 11th century, Lopburi was conquered by the Khmers, under whom the city became an important provincial capital of the Angkor empire. The Thais recaptured the city in the 13th century during the Sukhothai era.

Lopburi once again grew in prominence near the end of the 17th century under King Narai, who chose it as his summer capital when the Franco-Siamese alliance was at its height. French architects were hired, which explains the peculiar — and quite successful — mixture of Thai and European motifs in the decoration of many of the buildings.

It is a shame that many of the treasures here have not been restored as they deserve to be. Constantine Phaulkon's Palace (Chao Phraya Wichayen), for example, which was as large as the king's residence, is now overgrown with weeds. An exception to this neglect is an old locomotive, refurbished and displayed outside the railway station.

If you are driving, you may want to stop at the fish-curing centre just outside Lopburi on the road leading north. This is an interesting visual and olfactory experience (the fish are smoked or dried in the sun).

King Narai's Palace*** (Narai Radja Niwes)

Open daily 9am-noon and 1pm-4pm. Closed Mon., Tue., and holidays. Entrance fee. Remember to remove your shoes at the entrance. The palace originally consisted of several buildings surrounded by a wall. You enter its inner courtyards by way of well-preserved and majestic gateways. Leaf-shaped niches high in the walls served to protect the coconut oil lamps which were lit on ceremonial occasions. Two pavilions in the second courtyard serve as a museum; one of these was originally the residence of King Rama IV. The museum contains fine Lopburi and Dvaravati sculptures, along with furniture, pottery, etc.

Wat Phra Si Ratana Mahathat***

One of Lopburi's most important ensembles, with its *prangs* and *chedis* of different styles. The cloister that once surrounded it has now completely vanished but you can still distinguish the various stages of construction, along with the Sukhothai and Ayutthaya contributions to the *chedis*.

The Dusit Maha Prasad Hall*
This was built to receive the Chevalier de Chaumont, ambassador of Louis XIV, in 1685. It originally incorporated its own 'Hall of Mirrors', inspired by the one at the Chateau of Versailles in France. You can also see the residence of the Jesuit astronomers who accompanied the Chevalier Chaumont.

Hindu Sanctuary (Prang Khaek)
The central *stupa* here contains a phallus representation dedicated to Shiva, the Hindu god of regeneration. The sanctuary, which is situated in the middle of town, was built during the 10th or 11th century when Lopburi province formed part of the Khmer empire. It was restored by King Narai in the 17th century.

Monkey Temple (Kala Temple)
The ruins of this building are overgrown with banyan roots and inhabited by a large colony of monkeys. If you're in a car, close the windows, as the monkeys won't hesitate to hitch a ride. Nearby, a modern sanctuary houses a Hindu divinity.

Prang Sam Yod (three-spired pagoda)
A temple of Hindu origin built on an esplanade. The 13th-century architecture is Khmer-influenced and the temple was probably restored in the 17th century on the initiative of King Narai. It has become the symbol of Lopburi.

PHITSANULOK
308 mi/498 km north of Bangkok.

Access

Plane
Thai Airways offers daily flights from Bangkok at 6:40am and 4:10pm (35 min.) See also p. 126.

Train
See the times for Lopburi (p. 127), which is on the same line. If you come directly from Bangkok, the best train is the one which leaves at 9:30am and arrives at 6:10pm. All the others arrive in the middle of the night.

Bus
Departures from Bangkok's Northern Bus Terminal at 8:10am and 9:55pm (6.25 hours).

Accommodation
Telephone area code: 055
▲▲ **Phailin**, Baromtrilokenart Rd   Tel: 252 411.   175 rooms.
▲ **Amarin Nakhon**, Chaophya Phitsanulok Rd. Tel: 258 588. European food available.   150 rooms.
▲ **Nandhao**, 242 Baromtrilokenart Rd.   Tel: 259 511.   A comfortable, centrally located hotel.   115 rooms.
▲ **Rajapruk**, 99/9 Phra-Ong Dam Rd.   Tel: 258 477.   Swimming pool.   100 comfortable rooms.

Visit

Phitsanulok, a lively commercial town, is principally a stopping-off point on the way to Sukhothai. Entirely destroyed by fire in 1960, Phitsanulok itself has nothing of particular interest to offer but its site beside the Nan River and its floating houses are not without charm. You can enjoy yourself at Phitsanulok by taking one of the boats that ply the Nan River (these also serve meals; very romantic at dusk).

Wat Mahathat***

At a slight distance from the town, this remarkable *wat* fortunately escaped the great fire. It houses a much-venerated statue, known as the **Phra Buddha Chinarai.** The statue, which dates from the late Sukhothai era (mid-14th century), represents a seated Buddha in polished bronze. Its serenity is accentuated by the black background against which it is displayed. Note the fingers, which are all exactly the same length. This figure is kept in the main *bot* behind 18th-century doors encrusted with mother-of-pearl. A gilded Khmer-style *prang* dominates the ensemble; this was built during the Ayutthaya epoch, and is surrounded by cloisters containing statues of different styles.

▬ SUKHOTHAI***

290 mi/466 km from Bangkok.

Access

Car
The old capital is 7.5 mi/12 km west of the modern city (also called Sukhothai) on route 12 leading to Tak.

Bus
From Phitsanulok, there is a bus to Sukhothai that leaves from in front of the police station every 20 minutes between 5am and 5pm.
Direct from Bangkok (6 hours), there are daily departures at 10:30am (air-conditioned) and 11:35am (non air-conditioned).

Accommodation

▲▲ **Thai Village House,** 214 Jarod Vithi Tong Rd., Muang Kao, Sukhothai. Tel: 611 049. Situated close to the ruins, it consists of several wooden pavilions built around a small stream that is lit at night by torches. The bungalows are comfortable and the Thai restaurant is excellent. A small cultural centre, half museum, half shop, sells antiques and local crafts. In the evening, young people from the village present lively displays of folk and court dancing. 62 rooms.

Hotels in the new town that offer reasonable prices and quality include:

▲▲ **Pong Prasert,** 92/6 Nilornkasem Rd. 30 rooms.
▲▲ **Rung Fah,** 8 Singhawat Rd. 14 rooms.
▲▲ **Sukhothai,** 15/5 Singhawat Rd. 40 rooms.

If you plan to visit Sukhothai in Oct. or Nov., be sure to book accommodation well in advance. This is the time when the Loy Krathong festival (festival of light) takes place. The festival originated in Sukhothai and celebrations are particularly elaborate here.

Visit

Sukhothai was the first capital of Siam, from 1257 to 1379. Situated in a beautiful valley and protected on the west by wooded hills, it has symbolic value for the Thais because its creation marked the emergence of the Siamese nation. Among the eight kings who reigned there, Rama Khamheng is the best remembered as a just and compassionate ruler whose reign coincided with a time of prosperity and extraordinary artistic vitality.

A large part of the archaeological site has been developed into a park but the more adventurous will head towards the buildings still overgrown with wild flowers beyond the main border. The site stretches over 6 mi/10 km from east to west and the same from north to south; a tourist trail runs around the perimeter. Bicycles are not available for rental but it is sometimes possible to borrow one. If you limit yourself to the most spectacular ruins within the walls, half a day should suffice. There is a map at the main entrance that will help you find your bearings around the site, which is divided into five sections. There is a small entrance fee to each section.

The Rama Khamheng National Museum***
Open daily 9am-noon and 1pm-4pm. Closed Mon. and Tue. Entrance fee.

In a garden close to the Wat Mahathat and the main entrance to the site. Collections of objects found at Sukhothai, Si Satchanalai, and Kamphaeng Phet (another important site dating from the same era 50 mi/80 km to the south-west). The official tour, which is in English, will complement your visit. In the entrance hall you will discover one of the finest statues of the 'walking Buddha' in existence. This attitude, which was introduced by the artists of Sukhothai, represents Buddha just after his illumination, entering the world of men to show them the true way. On the first floor, there are Chiang Saen and Lopburi sculptures and ceramics. A copy of the Rama Khamheng *stele* is displayed on the mezzanine (the original is in the Bangkok National Museum).

Inside the walls

Wat Mahathat***
This huge building was once surrounded by nearly a mile of moats. At its centre stands a massive *chedi*, the base of which is decorated with stucco bas-reliefs representing a procession of monks (badly restored and disfigured by graffiti). Four Khmer-style towers are arranged at its corners. The strangest structures here are two monumental, symmetrical, standing Buddhas, enclosed in a kind of vertical brick wall sarcophagus. Their heads project above the top of the wall and they seem to stare straight ahead, each oblivious of the other. This temple, with its 185 *chedis* and many sanctuaries, was originally reserved for the devotional use of the royal family and is the earliest example of a royal *wat* in the Siamese tradition. (The idea was perpetuated at Bangkok by the Wat Phra Keo attached to the Palace.)

Wat Sra Si***
One of the most poetic of Sukhothai's temples, with its monumental Buddha seated on a dais and offset by six rows of columns. The *wat* is reflected in a pool, which makes it a favourite subject for photographers. The remains of other important temples may be seen within the perimeter, notably the Wat Chana Songkram, the Wat Trakuan, Wat Tha Pa Doeng, Wat Sorasak, and Wat Son Kao.

Wat Si Sawai*
This *wat* was founded during the era when the region lay under Khmer domination. It is in the Lopburi style. The three *prangs* (spires) were added in the 15th century. Here, if you have sharp eyes and plenty of imagination, you can see remains of mural paintings in the recess on the right-hand side.

Outside the perimeter

Wat Chetupon***
(to the south) Remarkable for its surrounding wall built of slate. The *chedi* here was once protected by four Buddhas, each in a different attitude (standing, seated, reclining, and walking). Although its head is missing, the walking Buddha is considered a model of its type. The curve of its shoulders still gives an impression of calm majesty.

Wat Sapham Hin***
(to the west) Contains a standing Buddha over 40 ft/12 m tall, with a beautiful view across the ruins of Sukhothai to the Si Satchanalai mountains.

Wat Si Chum**
(to the north) The seated Buddha, measuring no less than 49 ft/15 m high, is one of the largest in Thailand. A stairway hidden in the wall allows the visitor to climb to the level of the statue's head. This stairway is said to have enabled one of the Sukhothai kings to make the Buddha

> **The City of Contentment**
>
> 'Happy is the city of Sukhothai; its waters are filled with fish, and its fields abound in rice. No tolls are levied on those who travel the roads to bring their cattle to market or to sell the horses on which they ride. All men are free to trade in elephants, horses, gold or silver. When a dispute arises among the people, the nobles, or the princes of royal blood, the king orders an impartial inquiry and decides on his own high authority; he will not favour the thief, nor will he show mercy to the malingerer. For he harbours no desire for his neighbour's rice. At the gate of his palace hangs a bell. Any man who wishes to make some spiritual or temporal request to the king, may ring this bell. King Rama Khamheng will consider his case, and will tend a just and attentive ear to what he has to say.'
>
> *Stele* of Rama Khamheng

'speak' to his routed soldiers, thus permitting them to turn the tide of battle and defeat the enemy.

Wat Phra Pai Luang

(to the north) This is another vestige from the Khmer epoch. At its inception, the temple was located in the very centre of Sukhothai. The main edifice is a pyramid-shaped *chedi* inside which a number of Buddhas were once immured. (With regard to these, the antique dealers acted more quickly than the Department of Fine Arts, to the benefit of private collections.)

KAMPHAENG PHET***

220 mi/357 km from Bangkok.

Access

Car

Kamphaeng Phet, the former capital of the kingdom of Sukhothai, lies on the left bank of the Ping River, 40 mi/65 km south of Tak on Route 1. The archaeological site is about a mile from the present village of Kamphaeng Phet.

Bus

Direct from Bangkok (6 hours), there are daily departures at 10:45am (air-conditioned) and 7:37am (non air-conditioned).

Accommodation

Telephone area code: 055

▲▲ **Chakungrao,** 123/1 Thesa Rd. Tel: 711 315. 120 rooms.
▲▲ **Navarat,** 2 Soi Prapan, Thesa Rd., Kamphaeng Phet. Tel: 711 211. Comfortable establishment with reasonable prices, beside the Ping River. 155 rooms.
▲▲ **Phet Hotel,** 99 Wichit Soi 3. Tel: 711 283-5. Modern comforts and swimming pool. 234 rooms.

Visit

Kamphaeng Phet was one of the three capitals of the Sukhothai kingdom; it was built by King Li Thai (1347-1368). The last king of Sukhothai fled here before submitting to his Ayutthaya rivals in 1378. Prior to this event, Kamphaeng Phet was a centre for the porcelain trade with China. The remains here are impressive, spread over an area of 6 sq mi/16 sq km. They have been abandoned to the encroaching jungle ever since the end of the 1970s although the site had been protected before.

Of the 37 temples listed at Kamphaeng Phet, only three are maintained, but at the time of writing considerable work is in progress to extricate the Buddhas and the buildings from the jungle. A small **museum** *(open*

9am-noon and 1pm-3pm. *Closed Mon. and Tues.)* within the main perimeter gives the visitor an idea of the site's topography. Among the various objects displayed is a seated Buddha which is thought to be one of the masterpieces of the U Thong epoch.

The atmosphere of Kamphaeng Phet is somewhat eerie and ghostly, with its stone Buddhas in faded saffron robes and chaotic jumble of columns, stucco and weatherbeaten smiling heads. Within the ramparts stands the **Wat Phra Keo*****, with its two giant Buddhas (one heavily damaged) and the three *chedis* of the Wat Prathat (entrance fee; closes at 5pm). Outside, the most remarkable building is the **Wat Chang Rob*****, with its *chedi* resting on a platform supported by laterite and stucco elephants. Some of these elephants are very well preserved (a similar piece of architecture survives at the Wat Chang Lom at Si Satchanalai).

SI SATCHANALAI***
325 mi/524 km from Bangkok.

Access

Car
Si Satchanalai is 36 mi/58 km north of Sukhothai on Route 101. The simplest way to get there is to hire a taxi at Sukhothai, Sawankhalot, or Uttaradit.

Bus
The modern town is also served by regular buses from Sukhothai (timetables at the bus station). From here take a taxi to the ruins which are 9 mi/15 km away.

Accommodation

If you decide to spend the night in the area, you can do so at Uttaradit (modest, air-conditioned hotels). The Bangkok-Chiang Mai train stops here and an ordinary train leaves Uttaradit at 7:53am (arrival Chiang Mai 3:05pm).

Visit

Si Satchanalai, beside the Yom River, is much less known than its contemporary, Sukhothai. The city was founded in the 13th century for the viceroys of Sukhothai. The place was dedicated to the Buddha and, apart from one or two wooden houses, consisted almost exclusively of religious buildings. The river and the surrounding hills create an extraordinary natural setting for Si Satchanalai's forest of slender *chedis* and the ruins radiate grandeur and poignant solitude.

The heat is often oppressive here and there are poisonous snakes in the region; take care to make plenty of noise as you walk through the high grass. Ever since the Fine Arts Department cleared away the vegetation that partly covered the temples, the site has lost some of its mystery. The old ferryman has put away his boat and a new bridge now spans the Yom, which offers direct access to the ruins.

Wat Chang Lom***

Built between 1285 and 1291 on the initiative of Rama Khamheng, as we are informed by the monarch's famous *stele*. The *stupa*, in laterite and stucco, is adorned at its base by 39 elephant heads. Hence the name of 'temple surrounded by elephants'. The upper terrace originally supported statues of Buddha meditating, each in its own niche.

Wat Chedi Chet Thao***

This temple stands to the south of Wat Chang Lom and is distinguished by seven rows of *stupas*, one of which is flanked by a seated Buddha

This statue of Buddha at Kamphaeng Phet is an example of Sukhothai art.

and a superb *naga,* the presence of which is both protective and dominating. This piece is recognizably Khmer in style.

Wat Phra Si Ratana Mahathat***
This is one of the most handsome at Si Satchanalai, standing about 1 mi/1.6 km south-east of the old town at Chaliang. You can reach this site by boat. The *wat* is built on a kind of peninsula formed by a loop in the river. Its two main buildings are separated by a platform bearing a Ceylonese-style circular *chedi* and a fine Khmer-style *prang.* The temple houses several statues, including one very beautiful walking Buddha (south building).

Wat Khao Suwan Kiri
On the hills to the north of the above temples you will see the **Wat Khao Suwan Kiri** (the temple of the golden hill) with its harmoniously proportioned *chedi* and the **Wat Kha Thanom Plung** (the temple of the mountain of fire), which stands close to the river and contains a large seated Buddha. The magnificent view from this point is well worth the effort of the climb.

At Si Satchanalai vendors will offer you authentic Sawankholok ceramics found on the spot. These can be a good buy, provided you drive as hard a bargain as possible.

▬▬ *LAMPANG****
374 mi/604 km north of Bangkok, 58 mi/93 km south of Chiang Mai.

Access
Lampang is served by plane, train, and bus from Bangkok and Chiang Mai. For Bangkok information, see p. 34. For information in Chiang Mai, contact the TAT office, 135 Praisani Rd. Tel: 235 334.

Accommodation and food
Telephone area code: 054.
▲▲ **Tipchang Garnet Lampang Hotel,** 54/22 Takrao Noi. Tel: 218 078. Modern comfort, cafeteria, pool, sauna. 125 rooms.
▲ **Asia Lampang,** Bunyawat Rd. Tel: 217 844. Cafeteria. 71 comfortable rooms.

Visit
The town of Lampang grew along the south bank of the Wang River; it is reminiscent of a bygone era, with its tiled roofs and old carriages instead of taxis. Temple-lovers will stop at two Burmese-influenced *wats.*

Lampang Luang***
Enthusiastic sightseers must visit the temple at Lampang Luang, 12 mi/20 km to the south, which is one of the most beautiful in Northern Thailand. The hilltop setting alone is worth the trip, with the temple's *chedi* soaring above a cluster of trees.

Two majestic staircases, facing north and east, spill forth ferocious-looking protective *nagas* (snakes) in the form of balustrades. The sanctuaries, which date from the 16th century, are surrounded by a wall, all that remains of the former fortified town. A small museum on the site contains an Emerald Buddha behind an iron grille; tradition has it that this statue was carved from the same block of jasper as the one in Bangkok. Lacquered wooden bookcases and various wooden sculptures are also on exhibit here. The *viharn,* which is decorated with woodcarvings, contains two Chiang Saen-style Buddhas.

Wat Phra Keo Don Tao***
This temple stands on the opposite bank of the Wang, a short way outside the town. Note the ceilings and columns of its 18th-century *viharn,*

which are sculpted in wood and encrusted with tiny fragments of mother-of-pearl, porcelain, and enamel. The gilded *chedi* is elegant, and this temple is generally a peaceful place to visit.

Wat Phra Sang**
Here one can easily recognize the layered roofs which are the distinguishing characteristic of Burmese architecture. The massive white *chedi*, with its gilded summit, is surrounded by seven chapels (one for every day of the week) all of which house Buddhas of alabaster.

SOME OTHER NORTHERN ITINERARIES

It takes several days to visit Northern Thailand properly. In addition to the Bangkok-Chiang Mai route, the following itineraries include the region to the north-east of Chiang Mai. Trips on the Kok River and areas around Chiang Rai are discussed in detail at the end of the following chapter devoted to Chiang Mai.

Seven to nine days
Bangkok-Chiang Mai in three or four days (Lopburi, Sukhothai, Si Satchanalai); two days at Chiang Mai; Chiang Mai-Chiang Rai in three days (trip down the Kok River, the villages of the Golden Triangle); or a circuit of Chiang Mai-Mae Hong Son in two days.

Five days
Bangkok-Chiang Mai in two days (choose your own stopping points); one day at Chiang Mai; Chiang Mai-Chiang Rai in two days (by bus, or via the Kok River). Return to Bangkok by plane from Chiang Rai.

CHIANG MAI

Chiang Mai, the capital of Northern Thailand, lies on the northern bank of the Ping River, in a valley surrounded by wooded hills. It is a lively town, which appears at first sight to have more motorcycles in it than people (pop. 180,000). However, the survival of the pedal-powered *samlor* leaves room for hope that the battle against pollution is not yet lost. Chiang Mai was founded in 1296 by King Rama Khamheng and Mengrai, first sovereign of the kingdom of Lan Na. The city maintained strong links throughout its history with the kingdom of

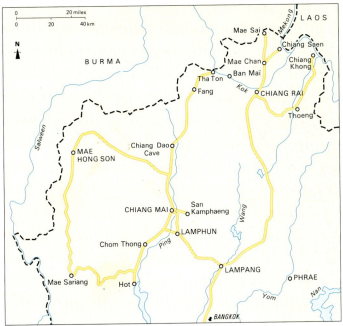

NORTHERN THAILAND

(*N.B.* To visualize the Bangkok-Chiang Mai itinerary, look at the map of Thailand pp. 8-9.)

Despite increasing contact with urban Thais, young Meos have not yet adopted jeans.

Luang Prabang (Laos) and was under Burmese rule for over two centuries (1586-1775). Its link to the modern Siamese nation is, therefore, a recent affair, which explains Chiang Mai's strong ethnic, historical, and artistic identity within Thailand. Until 1920 it could only be reached by river or on elephant back.

A city of temples

Chiang Mai possesses over a hundred temples, with architectural styles influenced by both the Mon and Burmese. Since construction of new modern buildings, the character of the town has changed, but one can still detect a strong flavour of the past in the many flower-decked *sois* (lanes) leading to old wooden houses, and in the peaceful temples just off the city's broad avenues. As a major tourist venue Chiang Mai offers glimpses of a new side to Thailand as well as its glorious past.

The population of the northern plains area is basically Laotian in origin. The mountain regions are occupied by Sino-Tibetan and Burmese-Tibetan minorities, relatively recent arrivals who belong to a totally different culture. Thus, Chiang Mai is also the gateway to a different Thailand, one which had not encountered Western influences until this century.

PRACTICAL INFORMATION

Telephone area code for Chiang Mai and the surrounding area: 053.

Access

For tourists who have little time to spare, there are three ways of reaching Chiang Mai directly from Bangkok.

Plane

Thai Airways operates the following flights from Bangkok (timetable subject to change). Daily: 7:30am, 9:40am (via Phitsanulok), 1:45pm, 6:30pm, and 9:30pm. Supplementary flight at 5:30pm, five days per week. The direct flight takes one hour (1.5 hours with stopover). Return flights Chiang Mai-Bangkok: 9am, 11:10am, 3:15pm (via Phitsanulok), 8pm, and 11pm, five days per week.

Train

The night express leaves Bangkok at 6pm (arr. 7:50am). Be sure to reserve sleeping berths at least one day in advance, especially during peak vacation periods.

Bus

Eight buses leave Bangkok daily, from 5:25am to 9:40pm. Avoid the 6pm bus, which takes the old road north, which is 500 mi/809 km instead of 440 mi/714 km. The trip takes about ten hours.

Getting around Chiang Mai

For the tourist, Chiang Mai is both the central focus and the springboard for forays into the surrounding region. The town consists of two sections: the old town, enclosed on all sides by moats; and the new section, which has spread to the north and the west along the left bank of the Ping River. Centres of interest are widely scattered because Chiang Mai is an open, airy place, full of gardens and low buildings, and you must be prepared for long hikes within the town. If you only have two or three days to spare, your best policy is to go to a travel agency, either to rent a car with a chauffeur-guide, or to sign up for planned tours.

If you have more than three days, you'll have time to get to know the local transportation system. The *tuk-tuks* and *song-teos* (short-haul share taxis) are very good value, but the best way to discover the inner city is by *samlor* or by bicycle, which are the only forms of transportation that match the setting. Bicycles (or motorcycles) can be rented at the east gate of the old town.

For details of the bus network, inquire at the TAT (see p. 32). There are several bus stations, each serving different destinations. (The main one is on Chotana Road, about 1 mi/1.6 km from the White Elephant Gate.) There is a regular bus service to all localities around Chiang Mai.

Accommodation

(Map coordinates refer to the map p. 141.)

Chiang Mai has excellent hotels, which cater to all tastes and pocketbooks. All of the major hotels have restaurants; those with special features are listed here.

▲▲▲ **Chiang Inn**, 100 Chang Klan Rd. (D2). Tel: 235 655. Right in the centre of town in a lively area. Excellent comfort without showy luxury. A good place to rest after a spell in the hills. 170 rooms.

▲▲▲ **Chiang Mai Orchid**, 100-102 Huey Kaeo Rd. (A1). Tel: 221 625. No doubt the best hotel in town from the standpoint of comfort but some distance from the centre. Five minutes from the airport by car. Pool. 267 rooms.

▲▲▲ **Chiang Mai President**, 226 Vichayanon Rd. (C1). Tel: 235 424. High standard of comfort. 140 rooms.

▲▲▲ **Dusit Inn**, 112 Chang Klan Rd. (D2). Tel: 236 835. Excellent location in the centre of town, close to the Night Market. 198 rooms.

▲▲▲ **Poy Luang**, 146 Super Highway Rd. (E2). Tel: 234 424. Located outside town. For admirers of Chinese kitsch. Pool, revolving restaurant on 16th floor. 230 rooms.

▲▲▲ **Rincome**, 301 Huey Kaeo Rd. (A1). Tel: 221 044. Good hotel, outside town. Two pools, pleasant garden, restaurants, discotheque. 158 rooms.

▲▲▲ **Suriwongse**, 110 Chang Klan Rd. (D2). Tel: 236 789. Excellent standard of comfort. Pool, tropical garden, restaurants serving local and Western food. 168 rooms.

▲▲ **Anodard**, 57-9 Rajamanka Rd. (D2). Tel: 235 353. In the old town, close to Wat Chedi Luang. Pool. 150 rooms.

▲▲ **Diamond**, 33/10 Charoen Prathet Rd. (D2). Tel: 234 155. Centrally located. Traditional meals *(khan toke)* in a fine teak house. 145 rooms.

▲▲ **Porn Ping**, 46-48 Charoen Prathet Rd. (D2). Tel: 235 099. Good location. French restaurant. Discotheque. 180 rooms.

▲▲ **Sumit**, 198 Rajpakinai Rd. (C1). Tel: 235 996. In the old town, close to Wat Chiang Man. 163 rooms.

▲ **Chaw Nua**, 53/4 Sittwong Rd. (C2). Tel: 235 117. 32 rooms.

▲ **Nakorn Ping**, 43 Taiwang Rd. (D1). Tel: 236 024. 23 rooms.

▲ **New Chiang Mai**, 22 Chaipoom Rd. (C2). Tel: 236 561. 43 rooms.

▲ **Thai Charoen**, 164-166 Ta Pae Rd. (C2). Tel: 236 640. 32 rooms.

Food

(Map coordinates refer to the map p. 141.)

It is possible to eat very well in Chiang Mai, not only Thai cooking but also every variety of 'foreign' cuisine. Strings of German sausages have invaded the restaurants and, without much trouble, you will find crêpes suzette, pizzas, tandoori chicken and all the Japanese dishes under the sun.

The food of Northern Thailand is different from that of Southern Thailand. For example, you will find 'sticky rice' everywhere: this gluten-rich bread substitute is rolled with the fingers and served in a little cylindrical basket which can be carried about like a sandwich. At meals, it is eaten in little balls, seasoned with sauces. The southern Thais make fun of northerners, calling them 'sticky rice eaters'; this term is also used for the Laos.

Thai traditional cooking is to be found in the small open-air restaurants around the Chiang Inn by the central market, near the east gate, or at the Nong Hoy market (on Route 106, near the Caltex service station). Many of Chiang Mai's restaurants are in old wooden houses, which gives them a special cachet.

Regional and mixed

Aroon Rai, 45 Khotchasarn Rd. (C2). Chiang Mai cuisine and Chinese cooking at very reasonable prices. Open for over 30 years, it has become something of an institution.

Mang Savirat, Chern Doy Rd., in front of the medical faculty building. Vegetarian Thai restaurant.

Old Chiang Mai, 185/3 Wualai Rd. (B3). Several restaurants attached to a complex that is a kind of living museum of the hilltribe minorities. The most interesting of these is the **Haw Muk** (Pearl Room), serving simple traditional meals known as *khan toke*. There are traditional dance performances nightly. Expensive.

Sandwich Bar, 3 Srak Rd. Thai-European cuisine. Excellent breakfasts.

Suthinan, near the train station (E2). Specializes in tasty breakfast food but also serves Thai, Chinese, and European dishes.

Tar Coffee, opposite the Chiang Inn (see p. 139). Chinese or Thai snacks. Ordinary and exotic ice cream.

Thai-German Dairy Products, corner of Ratchadamnoen Rd. and Mun Muang Rd. (C2). Something of an oddity, where you can get milk-based articles such as yogurt and cheese, rarities in Thailand.

Tip, 28/3 Chiang Mai - Fang Rd. (B1 north — in front of the Nong Haw Racecourse. Northern Thai cuisine.

Vilai Garden, 2 Super Highway (A1 north — near the National Museum). Thai cuisine open-air restaurant.

Whole Earth, 88 Sri Dornchai Rd. (C3). Thai and Indian cuisines.

French

Le Coq d'Or, Huey Kae Rd. (A1 — near the Rincome Hotel).

New Krua Thai Restaurant, Oom Muang Rd. (south-west of the old town). Magnificent seafood, pleasant atmosphere, and reasonable prices.

Italian

Babylon, 100/63 Huey Kae Rd. (A1). In front of the university. Pizza, pasta, and ice cream.

Pub

The Pub, Huey Kae Rd. (A1 — near the Rincome Hotel). In a superb Thai house. Lunches, dinners, and beer on tap.

Steak and grill

Pat's Tavern Grill, Chaya Poom Rd. (C2). For anyone who still hankers for Western cooking.

Shopping

You are bound to have noticed in Bangkok: lacquerware comes from Chiang Mai, celadon comes from Chiang Mai, old silver jewelry comes from Chiang Mai, opium scales come from Chiang Mai.... In short,

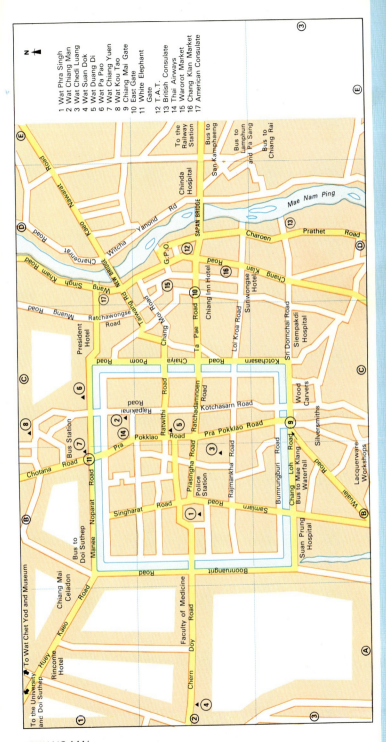

CHIANG MAI

Chiang Mai seems to be the main source of most of the handcrafts sold in Thailand. As for antiques, these are generally smuggled from Burma at great profit. An object which was originally obtained by a Shan trader somewhere in the jungle in return for salt or medical supplies eventually turns up in a Chiang Mai shop sporting a huge price tag. Apart from this steady and miraculous source, Chiang Mai also possesses a cluster of 'antique factories' that operate at great profit thanks to the effect of a little judiciously sprinkled dust and the inexperience of tourists.

The unit of weight used for silver is also called the *baht*. So don't be alarmed if you find yourself buying a *baht* (of silver) for a few *baht* more. Most of the shops engaged in the silver trade are in the Chiang Mai gate section and along the Wualai Road. Here you can buy objects made on the spot (bowls, dishes, jewelry) and superb older objects, usually from Montagnard villages (Meo necklaces, bracelets, earrings, belts, etc.). Prices are frequently marked in US dollars.

While the quality of traditional craftwork (lacquer, teak carving, ceramics) is still fairly high, its commercial significance is beginning to assume unhealthy proportions. The craftsmen's villages of not so long ago have become tourist supermarkets, where every product sold has a price stuck to it and where bargaining has become more and more incongruous. Although the workshops, like the living conditions of the people working in them, have changed very little, they are now hidden behind the gleaming shopfront of a rich boss. The tourist who buys here will invariably spend enough to keep the behind-the-scenes workman who sweats ten hours a day at a forge for one, three, or even six months running.

Among the objects produced by the hilltribes, woven fabrics and embroidery are of particularly fine quality. In the hope of giving the hilltribe populations a more profitable and honest source of income than opium poppy cultivation, the government encourages them to engage in handcrafts and assists them in selling their products. You can choose between Yao embroidery (cross-stitching on indigo fabric); Meo embroidery (layers of fabric superimposed for belts, aprons, skirt hems and the famous 'Meo squares' with geometric motifs); Karen woven fabrics (poncho-type smocks); Akha patchwork (marvellously intricate work involving the assembly of tiny pieces of cloth), etc. Articles of this type can be bought at the Chang Klan Road Market every evening, at handcraft shops in the commercial districts (Ta Pae Rd.) and in specialty shops.

Among the better known shops are the following:

Border Crafts of Thailand, 22 Huey Kae Rd. (A1). Tribal handcrafts.
Chiang Mai Art, 164/1-2 Rat Chiang Saen Rd. Lacquer, items in wood and silver, antiques, etc.
Chiang Mai Antique, 32 Wualai Rd. (B3). Antiques, silver jewelry.
Hudson Enterprises, 234-240 Ta Pae. Ceramics, fabrics, lacquer, tribal handcrafts.
Old Chiang Mai, 185/3 Wualai Rd. (B3). Hilltribe embroidery.
Saithong (centre of Old Chiang Mai). Various handcrafts, teak furniture.
Shinawatra, San Kamphaeng. Cotton and silk.
Thai Celadon Co., Fang Rd. (B1 north). Here you can watch celadon being made.

Festivals

All Thai civil and religious ceremonies are celebrated at Chiang Mai. Particularly spectacular are: the Carnival of Flowers (first weekend in Feb.); Songkran (Thai New Year, Apr. 13-15); Loy Krathong (the Festival of Light, at full moon in the 12th lunar month, i.e., Oct.-Nov.) and the Lichee Feast (May).

Entertainment and nightlife

Chiang Mai has recently begun to shake off its provincial lethargy and now offers entertainment and nightlife almost on the same level as Bangkok and Pattaya. There are plenty of bars and discotheques available to the tourist, but, in contrast to Bangkok, Chiang Mai tends to cultivate 'atmosphere', often thanks to Western residents who have fallen in love with its charm.

Music
Riverside, Charoengrat Rd. (opposite the Chinda Hospital), has Dutch management and the folk music here is anything but local. You can also sample delicious yet simple dishes from both Thai and Western cuisines in attractive surroundings by the river.
The Cabin, 239 Charoengrat Rd., in the same style, offers mellow guitar music and soothing songs.

Bars and discotheques
The 'in' discotheques are those of the big hotels: **Byblos** (Rincome Hotel) and **The Wall** (Chiang Inn). There is also a **'Playboy Bunny Club'**, like the original but with a distinctly Oriental touch.

Massage parlors
On the massage front, you will be glad to learn that far better value for money is to be had at Chiang Mai than at Bangkok (150-250 ฿ per hour, for 'professional' quality). You can also try a traditional herbal massage (**Rinkaew,** Wualai Rd., facing the Old Cultural Centre).

Chang Klan bazaar
The real 'must' of Chiang Mai by night has to be a walk around the Night Bazaar on Chang Klan Road, open every evening from 7pm to 11pm. The former street peddlers are now installed in boutiques where you will find everything the regular shops sell but at much lower prices.
For more complete information, consult *Chiang Mai Travel Holiday,* a magazine with local information and listings, at the TAT office or at your hotel reception desk.

Useful addresses and information

Banks
Open Mon. to Fri. 8:30am-3:30pm. The **central exchange,** in the middle of the Chang Klan Road Market (D2), is open until 10pm.

Emergencies
TAT Tourist Police, corner of Ta Pae Rd. and Charoen Prathet Rd. (D2). Tel: 235 334 or 235 490.

Hospitals
Chiang Mai Provincial Hospital, Suthep Rd. (A2). Tel: 221 122 or 221 544. Dentistry service also provided.
Lanna Hospital, Superhighway. (C1 north). Tel: 211 037-41.

Post office and telephone
Central Post Office, Charoen Muang Rd. (E2 east). Open Mon. to Fri. 9am-4:30pm; Sat., Sun., and holidays 9am-11am. Telegram counter open from 7am to midnight. International calls can be made from the first floor.
Telephone area code for Chiang Mai and the surrounding area: 053.

Tourist information and assistance

Immigration office
Fang Rd. (A1 north) or Airport (A2 south). Tel: 213 510.

Maps
On arrival, buy yourself Nancy Chandler's carefully annotated and illustrated street plan of Chiang Mai. Everything is included, from the colours of buses to good-value hairdressers, restaurants, public services, and tourist attractions. Sold in all hotels and news-stands.

Tourist office
TAT, 135 Praisani Rd. (D2). Tel: 235 334. Open Mon. to Fri. 8:30am to 4:30pm; Sat., Sun., and holidays 8:30am to 1pm.

Transportation

Chiang Mai Arcade Bus Station, Kaeo Narawat Rd. (E1). Tel: 211 586. For buses serving other provinces and Bangkok.
Chang Phuak Bus Station, Chotana Rd. (B1). Tel: 242 664. For buses serving Chiang Mai province.
Railway Station, Charoen Muang Rd. (E2 east). Tel: 244 795.
Thai Airways, 240 Pra Pokklao Rd. (C2). Tel: 236 011, 235 525 or 236 538.

VISITING CHIANG MAI

▬▬ THE TEMPLES OF CHIANG MAI

There is a splendid profusion of temples in Chiang Mai. Those of special artistic or historical importance are indicated on the Chiang Mai street map (p. 141), but there are also small, local *wats* of peripheral interest. If you think you can manage without a guide, hire a *samlor* for an hour or two. The driver will take you around the sights in his own way, which will be as good as any.

Wat Chedi Luang***

Pra Pokklao Rd. (B2). This temple was built by King Saen Muang Ma in 1391. In 1454, King Tilokaraj transformed it by building a *chedi* 280 ft/86 m high, and, during his reign, the Emerald Buddha, now in Bangkok, was placed in the eastern niche of this structure. A century later, the *chedi* was damaged by an earthquake and was never rebuilt. Also in the temple precinct are two fine old wooden pavilions. Wat Chedi Luang has a certain symbolic value for Chiang Mai because popular legend has it that the town's safety is somehow linked to the proper maintenance of the temple.

Wat Chiang Man***

Rajpakinai Rd. (C1). This temple is attributed to Mengrai, the king who founded Chiang Mai, and is the oldest in town. It is also one of the most charming, with wood carvings decorating the pavilions. The base of the *chedi* is surrounded by 15 elephants. One of the pavilions contains two remarkable statues of the Buddha. The first is a marble Buddha believed to be some 1200 years old. The second, made of rock crystal, was brought from Lamphun by King Mengrai. It is reputed to have the power of bringing rain and is carried through the town once a year at the start of the rainy season. This pavilion is only open on Sundays and Buddhist feast days.

Wat Phra Singh***

Phra Singh Rd. (B2). The 'Temple of the Lion Buddha', the city's largest, was founded in 1345. The statue which gave it its name — *singha* is lion in Thai — originally came from Sri Lanka; it is kept in a beautiful pavilion, the walls of which are decorated with 16th-century frescos. The original library contains remarkable decorations in carved wood.

Wat Chedi Jet Yod**

On the Lampang freeway, close to the museum (A1 north). This was built in the 15th century and modeled on a temple in Pagan, Burma, which itself was an imitation of an original in India. It has a seven-spired *chedi*, which is decorated with fine figurative bas-reliefs.

Wat Suan Dok**

On Sutness Rd. (A2 — opposite the school of dental surgery). 'The Flower Garden Temple' contains an ancient Chiang Saen-style Buddha. Unfortunately, successive restoration efforts have altered this

Chiang Mai markets offer a diverse abundance.

statue's original character. Behind the *chedi* are *stupas* which contain the ashes of the royal family of Chiang Mai.

Other temples

The above are Chiang Mai's most beautiful temples but if you have the time and energy, you should also visit the **Wat Duang Di*** (C2), noteworthy for its wood carvings and mirror-encrusted *chedi,* the Burmese-style **Wat Pa Pao** (C1), **Wat Chiang Yuen** (C1), **Wat Kou Tao** (C1), and any humbler buildings you may come across while walking around the town. They are all worth the detour.

*DOI SUTHEP*** (A1 off map)

The hill of Doi Suthep is 7 mi/11 km west of town. Take a taxi or a *song-teo* share pickup truck to get there. At an altitude of some 3300 ft/1000 m it is dominated by a superb temple, Wat Phrathat, which is Chiang Mai's most famous monument. Although there is a funicular railway, pilgrims habitually tackle the climb on foot. At the top is a flight of 290 steps, shaded by frangipani and protected on both sides by balustrades in the form of *nagas* with ceramic scales. The choice of this marvelous setting is attributed to a white elephant, to which King Kuena gave the task of finding a propitious site for a shrine to contain a relic of the Buddha in the 14th century. The elephant not only stopped at Doi Suthep — it died there. A *chedi* was built to house the relic, which was embellished two centuries later by the kings of Chiang Mai.

Wat Phrathat Doi Suthep*** is dominated by the 78 ft/24 m gilded *chedi*, which is surrounded by cloisters. It resembles Burmese temples, which embody the original Buddhist fervour that so many Thai *wats* seem to lack. Four graceful parasols in gilded copper stand beside the *chedi* and the cloisters contain Sukhothai and Chiang Saen Buddhas, some of which are very old. Nearby, a broad esplanade overlooks the valley. The continuous repairs have resulted in altering the artistic interest of the *wat*. Its chapels have been decorated with neo-realistic frescos of little merit, and the lovely sheen of the original murals, damaged by the weather, has been lost. As you go back down the steps, stop off at the **Rose Café** to the right of the parking lot; it is surrounded by a very pretty garden.

On the way back to Chiang Mai, you can visit the gardens of the king's Summer Palace **(Phu Bing Palace)** when he is not in residence, as well as the **Chiang Mai Zoo,** which has specimens of all the region's wild animals. Another much visited tourist attraction is the Meo village of **Doi Pui** (no entry fee, but you must pay to take pictures). On no account should you consider this village as typical or representative of the Meo nation.

▰ CHIANG MAI MUSEUM*** (A 1 off map)

Open daily 1pm-4pm. Closed Mon., Tues., and holidays.

The museum is located about 440 yds/400 m from Wat Chedi Chet. It contains a quantity of Buddhas and objects in the style of Chiang Saen, Sukhothai, Lopburi, U Thong, and Ayutthaya. There is also an interesting ethnological department that provides information about the hilltribe minorities and the peoples of the plain.

▰ CRAFTSMEN'S VILLAGES

Originally, the different crafts were divided up by districts or villages but with the proliferation of the tourist trade, the lines between them have become blurred. Handmade items are sold virtually everywhere in Thailand; you don't have to go to their source to find them. Visitors will probably be disappointed by what now passes for a 'craftsman's village'. With modern marketing, a workshop no longer sells its products directly; instead, you find yourself dealing with a boutique which may reveal how the product was made but will be resolute about fixed prices and will not bargain with you. It is, nevertheless, worth the effort to visit the craftsmen's villages if you can. Credit cards are welcome.

Celadon Village**

Past Bor Sang on the road to San Kamphaeng. Beautiful old-style ceramics in sea-green colours are made according to traditional techniques.

Lacquer workers' village**

Slightly further south, in Ban Tharam, on the road to Chom Thong (B3). The manufacture of lacquer is a tedious job; it can take several months to complete an object, using traditional techniques. The 'base', which is usually of teak or wickerwork, is painted with nine or ten successive layers of lacquer, then polished with a mixture of clay and ashes. The drying process takes about three months and requires humid conditions. A new technique which relies on an eggshell base has recently brought about a minor renaissance in the field. The gilding is done in the same way as batik, with glue replacing the wax. The antique lacquerware you will notice on sale in many Chiang Mai shops all comes from Burma.

Silversmiths' Village**

In the south end of Chiang Mai, on Wualai Rd. (C3). Only silver is worked on here: everything is done by hand, and the hammering of metal can be heard as soon as you enter the street. The most common items are jewelry, cups, belts, and dishes.

Umbrella Village**

In Bor Sang, 5.5 mi/9 km east of Chiang Mai on the San Kamphaeng road. Most of the inhabitants of this village are directly involved in this craft; those who aren't keep the shops. The spectacle of multicoloured umbrellas in the street is a magnet for photographers. Ever since 1978, the umbrella makers have been at pains to organize themselves, defending their craft, providing incentives to their workers, and improving their standard of living. (This explains the high prices they tend to charge.) The manufacture of an umbrella involves meticulous skill and several of the stages require a very delicate touch, for example the placement of the bamboo 'spokes'. The results are not always in the best taste, due to the general eagerness to please the tourist. Meanwhile, the umbrella painters will be happy to personalize a bag, garment, or camera in recond time and very cheaply. Favorite motifs are the lion, dragon or butterfly and a good buy is the local type of umbrella in treated paper, which will also protect you from the rain. Larger umbrellas can be packed and mailed home.

Weavers' Village**

San Kamphaeng, 4 mi/6 km farther on. This village is famous for its fine silk weaving. Here you will find raw silks and cottons, along with ready-made articles like shirts, skirts, and table linen. Most of the clothes sold in Chiang Mai come from here, and if you bring along an example or give instructions, you can have clothes made to measure in a single day. The weavers ply their looms in privacy behind their shops. A well-trained weaver can produce up to 5 yds/5 m of fabric in a day's work.

OLD CHIANG MAI**

To the southwest on Wualai Rd. (B3 south). Families belonging to various minority ethnic groups have been concentrated in this 'living museum' area, with instructions to carry on with their lives as if the tourists didn't exist. The result is better than you might imagine: the houses are authentic, built by their inhabitants, and you can at least familiarize yourself with the different ethnic costumes.

TRIBAL RESEARCH CENTRE

This centre (A1 north), which is part of Chiang Mai University, carries out studies on the ethnic minorities of Northern Thailand. Here you can find out about the location of villages and how to reach them. The centre also operates a small ethnographic museum which is open to the public; the two rooms containing costumes and traditional items are very small but the library contains a large amount of information, in English, on the subject.

OUTSIDE CHIANG MAI

Excursions to areas in the vicinity of Chiang Mai may be made individually by taxi, bus, or *song-teo* (share pickup trucks), as well as arranged through local agencies, which supply mini-buses and guides.

TO THE SOUTH

Lamphun**
16 mi/26 km south of Chiang Mai.

This little town, famous for its temple and as a centre for the cultivation of the *longane* (a fruit of the lichee family), is located on a tributary of the Ping River.

Wat Phrathat Hariphunchai

Between the river and the main street of the town. The present entrance is via the back of the temple, since the building was originally laid out to face the river. Within the temple precincts there is a juxtaposition of several styles, recent structures having been built to replace those which were destroyed. Thus the first sanctuary you will see when you enter the main courtyard dates from 1925, while the library (on the left) was built in the early 19th century. The central *chedi*, 167 ft/51 m tall, was built in several stages from AD 897 onwards. The *bot* contains two very fine bronze statues and the *viharn* gates are beautifully sculpted with gilded and lacquered pillars. The gong that hangs in the *sala* (open pavilion) is the largest of its type in the world. In front of the *wat* there is a small museum with a well-displayed collection of sculptures, furniture, and weapons. Entrance fee.

Pasang*

6 mi/10 km south of Lamphun. The people of Pasang, who are Mons by origin, specialize in the weaving of cotton. There are about 2000 looms in the district.

▰▰▰ TO THE NORTH

Elephants***

Chiang Dao Training Centre, 35 mi/56 km from Chiang Mai on the road to Fang. The camp, situated near the village of Ta Yaak, is in the forest by the Ping River. Daily performances (9:30am and noon) start with a bath in the river. Then the elephants gather in a clearing and are put through their paces by their *mahouts* (handlers). The baby elephants, which stay with their mother until they are two years old, sometimes cause chaos in the class.

The charm of the elephant

Elephants are intelligent, hard-working, and sweet-natured; their only drawback is their size. For centuries, the Thais have known how to make use of elephants, for both peaceful and warlike purposes. Today, there are still over 40,000 of these great beasts in Thailand, of which about half are trained. They are used for heavy work in the state-owned forests and they receive the same treatment as privileged employees: three days of work followed by three days of rest, three months' holiday per year, and retirement at 60 years of age. Moreover, they are officially registered in administrative documents under their own names.

It takes six years to train an elephant. Between the ages of three to four they learn to walk with short strides, with their feet chained together, then, from ages six to ten they are taught to shift logs and, finally, to stack them up and align them. Their working life begins at 11, with the most active years being between the ages of 16 to 50.

The elephant's trunk is used as an arm, a shower head and even as a radar instrument — during the war in Kampuchea, elephants were found to be excellent mine detectors. Contrary to popular belief, the elephant has no fear of mice but he dreads the ants which scurry up his trunk and sting him while he is chewing on trees and foliage. Indeed, he is so sensitive physically that in ancient times four soldiers were detailed to protect his feet in battle. History doesn't tell us what these soldiers did when their elephants charged the enemy.

An elephant's age is discernible by the notches in his ears. Males and females can easily be told apart because only the males have tusks and apparently it is possible to make a relatively accurate estimate of an elephant's height at the shoulder by measuring the circumference of his footprint and multiplying it by two. Finally, elephants are often used as babysitters; they dutifully rock cradles and will even fetch parents when their charges cry.

The omnipresent samlor.

For visitors, bungalows on stilts provide a base for exploring the surrounding countryside; whether by raft on the river or on elephant back through the villages of the Lisus and Meo hilltribes. The lodgings are simple but comfortable, with running water, mosquito nets, oil lamps, and a terrace. Information and reservations: Tourex, Chiang Mai Plaza Hotel, Tel: (053) 252 050.

Orchid Nursery at Sai Nam Phung**

On the road to Mae Sai waterfall, just after Mae Rim, 8.5 mi/14 km north of Chiang Mai. Orchids are parasite plants which usually require no soil and there are at least 100 species which flower at completely different times of year. Orchids are capricious plants which love attention: no less than 14 rules govern the care of the seedlings. This garden has been in existence for over a decade and was first opened to the public in 1978. Its owner, who works for the Border Police, has made it into a training centre for students of horticulture. Meals are available here and, if you wish, you can purchase astonishing jewelry made by dipping orchids into molten gold. Entrance fee.

Mae Sa Valley**

Down the road from the orchid farm, 3 mi/5 km from the falls, there is a small tourist complex in a superb setting. A comfortable stop-off, with possibilities for excursions (crayfish farm, orchid greenhouses, working elephants, etc.). Information at Hotel Suriwongse, Chiang Mai (p. 139).

Chiang Dao Caves**

42 mi/70 km from Chiang Mai, on the road to Fang. Access by bus or taxi. These caves contain a number of Buddha statues and constitute a well-known place of pilgrimage. Many stories are told of the site's magical virtues. In fact, no one has dared to explore all of the chambers and galleries cut into the chalk mountain. Prehistoric remains have been discovered, suggesting that the caves were inhabited. The main cave contains statues of Buddha of all sizes which you can illuminate with candles (on sale at the entrance), adding to the mystery of the experience.

MAE SARIANG AND MAE HONG SON

This itinerary skirts the edge of Burma, west of Chiang Mai, and will appeal to anyone who enjoys being off the beaten track. In a minimum of two days, you can visit an area that offers the magnificent spectacle of the jungle, the mountains, the teak forests, and the provincial world of small hill townships.

▬ PRACTICAL INFORMATION

Access

The itinerary covers 112 mi/181 km west from Chiang Mai to Mae Sariang, and 105 mi/170 km by a winding road that runs north-east from Mae Sariang to Mae Hong Son. There are regular buses along both of these roads but you can also hire a car with a driver, which will give you greater freedom of movement.

Because of the poor state of the direct road between Mae Hong Son and Chiang Mai (it is impassable during the rainy season), it is advisable to fly from Mae Hong Son to Chiang Mai (daily flight at noon, arr. 12:30pm).

▬ THE ITINERARY

Chom Thong**

This little town, 36 mi/58 km from Chiang Mai, is worth visiting for the remarkable 15th-century Wat Phra Thai Si Chom Thong in its centre. The main building is particularly elegant, with its tiered roofs and carved wooden façade. Its cruciform layout is unusual and the interior decor is in the Burmese style. Note the four richly garbed standing Buddhas, which frame the high *prang*. The oldest building in the ensemble is the Burmese *chedi*, which was built in 1451.

Hot*

54 mi/88 km from Chiang Mai. The road continues, fringed with trees: coconut, banana, mango, frangipani, teak, and kapok. The peasants cultivate tobacco, garlic, soy, and rice. Hot is a little market town which has kept the name of the old city which once lay farther south on route 1012. The site of the old city is now only of interest to archaeologists.

Ob Luang Gorges**

65 mi/105 km from Chiang Mai. You can stop here for a while to contemplate the gorges; nothing disturbs the peace of the landscape, except the churning waters of the Chaem River. Ob Luang is modestly referred to as 'Thailand's Grand Canyon', which is something of an exaggeration. At this point you enter Karen country, the abode of the Skaw Karen subgroup. Some of their villages can be seen from the road.

Mae Sariang***

116 mi/188 km from Chiang Mai.

Accommodation and food

Mae Sariang has only one hotel:
▲ **Mitaree Hotel,** near the bus station. Very inexpensive and impeccably clean.
The **Inthara Restaurant,** on the road entering town, serves delicious fried chicken and frog dishes.

Visit

Mae Sariang, in the valley of the Yuam River, is only a few miles from the

Burmese border. The district has a population of about 40,000 people who live off the teak forests and 'commerce' with Burma. (Since Mae Sariang is really the back of the beyond, the Thai government is not very interested in the precise nature of its local commerce.)

The little town itself is built along the roadside; with its wooden houses and occasional cars, it constitutes an infallible remedy for all forms of stress. In the market, you will see one or two women in traditional Burmese costume (which resembles the Chinese tunic, with buttons down one side), placidly smoking giant cigars. The temples, though not a significant part of the Thai cultural heritage, are nonetheless delightful with their tiered, Burmese-style roofs.

From Mae Sariang to Mae Hong Son, the road winds through wild and magnificent teak forests. If you are lucky, you may see elephants at work along here. Elephants or not, the road will supply sufficient excitement: take care crossing the jerry-built wooden bridges and watch out for huge trucks transporting teak logs that you are apt to meet coming from the other direction.

Mae Hong Son**

105 mi/170 km from Mae Sariang.

Accommodation and food

Most of the hotels and restaurants are on the main street, Khunlum Praphat Rd. Our particular recommendation:
Mae Tee Hotel, near the bus station. Very clean, some rooms with air-conditioning, near several restaurants, and right in front of the town market.

Visit

The little town of Mae Hong Son will surprise anyone who knows Luang Prabang, the royal capital of Laos. The similarity is particularly striking from the top of Wat Phra Doi Kong Mu, overlooking the valley. The Wat Chong Kham stands reflected in the waters of the lake where children fish from the bank. There you can see an interesting series of pictures in glass, originating from Burma, that depict the life of Buddha. As at Mae Sariang, the Burmese influence is shown in the women's costumes and the multicoloured gems on their fingers; it is also very apparent in the architecture of the temples.

Here, people await the airplane with great excitement. Even a trip to Chiang Mai is a tremendous adventure. The cinema is probably the most popular attraction in the district, especially for the Burmese, who cross the border to see terrible copies of soy westerns, worn out by constant use in these remote provinces.

BY PIROGUE FROM CHIANG MAI TO CHIANG RAI: ALONG THE KOK RIVER

If you do not intend to visit the hilltribes in the region, this trip can be made in one day — but it would be a shame to miss them. Allow three days to a week to get the most out of this expedition, the one limitation being your physical fitness.

PRACTICAL INFORMATION

Access

Although it is possible to travel independently with a guide, using the local buses and the regular boat service, we do not recommend it. You will get far more out of the visit if you join one of the organized expeditions offered by the many travel agencies in Chiang Mai (information is available at the TAT office there, see p. 143).

Itinerary for a three-day excursion

The following is a typical itinerary to give you an idea of what one of these expeditions involves. The time you might want to spend in Chiang Rai and/or your return to Chiang Mai are not included in the three days.

Day One: Leave Chiang Mai for Tha Ton; then take a *pirogue* (dugout canoe) downriver to Ban Mai. Two-hour walk to a Lahu village, where you will spend the night.

Day Two: Visit Karen and Akha villages; spend the night at the Kuomintang Chinese village (this circuit involves no more than 5 hours walking).

Day Three: Return to Ban Mai (3 hours) and take a pirogue to Chiang Rai (arrival in the afternoon).

Preparation

The best time to visit the region is between Nov. and Feb. as these months avoid both the hot season (Mar. to June) and the rainy season (June to Oct.), when mud and leeches would hamper you severely.

Take the least possible baggage (a very small rucksack, for example) because you will have to carry it over long distances. A sleeping bag is not indispensable because you can rent blankets in the villages but be sure to take along one warm garment. It can be very cold at night.

Purchase a straw hat if you don't already have one — the sun can be fierce on the river. You should also be fully protected against malaria (you will have seen to this before you left home) and have suitable footwear. Take your passport with you: there are frequent police checks in the region and you will have to show it at the Border Police post on your way up (and down) the Kok River. Finally, buy a few provisions before you leave Chiang Mai, because the 'supermarket' in Thamakeng has very little. Purchase anything you might need along the way as well as sweets and small items to give as presents in the villages.

GOING DOWN THE RIVER***

Leave Chiang Mai in the direction of Fang, 94 mi/152 km north of Chiang Mai, on Route 107. The small village of Tha Ton, which is 13 mi/22 km further on, is beside the Kok River, where there is a boat landing. If you are traveling independently and have not already hired a guide in Chiang Mai, you can find one here.

You will travel in a *hang yao* pirogue, which you will probably find narrow and uncomfortable. Chiang Rai is five or six hours away. As long as you don't do it during the monsoons, this trip is pure delight; the river winds through the wild jungle, from time to time enlivened by villages, children bathing and women doing their laundry. Occasionally you will see the vivid purple of a Yao woman's dress in a passing taxi boat, or sweep down a stretch of fast-flowing water. Most of the hilltribe villages lie to the north of the Kok (Lisus, Karens, Shans, Akhas, Yaos, Lahus, Meos, and Kuomintang Chinese), which is fortunate because the southern bank is much rougher and takes longer to cover.

Three riverbank villages are used as traditional departure points for excursions into the back country. The first is Thamakeng (1 hour by boat from Tha Ton), from where you can reach Lahu and Lisu villages in two or three hours. Ban Mai is the second access point to the hilltribe areas (45 minutes by boat from Thamakeng). From here you can easily reach Lahu, Karen, and Akha villages, as well as the Kuomintang settlement where you will spend the night. The last departure point is Mae Salak, which provides access to the villages on the south bank of the river (Lahus, Yaos, Lisus).

Your guide will know the villages well and because tourists are a welcome source of revenue and gifts, you will be greeted with hospitality and curiosity. Although the accommodation will be basic, they are bound to be the very best the villagers can provide and the village chiefs will make it a point of honour to receive you as personal guests.

The North-west, near Mae Hong Son.

CHIANG RAI AND
THE GOLDEN TRIANGLE***

Chiang Rai, like Chiang Mai, was founded by King Mengrai in 1262, or, as legend has it, by his elephant which, for no apparent reason, ran away from his kingdom in Chiang Saen and halted on the site. In Thailand, elephants are always right, so the choice was not questioned.

▬ *PRACTICAL INFORMATION*
208 mi/335 km from Chiang Mai.

Access
Chiang Mai to Chiang Rai:
Plane: Departure 8:50am, arr. 9:25am.
Bus: See timetables at bus station (5.5-6 hours).
Boat: See 'Going Down the River' p. 152.
Bangkok to Chiang Rai
Chiang Rai can be reached by plane, train or bus. See the general information given for access to the northern cities on pp. 126-135.

Accommodation
▲▲ **Wangcome,** 869/96 Pemaviaphat Rd. Tel: (054) 311 800. 221 rooms.
▲ **Wieng Inn,** 893 Pahol Yothin Rd. Tel: (054) 311 543. 160 comfortable rooms, restaurant, pool.

Visit

Surviving vestiges of Chiang Rai's past are limited to two 15th-century temples; both of which are well worth a detour. These are **Wat Phra Keo****, which once housed the Emerald Buddha of Bangkok, and **Wat Phra Singh****. Otherwise, the town itself has little of interest, with the exception of its marketplace, which is full of hilltribe people who descend from the mountains on shopping expeditions.

EXPLORING THE GOLDEN TRIANGLE

From Chiang Rai, you can explore the so-called Golden Triangle, where many of the hilltribes of Thailand live (see p. 62). The Golden Triangle gets its name both from the wealth amassed by those dealing in the international sale of the opium produced in the region, and from its shape: the area, indeed, forms an upside-down triangle with its point at Chiang Rai, one side formed by a line running north-east to Chiang Khong, the other by a line running northwest to Mae Salong, and the base formed by the Burmese-Laotian border. For maximum enjoyment in exploring the region you should go through one of the local tourist agencies. Some of them are highly imaginative and will offer you such adventures as a tour of the Golden Triangle on a bamboo raft (Chiang Mai Travel).

Mae Chan**

18 mi/29 km from Chiang Rai. Just before you reach the town of Mae Chan, you will notice a road leading off to the right. This will bring you to a Yao village, populated by Montagnards who have come down from the mountains to start up as rice farmers on irrigated land. The women do embroidery, while the men work in the fields. You will be hospitably received here. Outside this Yao village another side road to the right leads to a similar settlement inhabited by Akhas (the road is impassable during the rainy season). These two villages can be visited without undue exertion and are fairly typical.

In Mae Chan itself, it is worth stopping off at the market, where you are bound to come across Yaos and Akhas. After Mae Chan, 1 mi/1.6 km away, a road to the left leads to Mae Kam, where there is a centre to educate the hilltribes in basic hygiene and encourage them to cultivate crops other than opium. From here, the road continues to the Akha village of Ko Saen Chai, which stands on top of a hill. This delightful place is an ideal departure point for an expedition to other more distant villages, some of which are visible from Ko Saen Chai.

Chiang Saen**: the magic of the Mekong

20 mi/32 km from Mae Chan. A tiny cluster of houses on the Mekong River is all that remains of Chiang Saen. It contains a large number of ruins, of which the oldest date from the 10th century. Chiang Saen was razed at the end of the 18th century on the orders of Rama I, to prevent the Burmese from gaining control of it. Subsequently, it remained uninhabited for over 100 years. Before the revolution in Laos, Chiang Saen was a departure point for expeditions along the Mekong, upstream to the Yao villages, and downstream to Chiang Khong and Ban Houei Sai, the main border towns connecting this region with Laos.

Mae Sai**: the heart of the Golden Triangle

19 mi/30 km from Mae Chan. This is Thailand's northernmost village, a frontier post leading into Burma (closed to all except Burmese and Thai for the time being) and only a few hundred yards from Laos. From here you will have to retrace your steps to Mae Chan because you cannot go farther than Mae Sai. Its market is picturesque: Burmese mingle with Thais and hillpeople and exchange various products. The market is an important centre for jade and precious stones. The jade-carving workshop is worth a visit but the main attraction is the bridge which joins Mae Sai to the Burmese village of Tachilek. There is a constant flow of Burmese to this consumer's paradise in a forgotten corner of Thailand.

SOUTHERN ITINERARY: THE EASTERN SEABOARD

If you are looking for a vacation in the sun, Southern Thailand is the place to go. In recent years this area has undergone a spectacular tourist boom, mainly concentrated at Phuket. Long beaches of white sand are fringed with coconut palms and other exotic trees and the coastline is studded with charming islets bathed by crystal waters. It was inevitable that the time would come for Southern Thailand's humble fisherfolk to share their excellent resources.

Aside from the island of Phuket, off the west coast in the Andaman Sea, the major resort beaches of Southern Thailand are on the eastern seaboard in the Gulf of Thailand and the South China Sea. The island of Samui (Ko Samui) is the latest new paradise. With its 1240 mi/2000 km of coastline, there is no risk that peninsular Thailand will ever run short of beaches — or tourists.

Rich in natural resources, the 14 southern provinces control two of Thailand's key sources of wealth: the rubber and tin industries. The farther you go into the 'deep south', however, the more apparent the underlying cultural differences become. Buddhist temples give way to mosques; this is a Muslim area and many people here feel closer to Malaysia than to Thailand. The king, concerned by this situation, has built a palace at Narathiwat to remind his southern subjects of the need to maintain national unity.

Still, every opportunity is taken to defy the central government: bandits, communists, pirates, and secessionists all profit from the political situation and visitors are obliged to take special care on both land and sea. This state of affairs tends to limit tourism in the southern interior but the resort towns and their magnificent beaches remain perfectly safe.

The South's attraction is, therefore, totally different to that of the North. Instead of bygone civilizations and ethnographic riddles, you are enticed by a more relaxing, less challenging, kind of stay. If this is what you're looking for, forget any other projects: simply choose a point on the Andaman or China Sea coast, and go there for a real holiday. Don't worry about planning your time. You can improvise your activities on the spot to include the beach, short excursions by motorcycle, trips out to sea with the fishermen, or whatever you like.

PRACTICAL INFORMATION

Access

You should not lose sight of the fact that distances in Thailand are long: 930 mi/1 500 km separate Bangkok from Narathiwat, the country's southernmost city. Overland modes of transportation (train and bus) are the most suitable for anyone wishing to visit several places on their way south but they should be resolutely avoided by those who have come to Thailand for rest and relaxation in the sun.

Plane

Thai Airways operates regular services to Phuket, Trang, Hat Yai, Pattani, Nakhon Si Thammarat, and Surat Thani. The Hat Yai airport provides access to the beach at Songkhla, 18 mi/30 km away. If your schedule allows you to combine rest and exploration, you might consider arriving in the south at one airport (Phuket, for example) and leaving from another (Hat Yai or Surat Thani). For information, contact Thai Airways in Bangkok (p. 33).

Train

Rapid and express trains leave Bangkok's Hualampong Station in Thonburi daily for Hat Yai, stopping off in Nakhon Pathom, Ratchaburi, Phetchaburi, Hua Hin, Prach Uap Kiri Khan, Chumphon, Surat Thani, Thung Song, and Patthalung on the way. Departure times: rapid train, 12:30pm (19 hours to Hat Yai); express trains, 2:30pm and 4:10pm (18 hours to Hat Yai). On Mon., Wed., and Sat., the 4:10pm express continues on to Butterworth (Malaysia) where connections can be made for Ipon, Kuala Lumpur, and Singapore.

Bus

Ordinary and air-conditioned buses for the south leave Bangkok daily from the Southern Bus Terminal on Charan Sanitwong Road in Thonburi. Tel: 411 4978-9 for the air-conditioned buses. We strongly advise not taking the ordinary buses, which are very hot and umcomfortable. There are also express air-conditioned buses that leave from the Air Coach City Terminal on Pahol Yothin Road. Tel: 279 4484-7. (Check the timetables and see specific towns (pp. 157-164) for departure times, which vary depending upon the destination.)

ALONG THE COAST

You can take your pick of four charming resorts: Hua Hin, Prachuap Kiri Khan, Ko Samui, or Songkhla. Each of them is, in its own way, a kind of anti-Pattaya, with a much more natural approach to resort vacationing. Thailand's coasts have much more to offer than sand and sea, parachute gliding, and giant prawns: there are also pearl fishermen, swallow's nest gatherers, turtle farmers, monkeys who have been trained to pick ripe coconuts, and a host of other activities.

HUA HIN**: THE ROYAL BEACH

142 mi/230 km from Bangkok.

Access

Train

Daily departures from Bangkok's Hualampong Station at 12:10pm (arr. 4:35pm), 4:10pm (arr. 8:25pm), 5:30pm (arr. 9:45pm).

The South is paradise for beach-lovers and fishermen. Ko Samui.

Bus

13 departures daily between 5:50am and 5:40pm, from Bangkok's Southern Bus Terminal on Charan Sanitwong Rd. (4.5 hours).

Accommodation and food

▲▲▲ **Royal Garden Resort.** A new hotel complex. Reservations in Bangkok. Tel: 235 0522. Tennis, water sports (sailboards, skindiving), and the only authorized discotheque in the town. 177 rooms.

▲▲ **Central Hua Hin Resort Hotel,** Damnoen Kasem Rd. Tel: 511 012-5. (Reservations can also be made in Bangkok. Tel: 235 4424 or 235 4430.) The charming, original hotel building, which has recently been expanded to include a modern annex and bungalows, was used as a locale in the film *The Killing Fields*. The gardens are superb, with bushes sculpted into animal shapes. 260 rooms.

▲ **Chat Chai,** 59/1 Phetkasem Rd. Simple but comfortable. 35 rooms.

The best restaurants in Hua Hin are on Damnoen Kasem Road near the Central Hua Hin Resort Hotel; simply browse around and take your pick. Excellent food is also available at the central market, notably all kinds of fish, fried oysters, and other shellfish.

Visit

Hua Hin's role as a major resort dates back to the 1920s, when King Rama VI began going there. Soon after, everyone in Thai high society flocked to the place to hunt or play golf. In recent years, the flood of humanity has been diverted eastward with the rise of Pattaya as Thailand's principal resort town (see p. 122).

The name Hua Hin means 'Stone Head' in Thai, a reference to the great rock that stands at the entrance to the bay. The beach is 2 mi/3 km long and has very soft, fine white sand. A pleasant stroll will take you to Wat Kao Lad, which stands just beside the seafront.

You can also go riding, play 18 holes of golf, or a set of tennis — or simply relax. In the evening, be sure to go down to the port to see the arrival of the fishermen, who bring in impressive quantities of fish every day.

PRACHUAP KIRI KHAN**

198 mi/323 km from Bangkok.

Access

Train

Daily departures from Bangkok's Hualampong Station at 12:10pm, 2:30pm, and 5:30pm (6 hours).

Bus

Seven departures daily between 5:30am and 4:15pm, from Bangkok's Southern Bus Terminal on Charan Sanitwong Rd. (5 hours).

Accommodation and food

Although there are a few, very basic hotels in Prachuap, the best thing to do for accommodation is to rent a bungalow on the beach (contact the TAT for information p. 32). Food is generally good; we especially recommend the little restaurant by the jetty.

Visit

Prachuap is a small, attractive port located in a magnificent setting between the sea and the mountains of Burma. The bay is protected by strangely shaped islets, and the hill overlooking the town has a natural hole through which you can see the sky. The hill is known as Khao Chong Krachok, 'the mountain with the mirror'.

A flight of 400 steps, tenaciously defended by small monkeys, leads to a small temple and a heavenly view of the bay.

With easy access from Bangkok, Prachuap constitutes an economical alternative to overcrowded Pattaya. You can rent a boat to visit the islands, but no overland excursions are possible because all the roads in the area facing the sea are closed to foreigners.

KO SAMUI***

420 mi/677 km from Bangkok.

There's no such thing as a rainy paradise, so you should avoid Ko Samui during the monsoon months (particularly Nov.-Jan.).

Access

You should first go to **Surat Thani,** where transportation to the ports serving Ko Samui is arranged.

Plane

Daily flights leave Bangkok 11:40am (arr. 12:40pm).

Train

Daily departures from Bangkok's Hualampong Station between 10:30am and 6:25pm. This last train, which arrives at 7:03am, is the only one to take, however, because all the others arrive in the middle of the night. (12-13 hours.) Tel: Bangkok station 223 7010 or 223 7020.

Bus

Air-conditioned buses leave Bangkok's Southern Bus Terminal on Charan Sanitwong Rd. at 9am, 8pm and 8:30pm. The evening buses are to be preferred because the trip takes 11 hours. Private bus companies also offer a Bangkok-Surat Thani service; inquire for information at the local travel agencies in Bangkok.

From Surat Thani to Ko Samui

Ferries leave for the island from Donsak Pier, a port 40 mi/70 km from Surat Thani; the crossing takes 1 hour 20 minutes.

You can also catch an express boat which makes the crossing in 2 hours from Tha Thong Pier, 3 mi/5 km from Surat Thani.

If you arrive at Surat Thani by plane, you can easily buy a single bus-ferry ticket for 150 ฿ at the airport counter. The coach will board the ferry after a 1.5-2 hour journey at Donsak Pier. In all, counting waiting time and embarkation, the journey from the airport to Ko Samui lasts about 3 hours. If you arrive at Surat Thani by train or bus you can also take the bus-ferry or take a bus to the express boat port at Tha Thong Pier. In each case all access to Samui is clearly indicated and several companies compete for your business.

Accommodation

There are numerous small houses, or bungalows, with five rooms each, while the larger hotels rarely exceed 30 rooms. Some of the latter are represented at Bangkok, which makes it possible for you to book your room in advance, although it is not really necessary: you will always be able to find somewhere to stay on Samui, often for less than 200 ฿ per night. There are no real hotel addresses, simply an indication of the bay on which a given hotel is located. The greatest concentration of bungalows is on Chaweng Bay and Bo Phut Bay.

Chaweng Bay (East coast)

▲▲▲ **Imperial.** Reservations in Bangkok. Tel: 252 0450. Recently built, this hotel is a bizarre mixture of Mediterranean and Thai architecture, with a Hollywood-style pool looking directly out over the sea. 80 rooms.

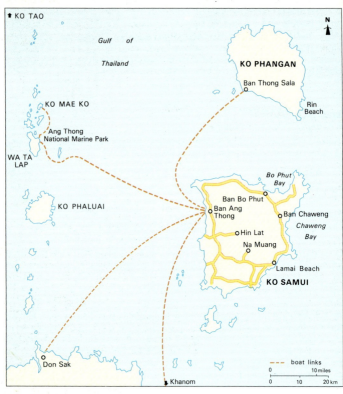

KO SAMUI

▲▲▲ **Pansea.** Reservations in Bangkok. Tel: 235 6075. 20 minutes from the ferry. Situated on the beach with 30 bungalows set unobtrusively back in the vegetation. Comfort (large bed, porch, shower) and plenty to do: sailboards, catamarans, diving equipment, bicycles, junk cruises (June-Oct.).

▲▲ **The Village.** For reservations, call Ko Samui. Tel: (077) 272 222 ext. 208. 20 minutes from the ferry. 17 charming palm-roofed bungalows, set in flower gardens extending down to the shore.

▲▲ **The White House.** Very pleasant and stylish hotel facing the beach, attractive wooden architecture. Good restaurant. 10 rooms.

Bungalows
▲ Chawang Guest House — 19 rooms.
▲ Kati Lodge — 6 rooms.
▲ Saengtip Villa — 24 rooms.
▲ Sun East — 10 rooms.

Thong Sai Bay (North-west coast)

▲▲▲ **Thong Sai Bay Hotel and Cottages.** Tel: Bangkok 252 0450. On the hillside overlooking a swimming pool and private creek. 56 luxurious bungalows with terraces. Mediterranean architecture and Thai decor in chic isolation.

Monkeys are trained to gather coconuts on Ko Samui.

Bo Phut Bay (North-east side)

▲ **Naia Lodge.** Reservations in Bangkok. Tel: 277 4240. 50 air-conditioned rooms, each with terrace. On the beach. A swimming pool and tennis courts are currently being added to this pleasant hotel.

Bungalows
- ▲ **Boon** — 13 rooms.
- ▲ **Island View** — 8 rooms.
- ▲ **Peace** — 28 rooms.
- ▲ **Sun Set** — 12 rooms.

Na Thon Bay (North-west side)

▲ **Chao Kao Bungalow.** Reservations in Bangkok. Tel: 252 8150. 22 rooms, restaurant.

- ▲ **Chinta** — 10 rooms.
- ▲ **Ni Nuan Court** — 20 rooms.
- ▲ **Samui** — 8 rooms.
- ▲ **Si Samui** — 14 rooms.

Thong Yang Bay (South-west side)

▲ **Samui Ferry Inn.** Reservations in Bangkok. Tel: 253 0510. 15 rooms, restaurant.

▲ **Sunflower.** Reservations in Bangkok. Tel: 235 6890. 20 rooms.

Visit

Ko Samui ('Ko' means 'island' in Thai) is the largest island of an archipelago of 80 islands and islets, of which six are inhabited. It is 15.5 mi/25 km long and 13 mi/21 km wide at its widest point. The main centre, Ban Ang Thong on the west coast, is a lively fishing port. Samui is a beautiful, romantic place with its forest-covered mountains, clear waterfalls, empty beaches, and coconut palms.

Coconuts

The 35,000 people who inhabit the archipelago have trained monkeys to pick coconuts for them with extraordinary success. The island exports some 2 million coconuts to Bangkok every month. The monkeys are taught to distinguish ripe coconuts from unripe ones but they are not always careful to check that there's nobody under the tree when they fling them down. You can go and watch them at work; they are kept on long leashes held by their owners.

There is also a **coconut fibre factory** here worth a visit (3-4 mi/4-5 km from the Hin Lad waterfall). The fibres processed are generally used as a reinforcement for foam rubber in the manufacture of car seats.

The beaches

Forget about the west coast of the island, which is a place of mud and shifting tides. The real paradise is on the east, where a succession of creeks and bays level off into broad beaches. Remember to bring masks and snorkels, as there is plenty to look at under the water.

After **Lamai,** to the south-east, you will discover the bay of **Chaweng,** with its high concentration of bungalows and hotels: don't worry, the beach is two miles long and there are no crowds. Further north is the bay of **Bo Phut,** with the constantly changing spectacle of **Ko Phangan** out to sea.

What to see

The sights of Samui are close together. Jeeps and motorcycles can be hired on the spot but the best way to see the island is a *songteo* (share taxi). There are the falls at **Na Muang**** (98 ft/30 m high, 65 ft/20 m wide), the falls of Hin Lad, the temple of the Big Buddha, and the fishing villages. The circular road around the island, which is in terrible shape, covers about 31 mi/50 km in all.

It is also worth visiting the other islands within range: **Ko Phangan**** (2 hours by boat), **Ko Mae Ko**** (2.5 hours), **Ko Tao**** (4 hours). You will easily find a boat to take you out for the day, with a picnic, to explore even more deserted creeks, remote villages, and untarnished landscapes. On the island of Phangan, you will find inexpensive bungalows to rent, on the beautiful beaches at Rin (Sunset, Sea View, Rolling Stone) and at Thong Sala Bay (Cookie, Watana, etc.).

Every Saturday, excursions are organized to the **Ang Thong National Marine Park*****. This is an archipelago of about 40 small limestone islands that extends over an area of some 96 sq mi/250 sq km to the north-west of Samui. You can spend the night on **Wa Ta Lap** island if you wish. Information at **Samui Holiday Tours,** Na Thon Pier. Tel: 421 043.

*SONGKHLA**

806 mi/1300 km from Bangkok.

Access

Via Hat Yai, 18 mi/30 km from Songkhla.

Plane
Between one and four flights daily from Bangkok (depending on the day of the week). From Phuket, five flights per week. Inquire at Thai Airways offices.

Train
Daily departures from Bangkok's Hualampong Station at 12:10pm (arr. 6:35am next day) and 4:10pm (arr. 10:18am next day).

Bus
Departures from Bangkok's Southern Bus Terminal on Chavan Sanitwong Rd. 6pm and 11:50pm. (20 hours).

Accommodation

▲▲ **Samila,** 1/11 Rajdamnoen Rd. Tel: (174) 311 310-4. Songkhla's most comfortable hotel, it is located only about 30 yds from the sea. It has a restaurant, a freshwater swimming pool, and air-conditioning. 150 rooms.

▲ **Chok Dee,** Wichiandhom Rd. Tel: (174) 311 158. A modest but comfortable hotel facing the lake.

Food

You can eat seafood on the restaurant terraces by the beach. In town, the **Kheng Nam,** like the other small restaurants on Saiburi Road, serves excellent food. The same may be said of the eating-houses on Nang Ngam and Sukhum Roads.

If you plan to spend the evening in Hat Yai, try the **Sukholta** (beside the tourist office). It has very good food and a pleasant atmosphere.

Visit

Songkhla and the nearby islands

Songkhla is about halfway between Bangkok and Singapore, and serves as a gateway for expeditions to Southern Thailand and Malaysia. The town stands on a kind of lagoon, between the sea and a huge lake. There are plenty of opportunities for excursions in the region but these take time as the area is not yet organized for tourism.

The first object of interest here is, naturally, the water: endless miles of deserted beaches, fishing villages built on pilings... an idyllic tableau which sadly became somewhat tarnished at the end of the 1970s with the arrival of the Cambodian 'boat people'. The refugee camp now standing on the beach at Songkhla has blighted any ambitions the city may have had to become a major tourist resort.

Songkhla itself has considerable style, with its blend of Chinese and Portuguese architecture, its lively market, its fisheries and temples. Wat Klong, for example, possesses a number of interesting frescos dating from the early 19th century, some of which represent the arrival of European navigators in the China Sea. (There is a small museum next door to the temple.)

Motorized boats may be hired on a daily basis. The main destinations in the area are:

The Cat and Mouse Islands (Ko Meow and Ko Non), 12 mi/20 km from Samila Bay.
The Malay village of Hua Ko.
The Bird Islands (1 hour by boat from Pattalung), where some of the famous swallows' nests are gathered.

If you really love the sea, try negotiating one or several days on a boat with the local fishermen.

Hat Yai and excursions inland

Hat Yai, the capital of Thailand's southern provinces, boasts a number of temples (notably Wat Mudchimmavert and Wat Ko-Tham), a university, plenty of shops (batiks, silk), and even a few nightclubs. Southerners love to gamble and cockfighting is a favourite sport here. In the past, Hat Yai organized buffalo fights which attracted fanatical crowds from all over the region and took place amid high excitement. Buffalo fights have now been banned but they are still held on an 'unofficial' basis.

If you like solitary landscapes and virgin tropical forests, you might want to take a bus to Trang, about 125 mi/200 km north-west of Hat Yai. Information: TAT office, 1/1 Soi 2 Niphat Uthit Rd., Hat Yai. Tel: (074) 243 747.

For a closer glimpse of Southern Thailand's cultural heritage, you might even consider a trip to Nakhon Si Thammarat, some 250 mi/400 km north of Songkhla. Nakhon Si Thammarat played a crucial role in the Dvaravati and Srivijaya epochs. **Wat Mahathat,** one of the oldest in Thailand, has a chedi 250 ft/77 m high, the upper section of which is covered in gold leaf. This chedi houses the famous statue of Phra Buddha Singh, and the nearby museum contains a number of splendid sculptures. For information on getting there, inquire at the Chok Dee Hotel in Songkhla, or at one of the tour-bus companies on Niphat Uthit Road in Hat Yai.

PHUKET

The island is in the Andaman Sea, 572 mi/922 km south of Bangkok. With its link to the mainland via the Sarasin Bridge, Phuket is the principal island of an archipelago which covers some 62 mi/100 km in the waters of Phangnga Bay. Measuring 31 mi/50 km from north to south, and 9 mi/15 km from east to west, Phuket alternates between ruggedness and tranquillity. The landscape changes from quiet coconut plantations to glimmering rice paddies, forests and endless deserted beaches. On the other hand, there are also green marshes full of mangroves and strange-looking limestone outcrops covered in jungle growth.

The charm of Phuket

Phuket is full of character; so are the women who live here, by all accounts. In 1785, the widow and the daughter of the island's governor managed to discourage a marauding Burmese expedition by dressing the local women folk as soldiers. Faced with this seemingly huge army, the invaders beat a hasty retreat. A statue in the village of Tha Rua, between the airport and the town of Phuket, still commemorates these two heroines.

Phuket's inhabitants have always been relatively prosperous. In the 17th century, the Dutch were attracted by the pearls found here, and a thriving pearl trade was developed. In 1900, following the discovery of underwater deposits of tin ore, the exploitation of tin began and the metal is now Phuket's principal resource, helping Thailand maintain its position as one of the largest tin exporters in the world. For six months of the year, in the dry season, a flotilla of ships drag the bed of the Andaman Sea for the ore, which is then carefully separated from the sand and processed.

Like Malaysia, Phuket has benefited hugely from the miraculous seed of the rubber tree, imported by the director of the Singapore Botanical Gardens in 1877. All along the island's roads you will see miles of rubber plantations. Among other resources, the coconut trees which so perfectly suit this landscape also produce quantities of copra (coconut fibre). Finally, the sea generously contributes crabs, lobsters, giant prawns, fish, and shellfish to Phuket's economy.

Vacationing in Phuket

Even though you may not have come to Thailand to lounge on a beach by the sea, you will certainly appreciate the chance offered by Phuket to escape your fast-paced itinerary as a tourist. Far from being a clone of Pattaya, full of fake exoticism, this island is like a free gift of nature, with a gentle, gracious approach to life comparable to that of Bali. If you keep away from the larger hotel complexes, you can spend days at a time on the beach in complete solitude.

The island's capital, also called Phuket, was built in the middle of the last century to replace Talang, which was destroyed by the Burmese in 1800. The town's older houses are a blend of Chinese and Portuguese styles, as in Malacca and Macao. The result, a small commercial centre with a lively market and thriving shops, lacks any particular value as a tourist attraction. An interesting Chinese Temple dedicated to Kuan Yin (**Put Jaw Temple,** on Ranong Rd.) is testimony to the size of the Chinese population on the island.

PRACTICAL INFORMATION

Telephone area code for Phuket: 076.

572 mi/922 km from Bangkok.

Phuket can be enjoyed at all times although it is best to avoid the monsoon seasons (May-June and Sept.-Oct.).

Access

Plane

Flights from Bangkok daily at 8am, 11:10am, and 5pm. There are other flights at 7:50am and 9am on certain days. (1 to 2 hours, depending upon whether or not there are stopovers.)

Bus

Daily departures of air-conditioned buses from Bangkok's Southern Bus Terminal on Charan Sanitwong Rd. at 8am and in the evening every 15 minutes between 6:30pm and 8:30pm. (13 to 14 hours.)

Getting around Phuket

If you really want to make the most of Phuket — that is, to see the countryside and leave ample time to relax — set aside at least four or five days for your visit. If you get restless, you can rent a motorcycle, a mode of transportation that has become something of an institution on the island. Thus equipped, you can go off in search of fishing villages and secluded beaches, or drive into town to do your shopping.

Other vehicles available are *tuk-tuks* (three-wheeled scooters), *songteos*, and buses — all excellent if you want to share transportation. The *song-teos* (share taxis) run on given routes and honk in each village to summon their passengers; they stop on request and their prices are fixed. If you would rather be independent, your best course is to hire a taxi — either at your hotel, or in town in front of the Thavorn Hotel. Taxi prices are set according to the time hired and distance traveled (minimum 300 ฿ for half a day).

If none of these options suit you, you can always join one of the excursion groups organized by your hotel.

Accommodation

All types of accommodation are available on the island — from the luxury hotel to the bamboo cabin. The two best hotels in the town of Phuket are the Pearl and the Thavorn, both of which have swimming pools. The only advantage to staying in town is that you are in a relatively central location for exploring the island. This is scarcely reason enough to deny yourself the pleasure of staying on the beach, surrounded by sand and coconut palms.

▲▲▲ **Pearl Hotel,** 42 Montri Rd. Tel: 211 1091 and Bangkok 251 6527. 221 rooms.

▲▲▲ **Thavorn Hotel**, 74 Rasada Rd. Tel: 211 333-5 or 211 339.

Generally, choosing a hotel means choosing a beach, and choosing a beach often means subscribing to a certain style. Thus, Patong could be called the 'chic' beach, Rawai the unpretentious one, and Kata the favourite of seasoned globetrotters.

On Pansea Beach (North-west coast)

▲▲ **Pansea Hotel.** Tel: 212 901 and Bangkok 235 6075. Located towards the north of the island on a very beautiful beach, part of which belongs to the hotel. 100 bungalows on pilings stretch up the hill behind, connected by bamboo walkways. Exclusively for people who like to keep to themselves — there's nothing anywhere near this hotel but woods and seashore. Plenty of leisure activities and water sports.

On Patong Beach (West coast)

▲▲▲ **Patong Beach Hotel.** Tel: 211 426 and Bangkok 233 0420. Very well-located and very comfortable.

▲▲ **Coral Beach.** Tel: 321 106 and Bangkok 252 6118. Well-located, in a quiet corner at the end of the beach. Pool facing the beach. 203 rooms.

▲▲ **Patong Merlin.** Tel: 321 070 and Bangkok 253 2641. Pleasant wooden building among the coconut palms but there is a road to cross between the hotel and the beach. 180 rooms.

Bungalows
Patong Beach. Tel: 321 213.
Patong Seaview. Tel: 211 346.
Phuket Cabana. Tel: 211 451.

Large numbers of new hotels appeared in the 1970s, profiting from the tourist rush to the white sands and crystal clear waters of Patong. Today, concrete continues to encroach on coral.

Kata and Karon Beaches (South-west coast)

Kata and its neighbouring beach of Karon are destined for rapid development in the years to come. There is already quite a wide range of accommodation.

Kata

▲▲▲ **Club Méditerranée.** Tel: 212 901, 902, 903 or 904. A new club, very chic, very attractive, in the midst of some 220 acres/90 ha of coconut groves. Tennis courts, water sports, martial arts courses, and many other activities for members. Restaurant. 300 rooms.

▲▲ **Kakata Inn.** Tel: 212 892 or 216 632 and Bangkok 214 4538.

▲▲ **Marina Cottage.** Tel: 211 432 or 213 604.

Karon

▲▲▲ **Meridien-Relax Bay.** Tel: Reservations through Bangkok 251 4707. A brand-new hotel in the luxurious style of the French Meridien Hotel chain, located at the far end of Karon Beach. 464 rooms.

▲▲ **Karon Inn.** Tel: 212 892 and Bangkok 214 4538.

▲▲ **Karon Villa.** Tel: 212 709 and Bangkok 250 1555-9.

In addition to the regular hotels, there are also cabins (somewhat pompously referred to as 'bungalows') for rent on these two beaches with standards that range from rustic to rudimentary. You will definitely need a mosquito net if you favour this option.

Naihan Beach (South coast)

▲▲▲▲ **Phuket Yacht Club.** Tel: 214 020 and Bangkok

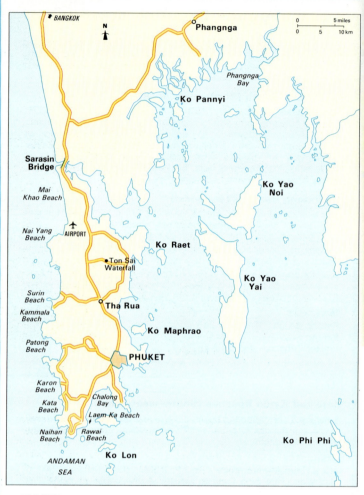

PHUKET

251 4707. The sophisticated architecture of this hotel contrasts oddly with the natural beauty of the site. 120 super-comfortable rooms (750 sq ft/70 sq m, with terrace). All services and water sports.

Rawai Beach (South-east coast)

▲ **Rawai Resort.** Tel: 212 943 and Bangkok 391 6440. Thai-style bungalows, with or without air-conditioning, set back in the woods or by the beach. Fine swimming pool.

▲ **Rawai Seaside.** Tel: 211 205 and Bangkok 585 5860. Situated in a coconut grove close to the beach. Friendly and unpretentious. 30 bungalow rooms.

Laem Ka Beach (South-east coast)

▲▲ **Phuket Island Resort.** Tel: 211 421 and Bangkok 251 5989. Top-class hotel on a hill overlooking the sea. Comfortable rooms, good view.

Despite the spectacular increase in tourism, Phuket has untamed and deserted beaches.

Food

The food in Phuket is uniformly good and generally enormous in size: green beans 23 in/60 cm long, giant black mussels, and gambas. The most common soups are made delicious with the addition of fresh coriander, peppers, and lemon grass. Fish and seafood are abundant, delicious, and well-cooked. Fried oysters are very popular and, between October and January, turtle eggs gathered on the Mai Khao beach are available.

Phuket's most famous restaurant is the **Lai-an**, 58 Rasda Rd. (close to the Thavorn Hotel), which is renowned for its lobsters.

Other good restaurants in the town are **Chao Fah** (Chao Fah Rd.), **Tai Fah** (opposite the Pearl Theatre), **Nai Yao** (opposite the Imperial Hotel), and **Jack and Joy** (near the Pearl Theatre on Pang Nga Rd.).

For a romantic evening, try the **Tun Ka Café**, on a hill overlooking town. The view from here is magnificent and the food is standard Phuket fare: seafood as well as Thai and Chinese dishes.

Even if you don't feel like eating away from your hotel, you will rarely have anything to complain about — most establishments serve excellent food. In the tourist areas, plenty of new restaurants have opened recently, most of them specializing in seafood. As a rule, you eat in the open air in the shade of the palm trees.

Lastly, do not hesitate to stop at any restaurant you like outside the known tourist spots. You will often find the cooking good and they are just as clean — sometimes more so.

Sports

Phuket is a paradise for deep-sea divers but the beauty of the ocean floor is also open to any swimmer with a mask and snorkel. For professionals, diving equipment can be rented on a daily basis at the Patong Beach Hotel (**Ocean Divers**, Tel: 321 166, and **Andaman Divers**, Tel: 321 155, have desks at the hotel) or at **Phuket Island Resort** (on Laemka Beach, 1 mi/1.6 km from Ranwai). Your best plan, if this appeals to you, is to join an organized expedition through these hotels, with qualified divers who know the most beautiful diving areas. The best places re by no means the nearest: Ko Phi Phi (4 hours by boat), Ko Dokmai (3.5 hours), the Similan Islands (10 hours). To see parrot fish and seafans around the islands opposite Rawai, an ordinary fishing boat is all you will need to hire. In all events, never go out on a diving expedition without someone who knows the local waters.

Deep-sea fishing excursions can be arranged through certain hotels, such as the Phuket Yacht Club.

All the more popular water sports, like wind-surfing, sailing, and parachute gliding, have made their appearance on the island.

Phuket by night

You will have trouble finding Bangkok- or Pattaya-style nightlife in Phuket. At the island's most fashionable club (the **Ratree**), you can learn the *lamvong*, in which the dancers are obliged to stay two feet apart at all times. Other nightclubs are concentrated on Montri and Bangkok Roads and Soi Poonphon, and all the large hotels have discotheques.

Useful addresses

Airlines
Thai Airways, Ranong Rd. Tel: 211 195.

Bus station
Pong Nga Rd. Tel: 211 480 or 211 977.

Hospitals
Wachira Hospital, Yaowarat Rd. Tel: 211 114. **Mission Hospital**, Thep Kassatri Rd. Tel: 212 386, 212 149 or 211 173.

Police
Yaowart Rd. Tel: 212 115.

Post office and telephone
Central Post Office, Montri Rd. Tel: 211 020.
Central telephone exchange, Pang Nga Rd. Tel: 212 299.
Telephone area code for Phuket: 076.

Tourist office
TAT, 73-75 Phuket Rd. Tel: 212 213 or 211 036. Open from 8:30am to 4:30pm weekdays, 8:30am to 1pm Sat., Sun, and holidays.

▬ THE BEACHES

The island's most beautiful beaches are on the west coast but unfortunately they are also very dangerous, especially during the monsoons, when there are huge waves and strong currents. If you go to these beaches, take care to follow the advice of those who know the area. The following is a brief description of each of the main beaches along the west coast and near the southern tip of the island.

Note: Nudity is strictly forbidden on the beaches, and the police are not gentle with offenders.

Mai Khao (North-west — the 'white wood' beach)

The longest beach on the island, where giant turtles lay their eggs from Dec. to Jan. No tourist facilities as yet.

Nai Yang (North-west — the 'airport beach')

A delightful spot for a picnic under the trees, or a spell of snorkeling among the sea anemones.

Pansea (North-west)

The junk anchored in the bay isn't just for show. It can take you on a cruise to the Similan Islands, 62 mi/100 km from Phuket, an archipelago where the only inhabitants are monkeys. The sea around these islands is ablaze from the coloured aquatic fauna. The junk can take up to ten passengers (five cabins and three bathrooms). Information at the Pansea Hotel.

Surin (West)

Come here at sunset — for the view only — because it is a very dangerous place to swim. Instead, try the golf course nearby.

Patong (West)

Considered the island's top beach, Patong was developed with spectacular speed during the 1970s — perhaps too quickly. At night, Patong's neon lights shine brighter than the stars, and the rustle of the jungle is drowned out by the blare of disco music. On the other hand, Patong offers an easy, comfortable holiday atmosphere.

Kata and Karon (South-west)

The backpackers who found this beautiful corner of Phuket in the early 1970s probably never dreamed they would be followed by Club Méditerranée, which has transformed the area by bringing in large numbers of tourists. Kata is now being developed as a resort.

Naihan (South)

Until the construction of the luxury Phuket Yacht Club, Naihan was a private, intimate beach with a few bungalows at its edge. The new Yacht Club's terraced architecture blends to some extent with the site but detracts from its original naturalness. Avoid bathing at Naihan beach during the monsoon period.

Rawai (South)

This is one of the most sheltered of Phuket's beaches, in a bay protected by several islets. Nothing spectacular in comparison to Kata or Naihan, but safe all year round. Unfortunately, you cannot swim here at low tide because the bay is too shallow. Rawai is still a relatively intimate, family-oriented beach with small seafood restaurants. There are no water sports, the main activity is sharing a day at the seaside with the shell fishermen of the village of Moken (the famous 'sea-gypsies'), which is at the end of the beach. You can also go and contemplate a natural oddity that is the coconut equivalent of Siamese twins: namely, a four-headed coconut palm that grows here. Kings have been known to make the pilgrimage to see this wonder.

OUTSIDE PHUKET

PHANGNGA BAY ***

The excursion to Phangnga Bay is the most beautiful one Phuket has to offer. All the island's hotels schedule this trip regularly, with an early departure (return at about 4-5pm). You begin by crossing the length of the island from south to north; then you rejoin the mainland via the Sarasin Bridge and continue for about 30 mi/50 km to a landing site just beyond the little town of Phangnga. After this, you get in a motor-powered pirogue, which takes you past mangrove swamps and nipa palms, over waters that seem to swarm with every form of aquatic life.

The boat forges its way through the waterways, from time to time passing a pirogue full of 'gypsies' that suddenly materializes from the shadows of this magnificent, weird forest. Suddenly you arrive in a fantastic bay studded with dozens of huge limestone formations vaguely resembling dogs, elephants, chickens, and other fabulous animals from Chinese mythology, some of which are 325 ft/100 m high. The water has eroded their bases, hollowing out caverns with ceilings spiked with stalactites.

After the mandatory halt at 'James Bond Island' where one of the most thrilling scenes from *The Man with the Golden Gun* was shot in 1974, you finally reach **Ko Pannyi*****, a Moken (sea-gypsy) floating village. Here, 900 people live in houses on pilings above the water, with a school, shops, restaurants, and private rooms all connected to each other by planks. Ko Pannyi may be distant from the rest of the world but here, too, the portraits of the royal family watch over the 200 school children in their impeccable uniforms. The village has become a favourite stopover for all tourists visiting Phangnga Bay; you can eat delicious seafood and buy all kinds of stuffed fish and trinkets made from pearls or shells in the thriving shops.

> ### Accommodation
>
> A sign of the changing times in the form of a luxury hotel (a kind of concrete ocean liner) has invaded this extraordinary place. Fortunately, the moment you reach the hotel's balcony and take in the view across the bay, you forget to disapprove.
>
> ▲▲▲ **Phangnga Bay Resort.** Tel: 411 067 and Bangkok 235 6488. 100 rooms.

KO PHI PHI**: SWALLOW'S NEST ISLAND

Ko Phi Phi is one of the most beautiful islands in the bay. Excursions to the island are offered by most hotels (allow an entire day). The cave where the nests are and which has given the island its name is in the south. Swallow's nests, made by these birds with their saliva, are to Chinese cooking roughly what caviar is to European tables. It is no surprise, therefore, to see the locals clambering about at dizzy heights on fragile bamboo ladders to harvest these precious articles (Dec. to Apr.). Ko Phi Phi is also a minor natural marvel with its wonderful beaches, transparent water, stunning coral reefs, and beautiful fish. You can hire a fishing boat to the outer islets, all of which are surrounded by astonishing coral formations.

THE NORTH-EAST: TOWARD THE LAOTIAN BORDER

North-east Thailand, a high plateau of 65,000 sq mi/170,000 sq km, is home to no less than 17 million people, or one third of Thailand's population. It includes seven of the country's 16 provinces, and the land is often very poor. Here nature is parsimonious to a fault, and the monsoon season is always too brief or too long. The 'ghost market' *(talat phi)*, as the poor provinces of the North-east are known, is not listed among Thailand's greater glories. The inhabitants are very close to the Laotians, and speak a similar language. They are unflatteringly referred to as 'sticky rice eaters'. It is, therefore, not a surprise that the North-east has a tradition of opposition to the central government and also that it has become the principal reservoir of the uprooted, embittered people who swell the suburbs of Bangkok.

During the Vietnam War, US military bases created a false prosperity in towns like Korat, Ubon, and Udon. When the war ended, the GIs packed up and left, leaving the population as poor as before but much more demanding. For this reason, the North-eastern provinces offer the most extreme example of contemporary Thailand's social imbalances.

From a historical perspective, some of these areas have been heavily marked by Khmer domination. Lovers of archaeology will be able to find echoes here of the splendours of Angkor, the capital of the Khmer empire.

Visiting the North-east

Tourism has never been very developed in the North-east, Chiang Mai and (more recently) Phuket having siphoned off most of the visitors from abroad. The fact is that (apart from one or two specific attractions) this region has little to recommend it by comparison. To combat this situation the TAT is encouraging travel agencies to organize tours along the Mekong, an excellent initiative that deserves to be followed through. Perhaps because it is isolated from tourism, the North-east often offers an adventurous dimension which is disappearing in more popular areas.

If you go to the North-east, you can be sure of one thing: total immersion into Thai life. You will find a Thai-English dictionary is indispensable.

174 The North-east

PRACTICAL INFORMATION

Access

Plane

Thai Airways flies to the towns of Khon Daen, Udon, Loei, Ubon, and Nakhon Phanom.

Train

The line forks at Nakhon Ratchasima (Korat), northwards toward Khon Kaen, Udon, and Nong Khai (on the Laos frontier), and eastwards to Buri-ram, Sisakhet, and Ubon. For a complete list of stations, go to Hualampong Station in Bangkok.

Bus

The North-east region is served by the North-east Bus Terminal on Pahol Yothin Rd. in Bangkok. Tel: 279 4484-7.

ALONG THE KHMER TRAIL

Three Khmer sites in this region are of particular interest: Pimai, Phnom Rung, and Muang Tham. The town of Nakhon Ratchasima (formerly called Korat), 158 mi/255 km from Bangkok, is the best base for excursions to these places. Buses and trains from Bangkok to Nakhon are frequent and the town has several good hotels including the following:

▲▲ **Chom Surang,** 270 Mahad-Thai Rd. Tel: 242 940. 119 rooms.
▲ **Karat,** 4014 Asdang Rd. Tel: 242 444. 121 rooms.
▲ **Sri Pattana,** Suranari Rd. Tel: 242 944.

On the way through Nakhon, take time to visit **Wat Sutatchinda** and its museum.

PIMAI***: ANGKOR ON THE HORIZON

33 mi/53 km north-east of Nakhon Ratchasima.

Access

Taxi

You can hire a taxi in Nakhon Ratchasima; allow a minimum of 500 ฿ for a three-hour circuit.

Bus

They leave Nakhon Ratchasima bus station at frequent intervals (you can take a *samlor* to the bus station from your hotel; tell the man 'Pimai', he will understand). Your ticket will only cost a few baht and the trip will take about an hour.

For most of this journey, the road runs beside canals and rice paddies. The temple of Pimai stays open from 8am to 6pm (tickets sold till 5:30pm only). It is best not to arrive too late, even though you may miss the sun setting behind the temple, which is often a glorious sight.

Accommodation and food

You will probably simply return to your hotel in Nakhon Ratchasima but if you do want to stay overnight in Pimai, there is one hotel in the town:
▲ **Pimai Hotel,** around the corner from the bus station. There is a restaurant next to the hotel that is quite good.

Visit

The **Khmer temple** of Pimai dates back to the early 12th century. A small town of the same name has grown up within the former perimeter of the temple and its modest wooden houses stand alongside one of the finest examples of Khmer architecture in Thailand.

The Pimai temple complex consists of a rectangular courtyard with four gates. The gates, or *gopuras,* are placed in such a way that their entrances converge on the centre of the sanctuary, providing an extraordinary perspective. The main building has been skillfully restored and has fine carvings inspired by mythology. Within the temple proper you can see the mastery of the Khmer architects.

The old town of Pimai was originally surrounded by a perimeter wall almost 1 mi/1.6 km long and .5 mi/.8 km, built on an artificial island; and the victory gate was intended to guard the road to Angkor — which is only 155 mi/250 km away! All in all, the harmony and sheer grandeur of Pimai is irresistible.

PHNOM RUNG**: A TEMPLE OF PINK SANDSTONE

62 mi/100 km south-east of Nakhon Ratchasima.

Access

This is a more rugged excursion than going to Pimai, because the temple itself is hard to reach. The best way of getting there is to hire a taxi. Local transport exists, but it involves taking a bus and a *song-teo,* and then walking down a dirt road for 4 mi/6 km — it's really not worth that much effort — in either direction.

Visit

The 11th/12th-century temple of Phnom Rung stands at the top of a hill on a picturesque site. It is a Hindu sanctuary in the Lopburi style, built by a Khmer king in honour of Vishnu (the Preserver in the Hindu trinity), and is thought to have been a stopping-off point between Angkor and Pimai. A majestic flight of steps, preceded by an avenue, leads up to the main terrace; the temple itself is built of pink sandstone and includes a Khmer *prang* (tower), *gopuras,* and ruins of galleries, some of which are still covered with foliage. Here, the somewhat cold rigour of Khmer architecture is even more evident than at Pimai but the destruction wrought on the stone by time and nature creates an almost tragic atmosphere. The sculptures and bas-reliefs are in good condition and of great purity: among them are shapes of elephants and Hindu divinities.

MUANG THAM PALACE**

Access

Muang Tham Palace is about 3 mi/5 km from Phnom Rung; the same taxi can take you to both places from Nakhon Ratchasima.

Visit

The palace was built in the 10th century for a Khmer king, and contains four *gopuras* located at the four points of the compass, three of which still retain their sculpted lintels. The first courtyard is remarkable for the *nagas* (snakes) that decorate its four symmetrical ponds. The main courtyard, further on, contains ruins of four brick *chedis,* and the ensemble gives an impression of harmony and expanse. Most of the bas-reliefs are in an excellent state of repair, perhaps because they are taken care of by monks who live in a nearby pagoda and are responsible for the well-being of the site.

SURIN***: THE GATHERING OF THE ELEPHANTS

279 mi/450 km north-east of Bangkok.

Access

The TAT organizes a special train from Bangkok for the gathering of the elephants. This usually takes place in Nov., but the exact date changes

Elephant festival at Surin celebrates the battles of ancient Siam.

every year. Contact the TAT in Bangkok for up-to-date information (see p. 32).

Accommodation

Surin has several simple but comfortable hotels; arrangements for staying overnight in Surin can be made through the TAT in Bangkok (see p. 32).

Visit

The town of Surin, which is built on the site of a former Khmer city, is the scene of an extraordinary annual gathering of elephants. At this gathering, all the ancient Thai traditions linked to the elephant are in evidence: the capture of the wild elephant, its training, its use in war, its labours in the jungle, and the elephant at play. No less than 200 elephants take part in the celebrations, at which you will see mock battles, parades, and traditional Thai dances and an unusual game of soccer played by elephants and their *mahouts* (handlers).

Full information can be obtained from the TAT in Bangkok (see p. 32).

KHAO YAI**: THE TAMING OF THE JUNGLE

127 mi/205 km north-east of Bangkok.

The **Khao Yai National Park** offers cool, fresh surroundings, comfortable bungalows, walks through the jungle, the most beautiful orchids in the world, and, if you're lucky, a glimpse through binoculars of a tiger or a bear. The park was created in 1959, having for many years served as a hideout for outlaws fleeing the police. It covers some 772 sq mi/2000 sq km, mostly at 2616 ft/800 m altitude, its highest point being 4316 ft/1320 m above sea level. The wild animals (deer, elephants, bears, tigers, gaurs [Asian bison], monkeys) are very reclusive, but with a little patience and cunning you can spot them in the full magnificence of their freedom. You can also observe them by night from behind spotlights. There are excursions by jeep or on foot to several spectacular waterfalls and an 18-hole golf course.

Information and reservations

Contact the TAT in Bangkok (see p. 32).

USEFUL VOCABULARY

For Westerners, the Thai language is extremely complicated. The short list of words and phrases below will probably bring you plenty of surprises, in particular that of not being understood. Thai is a tonal language; in other words, the same monosyllable can take on completely different meanings according to the tone of voice used. Thus the word Kao can mean hill, white, entrance, knees, news, or rice, depending on how you say it. The classic, of course, is the phrase 'mai mai mai mai', which, according to how it is uttered, can mean 'is the new silk burning?' or 'the new silk is not burning'. A system for the transcription of tones exists (there are five in Thai), but its use presupposes that one has already acquired a certain mastery of the language.

Phonetics

The words 'khrap' (used by a man) and 'kha' (used by a woman) are courtesy formulae which come at the end of most phrases. They also mean 'yes'.

The personal pronoun 'I' translates 'Phom' (masculine) and 'dichan' (feminine).

The pronunciation of vowels and dipthongs goes like this: 'ai', i as in eye; 'ae', e as in stem; 'e', ay, as in stay; 'oi', oy as in cowboy; 'u', oo, as in blue.

Consonants are pronounced like this: 'ch'-tch; 'h' is aspirate (even when it follows another consonant); and 'r' and 'w' are spoken as in English.

To know by heart

Good morning (goodbye)	sawatdi
Thank you	khop khun khrap (kha)
It doesn't matter	maï pen raï
How are you?	sabaïdi ru
I don't speak Thai	phut thaï maï daï
How do you say this in Thai?	thaï riek was araï?
I don't know	maï ru
Who?	khraï
What?	araï
Which?	anaï
When?	mua raï
Where?	tii naï

Health

I don't feel well	rouseuk maï sabaï
Hospital	rong phayaban
I want to see the doctor	tongkhan phop mo

Shopping

How much?	thao raï
How much is that?	ni raka thao raï
It's very expensive	phaeng mak
Can you make it less?	lot raka noï daï maï
Do you have change?	mi tang lek

Traveling

Bus station	thi chot rot bus
Train station	sathani rot faï
Airport	sanam bin
Boat	ruah
Airplane	ruah bin

Useful vocabulary 179

Train	rot faï
Coach	rot bus
Bus	rot mé
Bicycle rickshaw	samlor
Stop here	yout thi ni
Wait here	khroi thi ni
Straight ahead	trong paï
To the left	liao saï
To the right	liao khwa
Bank	thana khan
Where is the bank?	thana khan you thi naï
Where is the market?	talat you thi naï
Where is the central post office?	praisani klang you thi naï

Hotel, restaurant

The hotel	rung raïm
A room	hong
Where is the ladies' (men's) room?	hong nam you thi naï
I'm hungry	hiou mak
I'm thirsty	hiou nam
A good Thai restaurant	ran ahan thai aloi
A good Chinese restaurant	ran ahan chin aloi
A good French restaurant	ran ahan farangset aloi
Fried rice	khao phat
Shrimp fried rice	khao phat kung
Chicken fried rice	khao phat kaï
Beef fried rice	khao phat neua
Fried fish	plaa phat
Cake	khanom
Bread	khanom pang
Butter	neui
Water	nam plao
Ice	nam khaeng
Without ice	maï saï nam khaeng
Hot water	nam ron
Tea	chaa
Cold tea with milk	chaa yen
Cold tea without milk	chaa dam yen
Coffee with milk	cafae
Coffee without milk	cafae dam (sweetened)
Black coffee without sugar	dafae dam maï saï nam tan
A bottle of Mekhong	Mekhong Khouat neung
The food is excellent	ahan aloi mak thi sout

Numbers

1	neung	11	sip et
2	song	12	sip song
3	sam	16	sip hok
4	si	20	yi sip
5	ha	30	sam sip
6	hok	40	si sip
7	chet	100	neung roi
8	paet	500	ha roi
9	kao	1000	phan
10	sip	2000	song phan

Miscellaneous

Wait a minute	khoi diao
You're lovely	khun suaï mak
See you soon	phop kan maï na

Good luck	chok di na
Go away	paï
Stop!	yout
Watch out!	rawang
Quick!	reo reo noï
Help!	chuaï duaï
Danger	antaraï
Forbidden	ham
I'm in a hurry	phom (dichan) kamlang rip
Today	wan ni
Tomorrow	phrung ni
Every day	thuk wan

BIBLIOGRAPHY

Brennan, Jennifer : *Thai Cooking* (Futura Publications, London, 1984).
Cady, John F. : *Southeast Asia: Its Historical Development* (McGraw-Hill, New York, 1964).
Cooper, Robert and Nanthapa, *Culture Shock: Thailand* (Times Editions, Singapore, 1982).
Dhani Nivat, Prince, *A History of Buddhism in Siam* (Siam Society, Bangkok, 1965).
Diskul, M. C. Subhadradis, *Art in Thailand: A Brief History* (Silpakorn University, Bangkok, 1970).
Hall, D.G.E., *A History of South-east Asia.* Third edition (Macmillan, London, 1968).
Hudson, Roy, *Hudson's Guide to Chiang Mai and the North.* Updated annually. (Hudson Enterprises, Chiang Mai).
Ingram, J. C., *Economic Change in Thailand, 1830-1970* (Stanford University Press, Palo Alto, California, 1971).
McCoy, Alfred W., *The Politics of Heroin in Southeast Asia* (Harper and Row, New York, 1972).
Moffat, Abbot Lew, *Mongkut, the King of Siam* (Cornell University Press, Ithaca, New York, 1961).
Samudavanija, Chai-Anan, *The Thai Young Turks* (Institute of Southeast Asian Studies, Singapore, 1982).
Seidenfaden, Erik, *The Thai Peoples* (Siam Society, Bangkok, 1967).
Skinner, G. William, *Chinese Society in Thailand* (Cornell University Press, Ithaca, New York, 1957).
Smithies, Michael, *Old Bangkok* (Oxford University Press Pte. Ltd, Singapore, 1986).
Wells, K. E., *Thai Buddhism: Its Rites and Activities* (Police Press, Bangkok, 1960).
World Travel Map: Thailand (John Bartholomew & Son Ltd., Edinburgh, 1988).
Young, Gordon, *The Hill Tribes of Northern Thailand.* Third edition (Siam Society, Bangkok, 1966).

INDEX

Airlines
    Australia, 11
    Bangkok, 34, 96
    Chiang Mai, 138
    London, 11
    North America, 11
Airport: Don Muang (Bangkok), 11
Air travel (domestic flights), 33-34
    Eastern network, 33
    North-eastern network, 33
    Southern network, 33
    Traveling by air, 11-13
Akha: hilltribe population (Northern Thailand), 66
Ancient City (south-east of Bangkok), 121
Angkor: capital of Khmer kingdom at its height (12th century), 39, 101
Animal fights, 94, 124
Antiques, 30-31, 91
Ayutthaya: former capital (north of Bangkok)
    Art of, 52-53
    History, 39-40
    Visiting Ayutthaya, 117-118, 127

Bangkok: capital of Thailand, Krung Thep in Thai
    Art, 53
    History, 40-42, 53, 78-79
    Practical information, 82-85
Bang Pa In (north of Bangkok), 119-120
Bang Saen: beach (east of Bangkok), 122
Banks
    Bangkok, 96
    Chiang Mai, 143
Baphuon, 51
Bargaining, 30
Bayon, 51
Beverage, 25-26
Bhumibol Adulyadej: see **Rama IX**
Bibliography, 181
Boat
    Bangkok, 85
    Traveling by boat, 34-35
Bon Mai, 152
Boroma Trailokanat: King of Ayutthaya (late 14th century), 39
Bot: main chapel of a Wat, 48
Boxing (Thai), 93-94
Brass, 31
Bronze, 91
Buddhism: religion practiced by 90% of Thai population, comprised of two schools, Hinayâna and Mahâyâna, 71, 74-77
Bus
    Bangkok, 82, 83-85
    Chiang Mai, 138, 144
    Eastbound, 174
    Northbound, 127
    Southbound, 157
    Traveling by bus, 34

Business hours (shops, offices), 18

Car (rental), 35-37
Celadon, 31, 91, 140, 142
Chakri: name of the ruling dynasty, 21, 43-45
Chao Phraya: principal river of Thailand, 39, 40, 57
Chedi: religious monument, 48
Chiang Dao, 149
Chiang Mai: capital of Northern Thailand
    History, 137-138
    Practical information, 138-144
    Visiting Chiang Mai, 144-147
Chiang Rai (Northern Thailand), 151-154
Chiang Saen: also called Lan Na (north of Chiang Rai)
    Art, 51-52
    Visiting Chiang Saen, 154
Chinatown (Bangkok), 99, 115
Chinese (in Thailand), 58, 59-61, 78
Chinese opera, 94-95
Chom Thong (south of Chiang Mai), 150
Chulalongkorn: see **Rama V**
Cinema (in Bangkok), 95
Classical dance (Thai), 94
Climate: when to go, 11
    Golden Triangle, 152
    Phuket, 166
    Samui, 159
Clothes: what to take, 14-15
Crafts, 91, 146-147
Craftsmen's villages (Chiang Mai), 146-147
Crocodile farm, 124
Currency, 14, 18-19
Customs, 13

Damnoen Saduak: see **Markets**
Doi Pui: Meo village (Chiang Mai), 146
Doi Suthep (Chiang Mai), 145-146
Do's and don'ts, 19
Drinking water, 14
Drugs, 28, 69-70
Dusit Maha Prasad Hall (Lopburi), 128
Dvaravati: ancient kingdom of Central Thailand (6th-11th centuries), 30, 50

Electricity, 34
Elephant Kraal (Ayutthaya), 119
Elephants, 23, 66-67, 72, 123, 145, 148, 175-177
Embassies, 16
Emerald Buddha, 23, 45, 52, 100, see also **Wat Phra Keo**

Fang (north of Chiang Mai), 152
Festivals, 20-23, 142
Flowers, 92

Formalities, 13
Fruit, 25

Getting there (to Thailand), 11-13
Golden Triangle, 28, 69-70, 153-154
Guides (English-speaking), 88

Haadyai, 31, 163-164
Hang yao: literally 'long-tailed boats', pirogues, 35, 85, 115, 152
Health, 13-14, see also **Hospitals**
Hindu Sanctuary (Lopburi), 128
Hospitals
  Bangkok, 97
  Chiang Mai, 143
  Phuket, 170
Hot (south of Chiang Mai), 150
Hotels
  Ayutthaya, 118
  Bangkok, 85-87
  Categories, 17-18
  Chiang Mai, 139-140
  Lopburi, 127
  Pattaya, 122
  Phitsanulok, 128
  Phuket, 166-168
  Samui, 160
  Sukhothai, 129
Hua Hin: beach (southern coast), 157-158

Jataka, 48, 52, 104
Jewelry, 31, 92, 146
Jim Thompson's House (Bangkok), 86, 112

Kala Temple: see **Monkey Temple**
Kamphaeng Phet (Northern Thailand), 51, 131-133
Karen: hilltribe population (Northern Thailand), 62, 66-67, 142
Karon: beach (Phuket), 167
Khao Yai National Park, 177
Khmer: ancient civilization whose people are still present today in Eastern Thailand and Kampuchea, 38-39, 50
Khmer trail, 174-177
Khon: Thai traditional theater, 94, 124
King Narai's Palace (Lopburi), 127
Kite-flying, 20
Klong: canal, 57, 59, 78, 115-116
Ko: island
  Ko Dokmai (Phuket), 170
  Ko Khrok (Pattaya), 123
  Ko Larn (Pattaya), 123
  Ko Mae Ko (Samui), 162
  Ko Meow (Songkhla), 163
  Ko Non (Songkhla), 163
  Ko Phangan (Samui), 162
  Ko Hanniyi (Phuket), 172
  Ko Phai (Pattaya), 123
  Ko Phi Phi (Phuket), 170
  Ko Samui: see **Samui**
  Ko Tao (Samui), 162
Kok River, 152
Krung Thep: see **Bangkok**
Kwai River, 124-125

Lacquerware, 31-32, 92, 146
Laemka: beach (Phuket), 168
Lahu: hilltribe population (Northern Thailand), 68-69
Lakhon: Thai classical dance, 94, 124
Lakshana, 46
Lampang (Northern Thailand), 134
Lamphun (south of Chiang Mai), 147-148
Language, 26
Lan Na: see **Chiang Saen**
Lao: people of North-east Thailand and Laos, 58, 138
Lisu: hilltribe population (Northern Thailand), 67-68
Local time, 18
Lopburi: ancient summer capital (Northern Thailand)
  Art of, 50-51
  Visiting Lopburi, 127-128
Luggage: what to take, 15

Mae Chan (north of Chiang Rai), 154
Mae Hong Son (east of Chiang Mai), 151
Mae Sai (north of Chiang Rai), 154
Mae Salak (on Kok River), 152
Mae Sariang (south-east of Chiang Mai), 150-151
Mae Sa Valley, 149
Mai Khao: beach (Phuket), 170
Manners: see **Do's and don'ts**
Markets: talat in Thai
  Bangkrak: food (Bangkok), 114
  Banglampoo: fabrics (Bangkok), 115
  Charoenphoen: night (Bangkok), 115
  Coconuts (Bangkok), 115
  Damnoen Saduak: floating market (west of Bangkok), 123
  Din Daeng: night (Bangkok), 114
  Fish (Bangkok), 114
  Floating (Bangkok), 113-114
  Nakhon Kasem: Thieves Market (Bangkok), 115
  Pratu Nam: night (Bangkok), 90, 99, 114
  Sunday (Bangkok), 114
  Theves: flowers (Bangkok), 115
Massage parlours
  Bangkok, 96, 102
  Chiang Mai, 143
Mekhong: Thai whiskey, 26
Mekong River, 57, 154
Mengrai, 137, 153
Meo: hilltribe population (Northern Thailand), also called Hmong, 63-64
Mongkut: see **Rama IV**
Monkey Temple (Lopburi), 128
Monks (bikkus in Thai), 19, 75-77
Motorcycles (rental), 37
Muang Thai: Thai name of Thailand since 1939, 'land of free men', 39, 58
Muang Tham Palace: Khmer temple (Eastern Thailand), 51, 175
Mudra, 46
Museums
  Ayutthaya Museum, 118
  Chiang Mai Museum, 146
  Kamphaeng Phet Museum, 131-133
  National Museum, 106-112
  Sukhothai Museum, 130
Muslims, 61

184 Index

Naga: snake, 48
Naihan: beach (Phuket), 167-168
Nai Yang: beach (Phuket), 170
Nakhon Kasem: see **Markets**
Nakhon Pathom (west of Bangkok), 120-121
Nakhon Ratchasima (Eastern Thailand), 174
Nakhon Si Thammarat (Southern Thailand), 164
Nam Tok (west of Bangkok), 125
Narai Raja Niwes: see **King Narai's Palace**
Nightlife
    Bangkok, 95-96
    Chiang Mai, 142-143
    Pattaya, 123
    Phuket, 170
Nudism, 170

Ob Luang Gorges, 150
Old Chiang Mai, 147
Opium, 62-63, 69-70
Orchid nursery: see **Sai Nam Phung**

Palace (Bangkok), 104-106
Pansea: beach (Phuket), 167
Pasang (south of Chiang Mai), 148
Patong: beach (Phuket), 167
Patpong: centre of Bangkok nightlife, 95, 99
Pattaya: beach (outside Bangkok), 122-123
Phangnga Bay (Phuket), 171-172
Phitsanulok (Northern Thailand), 128-129
Phnom Rung: Khmer temple (Eastern Thailand), 175
Photography, 15-16
Phuket: island (Southern Thailand), 165-171
Pilok: village on Burmese border, 125
Pimai: Khmer temple (Eastern Thailand), 174
Postal services
    Bangkok, 97-99
    Chiang Mai, 143
    Phuket, 170
Prachaup Kiri Khan: beach (southern coast), 158-159
Prang: square-based tower used in religious architecture, 48
Prang Khaek: see **Hindu Sanctuary**
Prang Sam Yod: temple (Lopburi), 128
Pratu Nam: see **Markets**
Prem Tinsulanonda: general, since 1980 chief of government, 44
Press (and tourist publications), 28, 96
Pridi Phanomyong: principal leader of 1932 coup d'état, 41, 43

Rama I: king (1782-1809), founder of Chakri dynasty, first king of Siam, 41
Rama II: king (1809-1824), 41, 44
Rama III: king (1824-1851), 41, 44
Rama IV: king (1851-1868), Mongkut, opened Siam to modernization, 41, 44
Rama V: king (1868-1910), Chulalongkorn, architect of opening to the West, 42, 44
Rama VI: king (1910-1925), 44
Rama VIII (died 1946): Ananda, murdered at 21 without having taken the throne, 42, 44
Rama IX: King Bhumibol, king since 1946, brother of Rama VIII, 43-45
Rama Khamheng: principal figure among the kings of Sukhothai, inventor of the Thai script (late 13th century), 39
Ramakien, 48
Ramathibodi: first king of Ayutthaya (1350-1369), 39
Ratanakosin: Thai artistic period (late 18th century), 53
Rawai: beach (Phuket), 168
Restaurants
    Bangkok, 87-90
    Chiang Mai, 139-140
    Pattaya, 122-123
    Phuket, 169
Rose Garden (west of Bangkok), 124
Royal barges (Bangkok), 103

Sabre contests, 94
Safety precautions, 26, 28, 155
Sai Nam Phung: orchid nursery (north of Chiang Mai), 149
Saint Joseph's Cathedral (Ayutthaya), 119
Samlor: three-wheeled vehicle, 35, 83, 149
Samui (Ko), 159-162
Sanam Louang (Bangkok): heart of Bangkok, 90, 91
Sanuk: Thai expression for everything that is pleasant, 19
Shopping
    Bangkok, 90-92
    Chiang Mai, 140-142
    What to buy, 30-32
Siam Center (Bangkok), 90
Siam Society (Bangkok), 113
Silom Road (Bangkok), 90, 99
Similan Islands (Phuket), 170
Sirikit (Queen), 22, 44-45
Soi: small streets, often cul-de-sacs, 78, 79
Songkhla (Southern Thailand), 162-164
Spirit house, 75
Suan Pakkard Palace (Bangkok), 112-113
Surin (Eastern Thailand), 175
Surin: beach (Phuket), 171

Taxis (Bangkok), 82-83
Telephone
    Bangkok, 97-98
    Phuket, 170
Temples: see **Wat**
Thai cooking, 23-35, see also **Restaurants**
Thai cotton, 31, 148
Thais: people that make up the majority of Thailand, 58
Thamakheng (on Kok River), 152
Tha Ton (on Kok River), 152
Theatre (traditional): see **Khon**
Thonburi: part of greater Bangkok, on the right bank of the Chao Phraya River, one-time capital of Siam (1769-1782), 40, 57, 78, 113

Index

Tipping, 32
Toilets (Hong Nam in Thai), 32
Tourism Authority of Thailand (TAT)
  Bangkok, 90
  Chiang Mai, 143
  List of offices, 32
  Phuket, 170
Tourist Police
  Bangkok, 90
  Phuket, 170
Train
  Eastbound, 174
  Northbound, 126
  Southbound, 157
  Traveling by, 34
Tribal Research Centre (Chiang Mai), 147
Tuk-tuk: three-wheeled vehicles, 35, 83

Useful Vocabulary, 178-180
U Thong, 52
Uttaradit (Northern Thailand), 133

Vaccinations, 13
Viharn: chapel containing sacred objects in the centre of a wat, 48
Viharn Phra Mongkol Bopitr (Ayutthaya), 118-119

Wai: traditional gesture of greeting, 19
Wang Luang: royal palace (Ayutthaya), 119
Wat, 47-48
  Wat Arun (Bangkok), 102-103
  Wat Benchamabophit (Bangkok), 103
  Wat Bovornives (Bangkok), 104
  Wat Buddhaisawan (Ayutthaya), 119
  Wat Chang Lom (Si Satchanalai), 133
  Wat Chang Rob (Si Satchanalai), 133
  Wat Chedi Chet Thao (Si Satchanalai), 133-134
  Wat Chedi Jet Yod (Chiang Mai), 144
  Wat Chedi Luang (Chiang Mai), 144
  Wat Chetupon (Sukhothai), 130
  Wat Chiang Man (Chiang Mai), 144
  Wat Khao Suwan Kiri (Si Satchanalai), 134
  Wat Khao Thanom Plung (Si Satchanalai), 134
  Wat Mahathat (Bangkok), 104
  Wat Phra Keo (Bangkok), 100
  Wat Phra Pai Luang (Sukhothai), 131
  Wat Phra Sang (Lampang), 135
  Wat Phra Si Ratana Mahathat (Si Satchanalai), 134
  Wat Phrathat Doi Suthep (Chiang Mai), 146
  Wat Phrathat Hariphunchai (Lamphun), 148
  Wat Po (Bangkok), 101-102
  Wat Rachanada (Bangkok), 104
  Wat Rajabopitr (Bangkok), 104
  Wat Raj Burana (Ayutthaya), 119
  Wat Sakhet (Bangkok), 103
  Wat Saphan Hin (Sukhothai), 130
  Wat Si Chum (Sukhothai), 130-131
  Wat Si Sawai (Sukhothai), 130
  Wat Sra Si (Sukhothai), 130
  Wat Suan Dok (Chiang Mai), 144
  Wat Suthat (Bangkok), 103-104
  Wat Traymit (Bangkok), 104
  Wat Yai Chai Mongkol (Ayutthaya), 119
Wickerwork, 92
Women (Thai), 70-71

Yao: hilltribe population (Northern Thailand), 64-66
Yaowarat Road (Bangkok): see **Chinatown**

Notes

Notes